Renée Roll

Y0-DJO-574

SAMS
Teach Yourself

FileMaker™ 7

in **24** *Hours*

Jesse Feiler

SAMS   *800 East 96th Street, Indianapolis, Indiana 46240 USA*

Sams Teach Yourself FileMaker 7 in 24 Hours

International Standard Book Number: 0-672-32578-0

Library of Congress Catalog Card Number: 2003103987

Printed in the United States of America

First Printing: May 2004

07   06   05   04   4   3   2   1

Trademarks

Warning and Disclaimer

Bulk Sales

Sams Publishing offers excellent discounts on this book when ordered in quantity for bulk purchases or special sales. For more information, please contact

U.S. Corporate and Government Sales
1-800-382-3419
corpsales@pearsontechgroup.com

For sales outside of the U.S., please contact

International Sales
1-317-428-3341
international@pearsontechgroup.com

Acquisitions Editor
Betsy Brown

Development Editor
Scott Meyers

Managing Editor
Charlotte Clapp

Senior Project Editor
Matthew Purcell

Copy Editor
Geneil Breeze

Indexer
Chris Barrick

Proofreader
Elizabeth Scott

Technical Editor
Jim Kirkpatrick

Publishing Coordinator
Vanessa Evans

Designer
Gary Adair

Page Layout
Kelly Maish

Contents at a Glance

Part IV: Sharing FileMaker Solutions

Part V: Appendixes

Table of Contents

Part II: Modifying Templates and Databases

Part III: Creating FileMaker Solutions

About the Author

Jesse Feiler is the author of a number of books on Mac OS X, FileMaker, the Web-based enterprise, the Y2K problem, and home offices. His books on OpenDoc, Cyberdog, Apple Guide, and Rhapsody are now collector's items.

A member of the FileMaker Solutions Alliance, he regularly consults on FileMaker and develops FileMaker solutions for small business, non-profits, art, retail point-of-sale, publishing, marketing, and other markets. He has specialized in "rehabs"—updates to existing FileMaker solutions including FileMaker 7 conversions.

He has worked as a developer and manager for companies such as the Federal Reserve Bank of New York (monetary policy and bank supervision), Prodigy (early Web browser), Apple (information systems), New York State Department of Health (rabies and lead poisoning), The Johnson Company (office management), and Young & Rubicam (media planning and new product development).

His interests in new forms of technical training have led him to MediaSchool (http://www.mediaschool.com), for which he has authored several Mac OS X courses available over the Internet, as well as to Geek Cruises' Mac Mania cruises to Alaska and the Caribbean. He is also the first author of a technical book to be published both on paper and as an e-book.

Active in the community, he is past president of the Mid-Hudson Library System, Chair of the Philmont Comprehensive Plan Board, founder of the Philmont Main Street Committee, and treasurer of the HB Playwrights Foundation. He is a regular on public radio WAMC's Roundtable program.

Acknowledgments

The picture of an author sitting alone in a room day after day may be true for some authors and some types of books, but it's not true for this author or for technical books in general. Many people have provided invaluable assistance to the creation of this book.

First and foremost, the FileMaker team has worked for more than twenty years to combine the power of personal computing and database technology with an unequalled interface both for developer and user. Their choices have consistently struck the right balance between complexity and ease-of-use.

As always, Carole McClendon at Waterside Productions has nurtured this project into being (and completion).

At Sams, Betsy Brown first brought this book into being. As it was being written, technical editor Jim Kirkpatrick provided excellent feedback to help make the book as accurate and complete as possible. Under the excellent guidance of development editor Scott Meyers, they, the project editor (Matt Purcell), the proofreader (Elizabeth Scott), the copy editor (Geneil Breeze), and indexer (Chris Barrick) did a great job in shaping the book.

We Want to Hear from You!

As the reader of this book, *you* are our most important critic and commentator. We value your opinion and want to know what we're doing right, what we could do better, what areas you'd like to see us publish in, and any other words of wisdom you're willing to pass our way.

You can email or write me directly to let me know what you did or didn't like about this book—as well as what we can do to make our books stronger.

Please note that I cannot help you with technical problems related to the topic of this book, and that due to the high volume of mail I receive, I might not be able to reply to every message.

When you write, please be sure to include this book's title and author as well as your name and phone number or email address. I will carefully review your comments and share them with the author and editors who worked on the book.

E-mail: consumer@samspublishing.com

Mail: Mark Taber
Associate Publisher
Sams Publishing
800 East 96th Street
Indianapolis, IN 46240 USA

Reader Services

For more information about this book or others from Sams Publishing, visit our Web site at www.samspublishing.com. Type the ISBN (excluding hyphens) or the title of the book in the Search box to find the book you're looking for.

Introduction

Welcome to FileMaker 7! Whether you're new to FileMaker or an old FileMaker hand, FileMaker 7 is an exciting new adventure. Once again, the people at FileMaker have struck the right balance: FileMaker 7 provides major new features in every part of the application, yet most existing FileMaker solutions convert automatically.

The book uses many of the FileMaker Starter Solution templates to introduce you to FileMaker features. In addition, a number of FileMaker databases have been developed to demonstrate features. You can find the databases developed specifically for this book on the Web at the publisher's site (www.samspublishing.com) as well as at the author's site (www.philmontmill.com).

Who Should Read This Book

Whether you are just getting started with FileMaker or moving to FileMaker 7, this book shows you what you need to know to become proficient at FileMaker. It also introduces you to the capabilities of FileMaker: It's not enough just to know how to do what you want to do; you should also know what you can do that you never dreamed of doing.

How This Book Is Organized

The multitude of Starter Solution templates shipped with FileMaker lets you create databases for a variety of uses—business, home, education, and more. Without further ado, you can use them to enter, retrieve, sort, print, and otherwise manipulate your data. Part I, "Getting Started with FileMaker—Using the Templates," shows you how to do this.

In Part II, "Modifying Templates and Databases," you'll see how to modify the templates to customize them for your specific purposes.

Part III, "Creating FileMaker Solutions," addresses the most daunting task of all: starting from scratch to build your own FileMaker solution.

Finally, in Part IV, "Sharing FileMaker Solutions," you'll see how to share FileMaker databases and solutions.

At the end of each hour, some questions and answers discuss issues raised; you'll also find some quiz questions to recap the high points. Finally, some suggested activities will help you gain hands-on knowledge of FileMaker.

As you can see, the book is organized in increasingly complex sections. This structure means that some aspects of FileMaker are covered—with different degrees of complexity—in different parts of the book. If you want to jump around, feel free to do so.

PART I

Getting Started with FileMaker—Using the Templates

HOUR 1

Introducing FileMaker

What You'll Learn in This Hour:

▶ A Brief History of FileMaker—Two decades of history have spanned most of the personal computer age. FileMaker has grown along with technology from a single-user desktop application to a networkable powerhouse.

▶ The FileMaker Market—Along with other changes, FileMaker has come to dominate the workgroup market (ranging from 2 to 250 people).

▶ How FileMaker Works: Overview—FileMaker shares many features with other databases, but it introduces many of its own.

▶ Talking About FileMaker: A Guide to Terminology—Here are the major terms that you need to know to talk about FileMaker.

▶ Talking About FileMaker: The Product Line—There's more than one version of FileMaker. This section helps you pick the one that's right for you.

▶ Introducing the FileMaker Templates—Along with FileMaker come a number of templates that you can use as examples or right out of the box to get started with your database needs.

This chapter introduces FileMaker and provides a brief overview of the terminology and concepts described later in the book. It gives some examples of what you can do with the templates provided with each copy of FileMaker.

A Brief History of FileMaker

In 1984, the year the first Macintosh computer was sold, FileMaker emerged as one of the earliest applications on that platform. Like dBase, a database application on PCs, it was, indeed, a *file* maker: It let you easily create files with data in them. The data was not the continuous data you find in a word processing document; rather, it consisted of *records*, each one of which had identical *fields* such as name, address, or phone number.

FileMaker was an elegant and easy way to enter and retrieve this data; you could sort it at will, and you could create sophisticated reports for display onscreen or for printing on paper. Today, FileMaker can still do all that, and many people believe that it remains the most elegant and easiest way to manipulate data on a personal computer.

Over time, FileMaker expanded from the world of the Macintosh to the world of Windows. Today, it is equally at home on both platforms. In addition, FileMaker Mobile runs on PalmOS and Pocket PC.

In addition to the move to other platforms, a tremendously important change occurred to FileMaker in 1995 with the release of FileMaker 3. No longer tied to single files, FileMaker 3 allowed you to create *relationships* between multiple files.

In addition to the technical advances, FileMaker underwent a number of organizational changes over the years. Now a wholly-owned subsidiary of Apple Computer, Inc., FileMaker has been profitable every quarter since its formation as a separate entity in 1998.

During the late 1990s and early 2000s, FileMaker added support for industry standards including the Web and XML. FileMaker now runs quite happily both on Web servers and on local area network (LAN) servers.

FileMaker 7 brought a change that is as significant as the change in FileMaker 3 that allowed you to use relationships between files. With FileMaker 7, the database engine has been drastically rewritten to allow multiple *tables* within a single *database file*. The meaning and significance of this is discussed later in this hour in "Talking About FileMaker: A Guide to Terminology;" for now, just note that it is a significant event both for existing and new FileMaker users. (FileMaker 7 includes many other important changes, which are described throughout this book.)

The FileMaker Market

FileMaker started as a single-user desktop database. As it gained relational features and was implemented on both Macintosh and Windows, it started to be used by groups of people. FileMaker has identified its core market as *workgroups*— groups of people from 2 to 250 who need to manage their own data.

FileMaker makes it easy for people to implement database solutions. One of its goals is to allow people with *domain knowledge* (knowledge about a particular business or operation) to function on their own. Whereas corporate database pro- grams such as DB2, Oracle, and Microsoft's SQL Server require IT staffs for their care and maintenance, in many environments FileMaker solutions are developed and managed within a workgroup by non-IT people. (This is one of the reasons why FileMaker frequently shows up in "skunk-works" projects that fly beneath the corporate radar.)

This primary focus on self-supporting groups of people is not limited to large enterprises. FileMaker is a major force in small businesses where the "enterprise" itself consists of a group of people—sometimes only one—that does everything. In such an environment, ease of use and the ability to function without a corporate IT staff is critical.

FileMaker Solutions Alliance and FileMaker Developers Conference

Although FileMaker can be used to implement customized solutions by end users and domain specialists, some small businesses and workgroups hire consultants to set up a FileMaker solution that they can then manage themselves. An excellent source of such consultants is the FileMaker Solutions Alliance, which is sponsored by FileMaker. You can reach it by clicking on the Developers button on `http://www.filemaker.com`. You'll find listings of consultants from around the world.

Another important source of FileMaker information is the annual FileMaker Developers Conference. More information about this conference is also available from the Developers button on the FileMaker site.

FileMaker does not require IT support, but changes in the last several releases of FileMaker allow it to be easily integrated into the world of corporate IT. FileMaker Server Advanced, for example, functions with standard Web servers such as Apache and Microsoft Internet Information Services (IIS). Other integration tech- nologies such as xDBC and XML are key to FileMaker's life in a heterogeneous environment. Although the details of FileMaker Server are beyond the scope of this book, you will find a brief discussion of it in Appendix D. YxDBC, XML, and other integration technologies are discussed in Hour 11, "Importing and Exporting Data," and Hour 12, "Working with ODBC and JDBC."

How FileMaker Works: Overview

To understand how FileMaker works, it is important to distinguish it from other types of databases. In this section, you'll see how database management systems work as well as how FileMaker works and the ways in which it differs from database management systems. You'll also find a description of the difference between database programming and traditional programming. This is important for you to understand as you start to think about building your own FileMaker solutions.

Database Management Systems

Databases come in several varieties. Large-scale enterprise databases focus on data storage and retrieval. Except for basic browsing (usually of the sort done for diagnostic work), you need other software to manage the interface to the database. These systems are called *database management systems* (*DBMSs*), and they are exemplified by products such as Oracle, IBM's DB2, and Microsoft SQL Server. On a somewhat smaller scale, products such as OpenBase, MySQL, and Pervasive.SQL are important tools.

These DBMSs use *Structured Query Language*, also known as SQL (described in the following section), and they often run on mainframes or on servers—sometimes clusters of servers. They typically incorporate load management software. Because the database normally runs independently of the software that accesses it, people talk of "starting" or "stopping" a database.

In addition to storing and retrieving data, these DBMSs support data validation rules that require certain conditions to be true before the data can be stored. Most also support the concept of *relational integrity* in which values of one field must appropriately coincide with values in another.

FileMaker's Role

FileMaker is designed as a complete solution provider. It not only manages the data the way a DBMS does, but it also provides a customizable user interface for accessing the data. Although it is possible to use FileMaker much like a DBMS and have other software manipulate the data, the most common situation is for people to launch FileMaker and do everything they need to do with their data: enter, search, print, sort, and so forth.

FileMaker provides its own scripting language so that you can expand its functionality and customize its operation. It provides a wealth of features such as built-in spell checking and find/replace for text. Its layout tools let you devise screens and printed reports with great precision and sophistication.

Its built-in functions give you a range of tools to perform calculations on data; you can store these calculations if you want. It takes care of updating calculations as needed when you click out of a field.

The phrase *click out* refers to clicking or tabbing on another field or on the background of a window. The effect is to terminate editing on the first field; at that time, calculations are updated. Note that clicking out of a field is specific to a window. If you have two FileMaker windows open, each maintains its own *focus*—the field currently being edited. Thus, clicking on a field in the second window leaves the first window's focus unchanged, and a calculation for a field that you are editing in the first window will not be performed until you click out of it by clicking elsewhere in that window.

Database Programming

Traditional procedural programming is similar to the procedures and processes that people are familiar with in life. You execute a series of steps in a given sequence. At times, you evaluate the situation and choose what to do next. (This is precisely the same as a cook deciding whether the pasta is cooked enough.)

Database programming is different from procedural programming. In essence, it moves the decision points out of the process. Whereas an accounting program might examine each account in turn and then decide whether to send a bill, a database program would use the database to select all the accounts that fulfill the requirements for sending a bill and then do the same thing—send a bill—for each of the selected accounts.

It is not uncommon to find database applications that perform several sets of retrievals. You might select all accounts due for billing and then send their bills. You might next select all accounts that have had no activity for three months and send a reminder letter.

With FileMaker, you often perform such a retrieval and then use a customized layout to display all the returned data in one format or another. As you will see throughout this book, the ability to use data to construct such *found sets* of records is an important part of FileMaker (and any other database).

If you want to do traditional procedural programming, you can do that, too, using FileMaker's built-in scripting language. Nothing requires you to use the style of database programming, but it frequently makes it easier to build complex solutions.

One additional point about database programming needs to be made. You can sort databases as well as found sets of records. FileMaker is fairly quick at sorting a database, and it's easy to re-sort it as necessary. What's even faster is to select only the data you're interested in and then to sort that subset of the database.

Talking About FileMaker: A Guide to Terminology

You have already encountered some FileMaker and database terminology. This section provides definitions of the key terms used in the world of FileMaker. (In Hour 2, "Using FileMaker and Its Basic Templates," you'll explore the FileMaker interface and find still more terminology presented in that context.) Note that the definitions given here are for FileMaker; the terms may be used in other environments in slightly different ways.

- ▶ Column—This is alternative terminology for *field*; it comes from the world of relational databases. (A field can also refer to the formatted representation of a column in a layout.)

- ▶ Database—All the data for a FileMaker solution. It can be in one or more database files.

- ▶ Database file—A single file containing one or more tables of data. (Before FileMaker 7, a database file contained only one set of data; the concept of tables is introduced for the first time in FileMaker 7.)

- ▶ Field—A single data element that occurs throughout a table. Each field contains a value. For example, the field "First Name" might contain 432 values in a table with 432 entries.

- ▶ Record—A single entry in a table. Each record contains one or more fields. Every record in the table has the same fields, but each usually has different data values.

- ▶ Relationship—A means of specifying which record(s) in one table match up with record(s) in another.

- ▶ Row—This is alternative terminology for *record*. It, too, comes from the world of relational databases.

- ▶ Schema—This is the description of a table. It specifies the fields/columns, validation routines, and the like. It contains no data values.

- ▶ Solution—Most people use this word to describe the collection of database(s), reports, screen layouts, scripts, and other FileMaker features and customizations that are brought to bear on a specific problem. Sometimes people refer simply to a "database," but this term makes it clearer when the larger entity is being discussed.

▶ Structured Query Language (SQL)—This standard language for relational databases is widely used in products such as Oracle, Sybase, Microsoft SQL Server, and the like. FileMaker does not use SQL itself; however, it can communicate with SQL databases and other applications using the xDBC interfaces described in Hour 12. (Note that the changes to the FileMaker database structure in FileMaker 7 bring it much closer to the SQL standard.)

▶ Table—A set of data pertaining to a specific area—customers, projects, addresses, and so forth. Tables contain fields and records or columns and rows (see the following definitions).

Talking About FileMaker: The Product Line

FileMaker started as a standalone desktop product. It has now grown into a family of products.

FileMaker Pro

At its heart, FileMaker Pro is the desktop product. You can buy it as a shrink-wrapped product. However, with its emphasis on workgroups, FileMaker has provided volume licensing agreements (VLAs) that make up a significant part of its sales. Although the terms vary, if you are interested in buying several copies of FileMaker, check out a VLA. (This and all other product and pricing information is available at `www.filemaker.com`.)

FileMaker Pro allows you to share databases over a network. It also allows you to publish databases using Web technology. The difference is that if you share databases over a network, the people who use the shared database access it with their own copies of FileMaker. If you use Web technology, the users of the shared database access it with a Web browser.

FileMaker Pro limits the number of users who can share databases to five. If you need to exceed those limits, you need to move on to FileMaker Server.

FileMaker Server and FileMaker Server Advanced

These products let you share databases among many people on the Web or on a local area network. It is optimized as a server; you can't use it to design databases the way you can with FileMaker Pro.

FileMaker Developer

FileMaker Developer allows you to build customized solutions with tools more sophisticated than those in FileMaker Pro. FileMaker Developer allows you to build standalone solutions that can be distributed without a fee (at least without a fee to FileMaker—you may charge for your work, of course). These standalone solutions run on Macintosh or Windows and do not require users to have their own copies of FileMaker. These standalone solutions are not networkable.

FileMaker Developer also provides tools to help you manage the solutions that you create and that users access with FileMaker Pro. These include reports and a variety of database maintenance features. FileMaker Developer also includes a debugger and the ability to create custom functions.

FileMaker Mobile

Finally, FileMaker Mobile runs on Pocket PC and Palm OS. It lets you synchronize data with your FileMaker databases on a personal computer. Furthermore, i-mode compatibility is implemented for Japan.

Introducing the FileMaker Templates

FileMaker ships with a variety of templates for solutions ranging from contact management to scheduling and asset management. Many people use them as is and never do any FileMaker programming. Others modify them slightly to accommodate their needs.

As you will see in the final hours of this book, you can link two or more of the templates together. (In Hour 23, "Using FileMaker and XML with Other Applications," and Hour 24, "Using FileMaker, XML, and XSLT," the Asset Management and Contact Management databases are combined to track which assets are assigned to which people.)

> The templates provide demonstrations of FileMaker features as well as starting points for solutions you might want to use or modify. For many people, the templates provide useful guidance for the problem at hand—not just the FileMaker concepts, but the concepts behind an asset management system, for example.

The FileMaker templates are divided into several groups. Some are in more than one of these groups:

- Home
- Education
- Business—Finance
- Business—General
- Business—People & Assets
- Business—Projects

They are described briefly in the following sections. Some of the databases demonstrate FileMaker's relational model and the new multitable database structure of FileMaker 7. They are noted in the descriptions.

Home

These are mostly relatively simple databases that can be used on their own or with minor modifications for your own needs at home. The names are self-explanatory: Contact Management, Document Library, Event Planning, Family Medical Records, Home Budgets, Inventory, Lending Library, Movie Library, Music Library, Photo Catalog, Recipes, and To Do List.

Three of the databases demonstrate particularly powerful aspects of FileMaker 7; they are discussed later in this book.

Contact Management demonstrates the use of a self-join to find contacts with a similar address or name. This is a concept described in Hour 14, "Working with Relationships."

Photo Catalog demonstrates the use of two tables in a single database along with several self-joins. The use of multiple tables in a single database is new in FileMaker 7; it is discussed in Hour 13, "Creating a FileMaker Database."

Finally, Lending Library provides a demonstration of the combination of the Asset Management and Contact Management databases into separate tables within a single database.

Education

These databases are particularly useful in the education sphere. Many of them, such as Contact Management, are also provided in the Home collection.

Among the new databases in this collection are Expense Report, Faculty Staff, Field Trips, Registration, Research Notes, Student Emergency Card, Student Record, and Task Management.

Three databases in this collection also demonstrate the same relational features and new FileMaker 7 features. Registration combines Events and Contacts in a single database, whereas Task Management combines Projects, Tasks, and Contacts. Expense Report provides an interesting example of using a self-join to select data from a given table.

Business—Finance

In addition to databases in the other collections, you will find Time Billing, Purchase Orders, and Time Cards. Time Billing demonstrates the new relational model of FileMaker 7 in the same way as the databases previously cited.

Business—General

The databases in this collection have been described in the other collections where they also are placed.

Business—People & Assets

This collection includes Personnel Management, Asset Management, and People Management. People Management demonstrates the new multitable database feature of FileMaker 7.

Business—Projects

New databases in this collection are Issue Tracking and Resource Scheduling. Resource Scheduling demonstrates the multitable database feature of FileMaker 7.

In the first part of this book, you'll see how to use FileMaker. The examples given use the templates distributed with FileMaker, so you should be able to follow along with your own copy of FileMaker.

Summary

In this hour you were introduced to FileMaker: its history, its market, and the basics of how it works. If you're itching to get started, the time is at hand: The next hour gets you started with actually using FileMaker.

Q&A

Q *What is the practical difference between FileMaker and SQL-based databases?*

A For most purposes, there is little significance. FileMaker supports ODBC, which lets you interact fully with SQL-based databases. Further, with FileMaker 7, the new database structure using multiple tables per file closely resembles SQL.

Q *What are the limits of FileMaker?*

A The limits are generally based on hardware constraints. The primary FileMaker market is workgroups, which are defined by FileMaker as being from 2 to 250 people. That gives you one indication of scale.

Workshop

Quiz

1. What is the difference between a table and a database?

2. What do you use to create a relationship?

Quiz Answers

1. A database contains one or more tables.

2. You need to define a matching key to relate two tables.

Activities

Make a list of the projects you want to work on in FileMaker. This wish list of database projects will come in handy as you proceed through this book: You'll be able to work on concrete examples that will help you solve your data management problems.

HOUR 2

Using FileMaker and Its Basic Templates

What You'll Learn in This Hour:

▶ Exploring the FileMaker Interface—This is the top-level overview of what you see when you open FileMaker.

▶ Using the Status Area and FileMaker Modes—The status area at the left of each FileMaker data window lets you navigate through the database and its elements. It changes depending on the mode you're using. You can use it to work with modes that let you browse data, search for data, create custom layouts to view data, and preview data before printing.

▶ Using Basic FileMaker Menus—The basic menus are the same in each mode.

▶ Working with FileMaker Windows—In FileMaker 7, you can now have multiple windows open on the same database table.

▶ Working with FileMaker Views—In Browse mode, views let you look at data a record at a time, in a list, or in a table that resembles a spreadsheet.

▶ FileMaker Preferences—The basic preferences let you customize the way FileMaker behaves.

▶ FileMaker Toolbars—You can use FileMaker's toolbars to augment the menu bar and the status area for easy control.

▶ Entering Data—Finally, here are the basics of entering data into FileMaker.

Now that you have been introduced to the basics of FileMaker, it's time to explore the software—both the database itself and the templates that come with it. If you have a copy of FileMaker, you can follow along with this part of the book: You don't have to create any databases other than the ones that come installed with FileMaker. (If you haven't installed FileMaker, now might be a good time to do so.)

This hour helps you learn how to use FileMaker from the standpoint of someone who just needs to enter and view data. In Hour 3, "Finding and Sorting Data," you'll see how to search for data. Then things get more interesting as you learn how to customize your database with your own layouts and how to print. As you proceed through this hour, you see some of the features of FileMaker that you can work with later in the book. If you're impatient, you can jump ahead. Whatever you do, don't feel that the brief explanations of these features are the last word on them: This is only Hour 2!

By the Way

You can use the commands in the menu bar and the status area to navigate through your database. Many FileMaker solutions automate these commands with scripts and buttons so that you don't need to use these commands at all in many cases.

Exploring the FileMaker Interface

When you launch FileMaker, you are prompted to open an existing file or to create a new one. In this hour, the Contact Management template is used. Accordingly, when you are prompted to open a database, choose to create one based on Contact Management as shown in Figure 2.1. (Contact Management is available under the Business - People & Assets, Home, and Education items in the pop-up menu at the right of the dialog shown in Figure 2.1.)

FIGURE 2.1
Use the Contact Management template.

FileMaker creates a new database, and the window shown in Figure 2.2 opens.

FIGURE 2.2
FileMaker opens a
Contact
Management data-
base.

> Throughout this book, the figures may differ in minor ways from what you see on
> your own computer. (In the most obvious case, the figures show both Windows and
> Mac OS X versions of FileMaker; you're likely to use one or the other.) FileMaker's
> many preferences for toolbars (docked/floating, shown/hidden) and other features
> let you customize your interface and, thus, make it look somewhat different from the
> figures in this book. Don't worry about these minor differences. By the end of the
> book, you'll know how to change all those settings to make your interface look exact-
> ly the way you want it to.

Except for the vertical *status area* at the left of the window, most of the window is
taken up with a view of the database. This is a *layout*, and it is used to display
data as well as provide interface tools for you to work with.

If you click in a field to enter data, the warning shown in Figure 2.3 may appear.
You've created a database, but each record in the database needs to be created
with the New button at the upper-left of the layout or the New Record command
(discussed in the "Using Basic FileMaker Menus" section later in this hour).

> The menu commands are available for all databases to which you have appropriate
> access (for example, permission to create new records). Layouts differ from one
> database to another; there might not be a New button in the layout you are using,
> and it might not be in this location or look like this. In the FileMaker templates,
> though, all the layouts use the same basic format, and New buttons look like this
> and appear in this location in them.

FIGURE 2.3
Choose New
Record before
entering data.

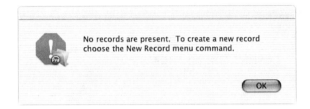

After you create a new record, you can enter data as shown in Figure 2.4. Click in the field and type. You can click in the next field or tab to the next field. (By default you tab left to right and top to bottom; the layout designer can modify this order.) The currently selected field is surrounded by a *focus ring*, a distinctive and darker border. In Figure 2.4, the field containing "Software Director" has the focus and is currently selected.

FIGURE 2.4
Enter data.

Each template layout is different, and you'll see in Hour 4, "Introducing Layouts," how to modify them and even create your own. It's worth pointing out a few features of the Contact Management layout shown here.

Buttons and Toolbars

At the top of the window is a toolbar containing the title of the database ("Contact Management") as well as a variety of buttons you can use to manipulate the database. Today, graphical user interfaces have many standard types of buttons—the Help button with its question mark is easily recognizable.

Icons for New, Delete, and Find are shown along with text identifying them. Depending on the application and the people who will use it, it's often difficult to come up with icons that are unambiguous and clear in their meaning, so a word is added to the icon.

In other cases, it's not worth trying to find an icon to represent a complex or abstract thought. At the top-right of the toolbar, the text "View Contact List" and "View Address Labels" is "hot"—you click on it as if it were a button (it technically is). In today's interfaces it is common to have such hot interface elements that contain text without icons. As long as the context—such as a toolbar—makes it clear that no data entry is allowed in this section, and because the pointer changes to a pointing hand when moved over the text, most people understand that they can click on the text.

Tabs

Tabs are a way to switch views of data within a single window. At the bottom, three tabs control what's visible in the bottom third of the window: the Main Address, Second Address, and Related Contacts. Clicking each one changes the display in that section of the window.

Three tabs also appear in the lower-right of the toolbar at the top of the window. They control the views of the main section of the window, and they are discussed later in this hour in the section, "Working with FileMaker Views."

Editable and Noneditable Fields

As you can see from Figure 2.4, as data is entered, the contact name is shown in large type above the data entry area. Data entry fields are usually bordered in some way to indicate that you can type in them. You can also display data in a window in noneditable forms. One way of doing so is to *insert* text fields into the layout just as you insert fields into a mail merge document. That is what has happened with the contact name in Figure 2.4.

Using the Status Area and FileMaker Modes

The *status area* is the vertical section to the left of the windows you have seen so far. The four buttons at the top control the modes in which FileMaker operates:

Browse, Find, Layout, and Preview. As you change the mode, the status area changes; also, the behavior of FileMaker changes.

FileMaker has four modes. One of them is active at all times:

▶ Browse mode is used to enter and view data on the screen.

▶ Find mode is used to specify data to retrieve; you then view it in another mode.

▶ Layout mode is used to design a layout that is displayed in one of the other three modes. The layout contains data, background text, and graphics, as well as buttons and other interface elements.

▶ Preview mode is used to display data as it will appear when printed. Not only does it use the page size that you've set for the layout being displayed, but also certain types of summary fields are calculated in Preview mode, whereas they are not in Browse mode.

Each of these is described in the following sections.

Browse Mode

You've seen Browse mode in the figures shown previously in this hour. Pay particular attention to the status area at the left in Figure 2.5. It lets you navigate through the data and change the layouts.

FIGURE 2.5
Select a layout.

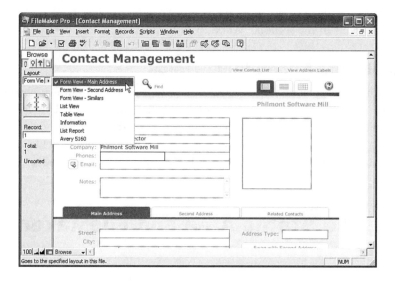

As usual, buttons at the top of the status area let you select the mode: The Browse button is on the left.

A pop-up menu lets you choose from among the layouts. A database can have a number of different layouts. One layout might be optimized for data entry, and another might be designed for analysis. Still another might be designed to print labels or preprinted forms.

Beneath the layout pop-up menu is a navigation tool called the *book*. Use the arrows to go back (left) and forward (right) one record at a time. The display in the main portion of the window changes appropriately.

The current record number is displayed beneath the book. You can type a record number directly into that field to go to a specific record.

Finally, two information items appear below these interface elements. You see the total number of records as well as whether they are sorted.

Sort status can be any of three states:

▶ Unsorted—You can use the Unsort command in the Records menu to return the records to the order of their creation.

▶ Sorted—The records are sorted according to criteria that you specify—see Hour 3.

▶ Semi-sorted—If you have sorted the data and then added some records, the table is semi-sorted.

In Browse mode, the Records menu lets you manage records. The first three commands—New Record, Duplicate Record, and Delete Record—are the most frequently used commands. Other commands let you manage found records (described in Hour 3), sort records (also in Hour 3), and manage field contents (described in Hour 19, "Finishing Up: Help, Testing, and Keeping Things Running").

Find Mode

Find mode lets you search for data. You use a layout to enter data just as you do in Browse mode, but in Find mode that data represents data to search for. Figure 2.6 shows the window in Find mode.

The status area lets you navigate through *find requests* rather than records. You'll see how to create find requests in Hour 3; they can be as simple or as complex as you want. In the most basic case, you enter one or more fields of data into the layout and click Find. If you check the Omit box, you'll find all the records that don't match the criteria. The records that are found are called a *found set*.

FIGURE 2.6
Find data.

When you perform a find, you return to Browse mode. As you can see in Figure 2.7, the status area now shows you not only the total number of records in the file but also the number of records in the found set that you're browsing. Using the book tool to navigate from one record to the next only moves within the found set (that is, it skips the unfound records).

FIGURE 2.7
The status area shows you how many records have been found.

You can sort the records within a found set; the other records remain unsorted. This can be an efficient way of displaying small sets of records from a large database.

In Find mode, the Records menu changes to a Requests menu. The first three commands on the Requests menu are similar to those on the Records menu in Browse mode: Add New Request, Duplicate Request, and Delete Request. You can use the Requests menu to perform finds and to specify how multiple requests are processed. You can also use the Show All Records to see all the records in the database again. You find out more about the Requests menu in Hour 3.

Layout Mode

The layouts that you see in the FileMaker templates and throughout this book are not complicated to create. You use Layout mode as shown in Figure 2.8 and as described in Hour 4 to do this.

FIGURE 2.8
Create and edit layouts in Layout mode.

In Layout mode, you have a Layouts menu instead of a Records menu (Browse mode) or Requests menu (Find mode). The first three commands should be familiar: New Layout/Report, Duplicate Layout, and Delete Layout. The other commands are described in Hour 4 and Hour 15, "More About Layouts."

The status area in Layout mode has a variety of editing tools to edit fields as well as graphics in the background of the layout. The book in the status area lets you move from one layout to another; you also can use the pop-up menu to select specific layouts.

Preview Mode

Finally, Preview mode lets you see how your database will look when it's printed according to the currently selected layout. Figure 2.9 shows Preview mode in action.

FIGURE 2.9
Preview data before printing.

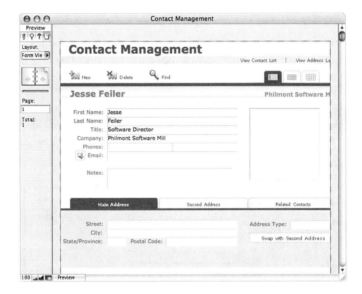

In Preview mode, the status area changes yet again. Now, the book is used to move from page to page of the output; that might be from record to record, but you may also choose to have many records per page (or many pages per record). The scroll bar moves you up and down on an individual page if it is wider or taller than the window.

The formatting in Preview mode should match what is printed. Some features are only implemented at this point. For example, you can set layouts to slide fields up or to the left: This lets you get rid of blank space in large fields. Sliding is only done when you print or go into Preview mode. In addition, summary fields are only calculated in Preview mode or when printing.

Other features are disabled in Preview mode. Most significantly, you cannot enter data or use buttons in the layout: What you see is the noninteractive representation of a printed page.

Preview mode is discussed further in Hour 5, "Printing Data."

Using Basic FileMaker Menus

The FileMaker menus change depending on the mode that you're in. Six basic menus stay the same; they are at the left of the menu bar. Their commands—or even the menus themselves—may be dimmed depending on what is selected and what type of window (if any) is open, but the menus are there. Most of the commands are standard commands available in any application. The standard commands are listed here; FileMaker-specific commands are discussed elsewhere, and references to those discussions are provided as well in this list.

▶ FileMaker application menu (Mac OS X)—The FileMaker-specific commands are Preferences and Sharing. Preferences are discussed later in this hour as well as in other sections to which they are relevant. Sharing is discussed in Part IV, "Sharing FileMaker Solutions."

▶ File—In addition to standard commands such as Open, Print, and Page Setup, you find other commands as well. The following list shows these commands and what part of the book gives more information on them:

New Database	Part III, "Creating FileMaker Solutions"
Open Remote	Part IV, "Sharing FileMaker Solutions"
Define	Submenus here let you define databases, value lists, file references, and accounts and privileges. Part III, "Creating FileMaker Solutions"
File Options	Hour 13, "Creating a FileMaker Database"
Change Password	Hour 18, "Securing Your Solutions and Databases"
Importing and Exporting	Hour 11, "Importing and Exporting Data"
Recover a database	Hour 6, "Validating and Auto-Entering Data"

▶ Edit—Standard commands such as Cut, Copy, and Paste are here along with Find/Replace and Spelling. The Export Field Contents command lets you export the contents of a field to a file that you can select. It's particularly useful for long text fields as well as for fields that contain graphics. On Windows, the Preferences and Sharing commands that are in the FileMaker application menu on Mac OS X are located in the Edit menu.

▶ View—This menu lets you select modes and views (described later in this hour), zoom in and out, show and hide the status area, show and hide the toolbars, and show and hide the Text Ruler (described in the data entry section later in this hour).

▶ Insert—This menu lets you insert files and graphics as well as constants such as the current date and time. Its From Index and From Last Visited Record commands are discussed in Hour 6. This menu and its commands are enabled depending on what type of data entry field (if any) is currently active.

▶ Format—The Format menu provides standard text formatting commands when a text field is selected (or when the text tool is selected in Layout mode).

By the Way

> Throughout this book, all the FileMaker commands are described. In some custom FileMaker solutions, access to certain commands in menus and toolbars is limited.

Working with FileMaker Windows

One important new feature in FileMaker 7 is the capability to open the same database in more than one window. With any window selected, choose Window, New Window from the menu to open a copy of it. After it is open, you can manipulate its data or layouts independently of the first one. This lets you see the same data in two different ways.

FileMaker keeps track of what is open where. If you are editing a field in one window, you can't start to edit that field in another window; you have to click out of the field in the first window before you can continue. To click out of a field, you can click in another one—but that simply repeats the problem. Clicking on the background or some other non-data-entry part of the window clicks you out of a field without clicking into another. If you do attempt to edit the same record from two windows, the error message shown in Figure 2.10 appears. Note that merely clicking in a field does not start the edit. As soon as you click in a field and press any key, you have started the edit and locked the record from other people.

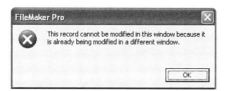

FIGURE 2.10
FileMaker warns
you about editing
the same record in
two places.

At the left of the horizontal scroll bar at the bottom of each window are four small icons. The one at the left displays the degree to which the window is scaled; the windows shown so far have been scaled to 100%. Clicking the next two icons decreases or increases the scale of the window, making the contents appear smaller or larger. If you click on the leftmost icon (which displays the current scale), it returns to 100%. The fourth icon from the left toggles the status area; you can show or hide it as you see fit. The window as a whole remains the same size; when the status area is hidden, more space is available for data.

Next to these icons is a pop-up menu that lets you choose the mode—Browse, Find, Layout, and Preview. This duplicates the functionality in the buttons at the top of the status area, but if the status area is hidden, those buttons are not visible, so you either need to use the command in the View menu or this pop-up menu.

Working with FileMaker Views

FileMaker supports three types of views in Browse mode. You can switch among them using the View menu. When you create a layout, you can limit the views available to it, but frequently all three views are available for any given layout. (You learn more about views in Hour 4.)

Form View

Form view is the view that you've seen so far in this hour. A single record is shown in the window. If the layout is too big, scroll bars let you scroll up and down or back and forth. To go to the next record, you use the book control, create a new record, find records, and so forth.

List View

In List view, records are shown in a scrolling list. To go to the next one, you can use the book or use the scroll bar. Figure 2.11 shows a List view. The views in the

Contact Management example are controlled by the tabs at the upper-right of the window. (The pointer is over the List view tab in Figure 2.11.) Compare Figures 2.11 and 2.12 to see how they differ.

FIGURE 2.11
Use a List view to see more than one record at a time.

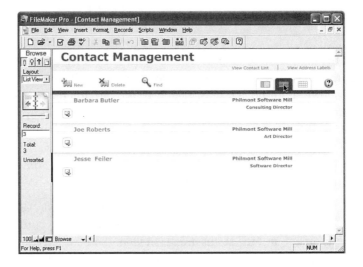

Table View

Finally, the Table view lets you view the data in much the way you see it in a spreadsheet. Figure 2.12 shows a Table view.

FIGURE 2.12
A Table view resembles a spreadsheet.

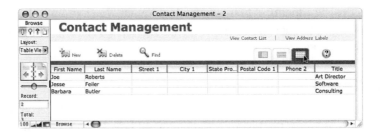

FileMaker Preferences

Like most applications, FileMaker allows you to set preferences for the way the application behaves. For most people most of the time, the default preferences are just fine. However, occasionally you need to change them—or you need to understand why FileMaker is behaving differently from the way you expected it to.

Thus, instead of treating preferences as an advanced topic, some of them are described here. You can safely come back to them later if you want. (The others are described in other hours where they are specifically relevant.)

The tabbed window shown in Figure 2.13 lets you control preferences. The first tab, as shown, is for General preferences.

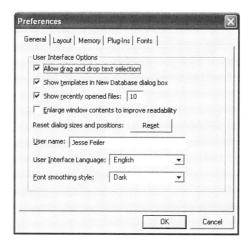

FIGURE 2.13
General prefer-
ences control basic
FileMaker behavior.

Drag-and-drop is a convenient way of moving data around: You select the data, drag it to where you want it, and drop it by releasing the mouse. Some people find drag-and-drop distracting because they're automatically dragging data they didn't intend to. You can turn drag and drop on and off in this tab.

Perhaps the most important feature here is the User Name. It can be obtained from the system automatically; however, you can also specify another username if you want. As you will see in Hour 18, security is implemented more stringently in FileMaker 7 than it was before.

Memory settings are key to *tuning* a database for best performance. The more data that is kept in memory, the faster the performance (memory access is faster than disk access). However, the more memory your application uses, the less there is for other applications. And, if your operating system supports virtual memory, the "memory" that you're using might be written out to disk periodically—so your fast memory access becomes slower disk access.

Another problem with using a large cache is that data can be left here unsaved; therefore, the cache is periodically flushed to disk. You can control how this happens, as shown in Figure 2.14.

FIGURE 2.14
Memory prefer-
ences affect
FileMaker perform-
ance.

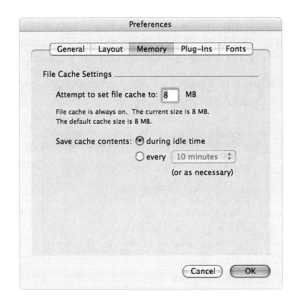

FileMaker Toolbars

Like many other applications, FileMaker provides optional toolbars. These group various commands in a toolbar that you can move around the screen. As you bring it close to the side or top of the screen or window, it snaps into place. You can use the slightly roughened edge at the left to drag it out of the window where you can position and size it exactly as you want. You show and hide the toolbars from the Toolbars subcommand in the View menu. (You can also close them with their own close boxes.)

On Windows, toolbars dock at the top of the window, underneath the menu bar. On Mac OS X, toolbars dock at the top of the screen, underneath the menu bar.

Standard Toolbar

FileMaker has two toolbars: the Standard toolbar and the Text Formatting toolbar. Figure 2.15 shows the Standard toolbar.

The Standard toolbar varies depending on the mode currently in use. Just as the menus change with modes, so, too, the toolbar changes. This section describes the constant commands on the Standard toolbar. The others are described later in this book.

FIGURE 2.15
The Standard tool-
bar brings together
useful commands
from a variety of
menus to help you
work with
FileMaker.

Starting from the left of Figure 2.15, the commands are identified. The menus in which they are located are shown in parentheses after the command.

- ▶ New Database (File)
- ▶ Open (File)
- ▶ Open Recent (File)
- ▶ File Options (File)
- ▶ Print (File)
- ▶ Spell Check (Edit/Spelling)
- ▶ Cut (Edit)
- ▶ Copy (Edit)
- ▶ Paste (Edit)
- ▶ Undo (Edit)
- ▶ New Record/Request/Layout (Records/Requests/Layouts)
- ▶ Duplicate Record/Request/Layout (Records/Requests/Layouts)
- ▶ Delete Record/Request/Layout (Records/Requests/Layouts)
- ▶ Sort (Records)
- ▶ Show All Records (Records)
- ▶ Omit Record (Records)
- ▶ Omit Multiple (Records)
- ▶ Show Omitted (Records)
- ▶ Help (Help)

The remainder of the commands are mode-specific and are described later in this book.

Text Formatting Toolbar

The Text Formatting toolbar, shown in Figure 2.16, lets you format text. It can be used to format text within a data entry field as well as text in the background of a layout.

FIGURE 2.16
Use the Text
Formatting toolbar
to format text.

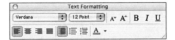

Most of the commands in the Text Formatting toolbar are found in the FileMaker menus and submenus; these are indicated in parentheses in the following list. Starting from the left of the first row, the commands are

- Font (Format/Font)
- Size (Format/Size)
- Decrease Font Size
- Increase Font Size
- Bold (Font/Style)
- Italic (Font/Style)
- Underline (Font/Style)
- Align Left (Format/Align Text)
- Align Center (Format/Align Text)
- Align Right (Format/Align Text)
- Align Full (Format/Align Text)
- Single Space (Format/Line Spacing)
- Double Space (Format/Line Spacing)
- Custom Space (Format/Line Spacing)
- Font Color (Format/Text Color)

Entering Data

Entering data in FileMaker is as simple as clicking in a field in Browse or Find mode and typing away. All the tools you expect to find for data entry are available to you in FileMaker. This section shows you what you can do. It covers text, spell checking, and other types of data that you can enter such as movies, graphics, and files.

> Hour 4 shows you how to enter and format text on layout backgrounds as well as in data entry fields. The full range of text editing tools is described there.

By the
Way

Entering Text

Click in a field to enter data. If you don't have an insertion point, the field is not editable. You can type whatever you want; use the Format menu or the text toolbar to apply formatting such as font and colors to the text. You can also align it as you see fit. You can tab from one field to the next; to back up use the combination Shift+Tab.

> Because the Tab key is used to navigate from one field to another, if you want to enter a tab into text, you need to use the combination Ctrl+Tab (Windows) or Option+Tab (Mac OS).

By the
Way

Some fields, such as date and numeric fields, format data for you after you have clicked out of the field. Currency symbols, standard numbers of decimals, and the like can be added. In addition, validation edits can be applied to some fields: You may hear a beep and see a message indicating that the data is invalid. If this happens, you are given an opportunity to correct the data or revert to the previous value (even if it was blank).

Spell Checking

You can use FileMaker's built-in spell checking to check your spelling. It's in the Edit menu. You can check a selection or the entire record. You can use the File Options command to set spelling options for the entire file, as shown in Figure 2.17.

FileMaker allows you to use a custom dictionary in addition to its own main dictionary. To add your own dictionary, choose Select Dictionary from the Edit/Spelling menu to open the window shown in Figure 2.18. If you choose the second radio button, you are prompted to select the dictionary you want to use. You can also use the New button at the bottom to create a dictionary for yourself. Many people find it useful to create such a dictionary; you can then share it among members of a workgroup. If you are creating a solution, the dictionary can be included with it to handle specific terminology relevant to the solution.

FIGURE 2.17
Use File Options to
select spelling
options.

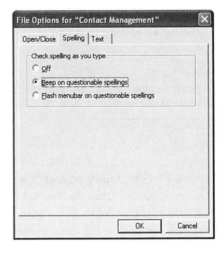

FIGURE 2.18
Add a custom dic-
tionary to
FileMaker's main
dictionary.

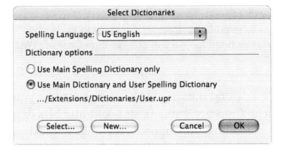

Working with Containers, Graphics, Movies, and Files

FileMaker supports *container* fields, which can contain graphics, movies, and other objects including files. To insert such an object into a container field, click in the container field and use the appropriate command from the Insert menu.

Summary

This hour provided an introduction to FileMaker. Almost everything you need to know for basic operation and entering data was presented. You learned about modes and views, menus, the status area, toolbars, and data entry. Don't worry if it seems like a lot: The following hours will focus on specific functionality, and you'll have plenty of opportunities to explore each of the topics described here.

Q&A

Q *What is the best way of working with FileMaker—toolbars, commands, or something else?*

A The best way is whatever is comfortable for you. You can use the toolbars, commands, and scripts that you or a developer write, or buttons placed on layouts. You can vary your choice of method depending on the data involved, the database, and your mood. FileMaker and database developers give you a choice.

Q *Why is some data reformatted?*

A Instead of forcing you to enter data in a specific format (day-month-year, for example), FileMaker provides options that let you enter data in a convenient way and then have it formatted automatically. This makes for more attractive reports and makes it easier to search for data. (Note that in entering dates, if you omit the year, FileMaker assumes the current year.

Workshop

Quiz

1. What can you put in container fields?

2. What is the difference between modes and views?

3. How do you set spelling options for a file?

Quiz Answers

1. Files, images, and movies. (You can put a FileMaker file into a container field!)

2. Modes control FileMaker's behavior—Browse, Find, Layout, and Preview. Views determine how data is displayed in Browse mode—Form, List, or Table.

3. Use the File Options command in the File menu.

Activities

Start to explore the FileMaker templates. Set Preferences to include the templates in the New Database dialog (with the General tab), and create your own database based on one of the templates. You should be able to enter data based on the information in this hour. Pick a database that interests you and use real data.

HOUR 3

Finding and Sorting Data

What You'll Learn in This Hour:

▶ Overview of Finding Data—The basic procedures and terminology are described.

▶ Creating Find Requests—This section provides the details on selecting data for retrieval.

▶ Omitting Data—Instead of creating complicated negative selections, you can find the data you don't want and then view the rest using Omit.

▶ Sorting Data—It's much faster to sort only the data that you're interested in rather than an entire database table.

In Hour 2, "Using FileMaker and Its Basic Templates," you explored the basics of FileMaker and saw how to enter data. In this hour, you'll learn how to find data that you've entered.

Overview of Finding Data

Databases let you manage data: store it, retrieve it, and manipulate it in various ways. In Hour 2, you saw how to store data, and in this hour you'll see how to retrieve it. (Manipulation is covered in Part II, "Modifying Templates and Databases.")

When you store data, you need to store it with an eye to retrieving it. Just as the folders in a file cabinet are set up to help you retrieve data, so, too, a good database is designed with that end in sight. (If your objective was only to store data, not to retrieve it, you could dump everything into one file drawer with no folders in it.)

This section provides background information that applies to all databases, not just FileMaker. It covers

▶ Reasons for finding data

▶ Mechanisms for finding data

▶ Setting up data for retrieval

▶ Steps for finding data

Reasons for Finding Data

There are two reasons for finding data, and they involve different processes. The first reason for finding data is to look up information that you know is present: a person, an invoice, the students in a class, and so forth.

The second reason for finding data is to search for information that might be present or that is calculated on-the-fly. This is what you do when you're doing research (or browsing the Web in many cases). Often, this type of searching involves summaries and calculations.

The two different reasons for finding data are exemplified in the following two-step search example:

1. Find all the people who live in a certain city.

2. Calculate the average income for these people.

When you're trying to understand data, you frequently use the second reason to massage the data and try to get it to yield patterns you can recognize. The first type of searching is much more specific.

When you set up data for retrieval, consider both reasons if they are likely to be used. As you'll see in the section on setting up data for retrieval, the ultimate use of the data determines how you store it.

Mechanisms for Finding Data

There are two basic mechanisms for finding data:

▶ You can find data as you need it based on whatever criteria matter to you at the time.

▶ You can set up relationships so that related data is automatically found as you browse records from a given table. (Relationships are discussed further in Hour 14, "Working with Relationships.")

Setting Up Data for Retrieval

It is not an exaggeration to say that the design of your database determines how easy it is to use to retrieve data. Fortunately, with FileMaker, it's not difficult to modify the database design. As a result, you can make changes over time to accommodate new data, as well as new search requirements. (Hour 14 discusses *normalization*, a process used to organize data storage and to make retrieval easier.)

Here are three important tips for organizing data:

▶ Create searchable fields—FileMaker can search for text within fields, but it's always easier to search on an entire field. For this reason, many databases store first and last names separately, with a third field for the name as it appears when it is all put together. To search on the last name, you search the last-name field, not part of the full-name field. With FileMaker, you can create calculation fields; they are often used to create search fields (see Hour 7, "Working with Calculations, Formulas, Functions, and Repeating Fields").

▶ Use meaningless IDs—One of the most common mistakes people make in setting up databases is to include identifying information in IDs for records. If you use a meaningless ID (such as a unique serial number that FileMaker can generate; see Hour 6, "Validating and Auto-Entering Data"), you can change any of the data in the record without changing the ID. If the ID contains information that indicates a person's status, name, or other identifying information, when that identifying information changes, so must the ID—and you lose any links to previously stored data.

▶ Game-plan your data storage—When you design a database, think not only of what you want to put in it, but also of what you want to get out. What sort of reports are required? How should they be sorted? Create search fields that allow you to retrieve and sort the data.

Steps for Finding Data

Finding data in FileMaker consists of two steps:

1. Create one or more *find requests*, which specify the data to be retrieved.

2. Perform the find to create a *found set* of the records that satisfy the find request. To actually perform the find, you can click the Find button in the status area or use any of the Find commands in the Requests menu: Perform Find, Constrain Found Set, or Extend Found Set.

At that point, you have various choices:

► Browse the record(s) returned.

► Sort the records returned. (Sorting a found set is faster than sorting the entire database; if the found set is substantially smaller than the entire database, the sorting is extremely faster.)

► Use the Omit command to see the record(s) that don't match the find request. (This is an easy way of performing "not" finds.)

► *Expand* the found set: Perform another find and add those records to the found set.

► *Constrain* the found set: Perform another find against the found set using new criteria so that only the record(s) matching both find requests remain in the found set.

All these choices are explained in the following sections.

By the Way

Each find request specifies all the criteria that must be met: If you specify a price and a color for an inventory item, both must match the data. (This is called a *logical and* or *anding*.) If you specify more than one find request, those requests are *logical ors*, or they can be described as *oring*. Within a request, all criteria must be met; across multiple requests, any of the requests can be satisfied, although within each one all must be satisfied. Thus, if you have two requests, and you specify a price in the first one and a color in the second, you will retrieve all data that matches either the price or the color.

Creating Find Requests

Begin by entering Find mode either from the command in the View menu or from the button at the top of the status area. (Custom layouts may provide Find buttons and other interface elements that automatically place you in Find mode.) This section shows you how to create a find request.

Creating the Simplest Find Requests

The simplest and most intuitive find requests are sufficient for many people. After you've entered Find mode, type a word or phrase into the field you want to search, and then perform the find. FileMaker locates all records in which the word or phrase appears at the beginning of words in the field into which you've typed it. (More complex searches are described in the following sections.)

The same simple method works for numeric, date, and time fields: Type the number, date, or time into a field, and FileMaker finds it.

Here's where your database design is important. If you've created a composite field containing city, state/province, postal code, and country, you're out of luck if you want to do a simple find. On the other hand, if you have created four separate fields (city, state/province, postal code, and country), typing "Ant" into city immediately finds Antwerp, just as typing "Italy" into country immediately finds all records for Italy. You might get unexpected results from searching on a composite field: Searching for "India" might match a country, a U.S. state (Indiana), and a city (Indianapolis).

Finding Duplicates

FileMaker provides a quick way of searching for duplicate values in a field. If you type !! in a field and then perform a find, you will retrieve all records that have duplicate values in that field (no matter what those values might be). If you need unique values (such as ID numbers), you can enforce uniqueness with validations as discussed in Hour 6.

Finding Text

FileMaker provides a number of more sophisticated searching tools for text. They're simple to use:

▶ Use quotes to match one or more characters anywhere in the text field (not just at the beginning). "werp" finds Antwerp.

▶ Use @ to indicate any single character (a *wildcard*). @arlton matches carlton, but it does not match Ritz-Carlton.

▶ Use * to indicate any number of characters (0 or more) to match. *arlton finds Ritz-Carlton.

▶ Use = to search for whole words. =Paris finds Paris but not Parisian.

▶ Use == to search for an exact match. ==Tokyo Japan finds Tokyo Japan but not Tokyo, Japan (note the comma) and not Tokyo Japan Pacific Rim.

▶ Use quotes around special characters such as @ and * to search for those characters. "*arlton" finds *arlton but does not find Ritz-Carlton.

▶ To perform a case-sensitive search, you need to change the default language for indexing and sorting text in the field in question. You can do this when you want to conduct a search, or you can set up the field to always use case-sensitive searching. (Normally, you either use case-sensitive searching all the time on a particular field or not at all, so setting up the field to use or not use case-sensitive searching, instead of adjusting it for individual searches, is generally the way to go.) Use the Options button in the Define Database dialog to set the language to Unicode rather than English, French, or whatever language you are using. Figure 3.1 shows the Unicode setting. This forces FileMaker to treat lowercase and uppercase letters differently. If you use a natural-language setting (such as Italian), FileMaker uses the rules of each language to determine which characters are to be treated similarly. The Define Database dialog is discussed in Hour 13, "Creating a FileMaker Database."

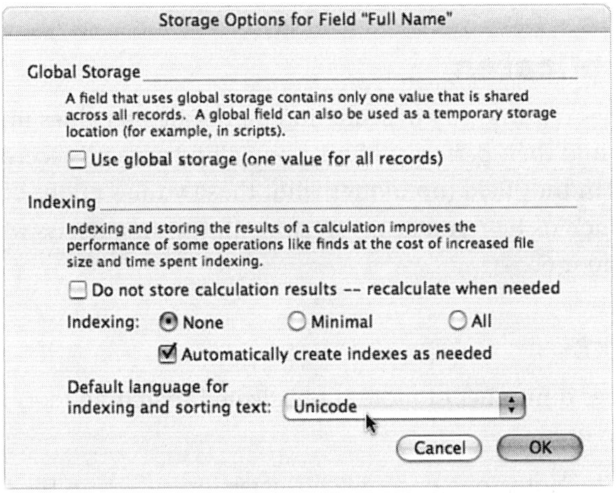

FIGURE 3.1
Set the language of a field to Unicode to do case-sensitive searching, sorting, and indexing.

Finding Numbers, Dates, and Times

Before starting to find numbers, dates, and times, it's important to note that FileMaker can apply various types of formatting to these values. (You'll see how to do that in Hour 4, "Introducing Layouts.") In a numeric field, the currency and percent symbols, as well as the number of decimal points, are determined by the format, which is stored separately from the value. Thus, the value 1.25 can be represented with various formats, as $1.25, 1.25%, 1.3, or 1.250. When you search, you find based on the value, not the formatted value. Searching for 1.25 finds all these values. (In a text field, however, the text is what it is. $1.25, 1.25, and 1.25% are different values when stored in a text field.)

The same principle applies to dates and times: The formatting is stored separately from the value. Thus, April 4, 2003 has the same value as 4/4/2003.

By the Way

Prior to FileMaker 7, it was possible to automatically coerce Boolean values to numeric ones, placing values such as yes or no in a numeric field. That is no longer possible. The `GetAsNumber` function converts such values to 0 (false) and 1 (true).

Just as with text, you can use some additional features for finding numbers, dates, and times:

▶ //—Used to indicate today's date in a field that you are searching on.

▶ ?—Used to search for an invalid date or time. Note that if you set automatic validation options, you may not have invalid dates and times, but if you set the option to allow a date or time to be formatted as entered, such anomalies can occur. (There is more on this in Hour 4.)

Ranges of Data

You can find ranges of data by inserting symbols into the field(s) on which you are searching. Figure 3.2 shows the Symbols pop-up menu. (You can also type these symbols into a field manually.)

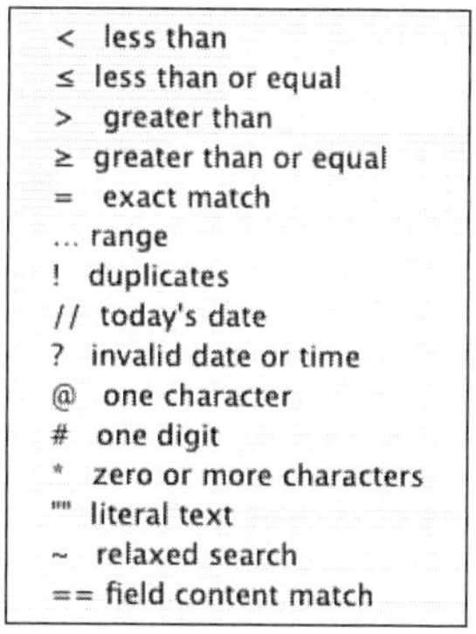

```
<    less than
≤    less than or equal
>    greater than
≥    greater than or equal
=    exact match
...  range
!    duplicates
//   today's date
?    invalid date or time
@    one character
#    one digit
*    zero or more characters
""   literal text
~    relaxed search
==   field content match
```

FIGURE 3.2
Insert symbols to search ranges of data.

The first five symbols are normal relational operators. For a field that contains a price, the entry

<5

finds all records that have a price of less than five (dollars/Euros/Yen or the like).

Ranges and relations also apply to text. The entry

<f

finds names such as Edgardo and Diana.

The language option described previously applies to ranges. If you use Unicode for the language, upper- and lowercase characters are treated differently. You can use two or three dots to specify a range of data. To find dates in the month of April (using standard U.S. month/day/year order), you can search on this entry in a date field:

```
4/1 .. 4/30
```

FileMaker assumes the current year if no year is supplied.

The other symbols in the Symbols pop-up menu were described previously in this section. You can either type them into fields or insert them into the currently selected field by using the pop-up menu. (The ~ for relaxed searching is used in Japanese.)

Omitting Data

Often it is useful to find records that do not fulfill your find request; you do this by clicking the Omit checkbox in the status area before performing the search. Alternatively, after you complete the search, you can use the Show Omitted Only command in the Records menu to switch the found set from those found to those omitted.

You can manually omit records with the Omit Record command in that menu or with the Omit Multiple command. Omit Record omits a single record, whereas Omit Multiple presents a dialog that lets you choose how many records (including the currently viewed record) should be omitted.

Omitting records is useful in a number of cases. Two of them are described here:

▶ If a certain value (or absence of data) is to be excluded from analysis, search on that value and omit those records. The entry = finds blank values in a field and can be useful in this case.

▶ If data is categorized in a number of categories that you want to retrieve, it may be easier to use Omit. If you want to examine all inventory items that are in stock or on order, it may be easier to retrieve all out-of-stock items and omit them.

By the Way

Once again, the design of your database helps you retrieve data. Considering the types of searches you want to conduct should affect the fields and values you choose for the database.

Sorting Data

Often you want to sort data after you retrieve it. Choose Records, Sort from the menu to open the window shown in Figure 3.3.

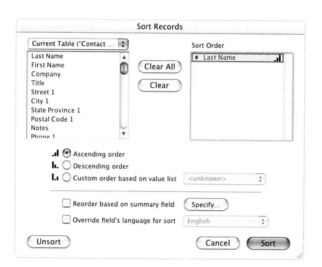

FIGURE 3.3
Use the Sort command to sort data.

> Sorting can be expensive in terms of computer power; if you need sorted data, it is best to perform any finds first so that you can sort only the found set.

By the Way

To set up a sort, double-click the first field on which you want to sort from the scrolling list at the left. When it appears in the right-hand list (Sort Order), you can use the radio buttons at the bottom to choose how to sort it: ascending order, descending order, or a value list. (Value lists are discussed in Hour 4; they let you sort on an arbitrary order that you define.) To perform a complex sort, select each of the fields you want to sort by in turn, and choose the sorting option for it.

The two checkboxes at the bottom let you use a summary field for ordering data (more on this in Hour 5, "Printing Data") and to override the sorting language.

You can add more fields to the sort using the same process. Drag each field up or down in the right-hand scrolling view to order the sort. FileMaker properly handles sorting for text, numbers, dates, and times. If, for example, the topmost field is Name and the next one is Birthday, you sort the found set alphabetically and by birthday within that order.

Summary

In this hour, you saw how to find data. You saw not only what methods are used for finding data but also how thinking about data retrieval can help you organize your database and its tables and fields.

You saw how to enter data (in Hour 2) and retrieve it. In Hour 4, you'll see the basics of using layouts both for data entry and retrieval.

Q&A

Q *What is probably the biggest waste of computing power and time in using FileMaker?*

A Sorting entire database tables when sorting only the relevant found records would suffice.

Q *How does the FileMaker find mechanism compare to that of SQL?*

A SQL is used not just to create database queries but also to manipulate the database. Through its xDBC interface, FileMaker can respond to SQL queries. It's easy to build up complex retrieval requests through FileMaker requests. Each request is fairly simple, and FileMaker combines them into a complex retrieval. In this way, many people find FileMaker easier than SQL.

Workshop

Quiz

1. How do you find a non-blank field?

2. How do you find a blank field?

3. What do you call the results of a find?

4. Can you mix find requests that have the Omit option checked with those that don't?

Quiz Answers

1. The * character matches one or more characters of any kind, so you can simply search on * in the field.

2. Use = to match what is in the text field: If nothing follows =, that's what will be found—empty fields.

3. A found set.

4. Yes.

Activities

Take one of the templates that you're interested in and enter some test data. Practice finding data that you know you've entered. Also practice searching for data that you know is not present. Experiment with the wildcard characters (@ and *).

HOUR 4

Introducing Layouts

What You'll Learn in This Hour:

▶ About Layouts—This is a brief introduction to layouts, the FileMaker mechanism for entering and displaying data.

▶ Using the Layout Status Area—As in other modes, the status area changes when you're in Layout mode. A variety of tools is available.

▶ How to Add and Format Fields—You may want to use formatting options to customize the templates. This section shows you how.

Layouts specify the formatting of data in FileMaker. All the data that you've seen in this book has been in one layout or another. FileMaker comes with a variety of templates. This hour introduces you to templates in ways you're most likely to work with them to start. You'll see how to modify existing templates and customize them for your own use.

In Hour 15, "More About Layouts," you'll see how to create layouts from scratch and how to use more advanced techniques for your custom solutions.

Value lists, actually elements of databases that you create, are described in this hour rather than in Part II, "Modifying Templates and Databases," because they are used to support interface elements, such as pop-up menus, radio buttons, and checkboxes.	**By the** Way

About Layouts

Layouts display all the data that you see in FileMaker. They can be as simple or as complex as you want; the layouts in the FileMaker templates provide examples of the range of features available to you.

A layout is always based on a single table. You can display data from other tables in the layout by using relationships. (Individual fields can be displayed, as well as lists of related records in interface elements known as *portals*, which are discussed in Hour 15.)

Layouts have one or more *parts*. The main part of a layout displays detailed data and is called the *body*. The other layout parts are as follows:

- ▶ Title—Text, graphics, and data fields that appear only on the first page or screen of a layout.

- ▶ Title footer—Text, graphics, and data fields that appear only on the last page or screen of a layout.

- ▶ Header—Text, graphics, and data fields that appear at the top of each page or screen of a layout.

- ▶ Footer—Text, graphics, and data fields that appear at the bottom of each page or screen of a layout.

- ▶ Leading grand summary—Text, graphics, and data fields (including calculated summaries) that appear before the detail data.

- ▶ Trailing grand summary—Text, graphics, and data fields (including calculated summaries) that appear after the detail data.

- ▶ Subsummary when sorted by—Text, graphics, and data fields (including calculated summaries) that appear before or after each section of sorted data.

Not all the parts appear in all summaries; at least one part must appear, but it can be any part. (Many short reports have no body data, but only present one or another form of summary. Hour 15 has more information on summaries.)

To work with a layout, you enter Layout mode in any of the standard ways: from the View menu, from the buttons at the top of the status area, or from the pop-up menu at the left of the horizontal scroll bar at the bottom of the window. Figure 4.1 shows Layout mode and the Layout status area.

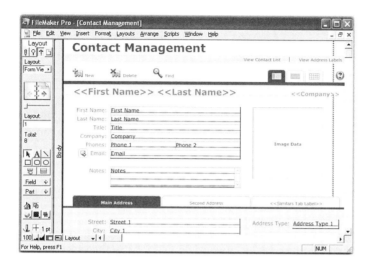

FIGURE 4.1
Use Layout mode
to design your data-
base interface.

Using the Layout Status Area

The tools in the status area are a combination of FileMaker-specific tools and
tools that might be familiar to you from other applications. From top to bottom,
they are described in this section.

Mode Buttons

At the top, the four standard buttons let you switch among Browse, Find, Layout,
and Preview modes.

Navigation Tools

Next, the book and its associated interface elements appear. It enables you to
browse the various layouts sequentially (with the book) or choose a layout that
you want to work with from the pop-up menu. The behavior is exactly the same
as in Browse mode (where these interface elements control records) and in Find
mode (where these interface elements control find requests).

Tool Panel

Beneath these you'll find the *tool panel*, a set of 10 tools for designing layouts. The
tools in the tool panel are also available in the Tools toolbar (available in the
View menu in Layout mode), which is shown in Figure 4.2.

FIGURE 4.2
The Tools toolbar
contains Layout
tools.

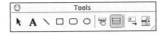

Use these tools to make your layout easier to use and more attractive. You can add text to the layout to identify fields or to provide brief instructions, but see Hour 17, "Working with Summaries and Layout Parts," for many more possibilities. When you group fields together for readability or convenience, you can enclose them in boxes to emphasize the grouping.

The first six of these may be familiar to you from other applications that let you manipulate graphics:

▶ Click the *arrow pointer* to select items in the layout. When they are selected, small rectangular handles appear; you can resize the object using the handles, and you can drag the object by dragging on the interior of an interface element. Multiple selections can be obtained by Shift-clicking with the arrow pointer or by dragging a selection rectangle around the objects on the layout you want to select after you have selected the arrow pointer.

▶ The *text tool* (letter A) is used to enter text on the layout. Click it, and then click on the layout and type the text you want to enter. You can use the Format menu to style the text. After the text is entered, you can use the pointer tool to move it or resize and reshape its box.

▶ The *line tool* enables you to draw lines. To constrain lines to being horizontal or vertical, hold down the Shift key while drawing; to constrain them to 45 degrees, hold down the Ctrl (Windows) or Option (Mac OS) key while drawing.

▶ The *rectangle tool* draws rectangles. To constrain it to a square, hold down Ctrl (Windows) or Option (Mac OS) while drawing.

▶ The *rounded rectangle tool* draws rectangles with rounded corners. To constrain it to a square, hold down Ctrl (Windows) or Option (Mac OS) while drawing.

▶ The *oval tool* draws ovals. Using the same key combinations, you can force it to draw circles.

The next four tools go beyond simple graphics. Each is discussed in more detail in Hour 15.

▶ The *button tool* enables you to draw a button anywhere in the layout. When you finish drawing, a dialog prompts you for the behavior that button should have.

▶ The *portal tool* enables you to draw a portal through which related records can be seen.

▶ The *field tool* enables you to insert a field into the layout. Drag it to the approximate location that you want and release it. From the pop-up menu, you can select the field you want to add. Then, you can use the arrow pointer tool to resize, reshape, and move the field.

▶ The *part tool* enables you to insert a new part into the layout. Parts are designed to show information on each page (headers and footers) or information for specific groups of records (summaries, for example). There is more on parts in Hour 17.

Using Graphics Controls

Beneath the tool panel are two sets of palettes: the Fill controls palette and the Pen controls. Both function in somewhat similar ways. If one or more objects in the layout are selected, the settings of these controls affect those objects. If no objects are selected, the settings become defaults and are used for new objects until they are changed.

Figure 4.3 shows the palettes.

FIGURE 4.3
Palettes are located toward the bottom of the status area.

Using the Fill Controls

The first row of the Fill controls contains a paint bucket icon identifying it; next to it a sample of the current fill pattern and color is shown.

The three buttons on the second row have the functions discussed in the following sections (from left to right).

Using the Fill Color Palette

The first button enables you to select the color to use. The default colors are set in the Color Palette area of the Layout tab of the Preferences dialog, as shown in Figure 4.4.

If you want to use another color, you can select it from the system palette by clicking Other Color at the bottom of the palette, but that defeats the notion of a constrained palette of colors.

FIGURE 4.4
Set the default palette in Preferences.

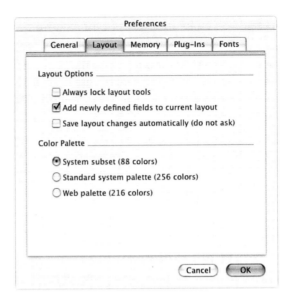

Using the Fill Pattern Palette

The second button enables you to select the fill pattern to use for the interiors of rectangles, ovals, and data entry fields. Figure 4.5 shows the Fill pattern choices.

FIGURE 4.5
Set the fill pattern.

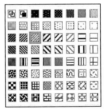

At the upper left, the first two icons have special meanings. The first one is a transparency tool; objects using this fill pattern pick up whatever color or background is behind them. This is useful for layouts that do not have a white background. The next icon to the right sets the fill color to the currently selected color. The remaining patterns use the fill color in various patterns to fill objects.

Three-Dimensional Effects

The third button enables you to select 3D effects for object borders. The effects are all achieved using an assumption of light coming from the upper-left of the screen. The three effects are

▶ Embossed—The object appears raised above the plane of the layout. It is lighter on the top and left outside edges and slightly shadowed on the right and bottom.

▶ Engraved—The object appears depressed into the plane of the layout. It is slightly shadowed on the inner edges of the top and left and slightly lighter on the bottom and right sides.

▶ Drop shadow—This effect is the traditional effect achieved with a dark line shadowing the right and bottom edges of an object.

Using the Pen Controls

The Pen controls are located beneath the Fill controls. You use the same types of tools to set colors and patterns. In addition, instead of setting 3D effects, you can set the line width for the pen.

The pen is used to draw lines and borders around objects. (Three-dimensional effects are drawn in the pen's border area around objects, and they work best when the pen is set to transparent and a width of 2 points.)

How to Add and Format Fields

Much of what you may want to do with layouts at first has to do with formatting data entry fields. You may want to change the format and behavior of existing fields, or you may want to add new fields to the layout. This section shows you how to do both.

Format Painter, discussed in Hour 15, is a convenient way to copy format attributes from one field to another—or to many others. Don't think that you have to manually set each of the formatting elements described here for each field!

By the Way

Adding Fields to the Layout

Adding fields to the layout couldn't be easier: Drag the Field tool from the status area to the approximate place where you want the field to be, or click the Field tool on the Tools toolbar. The Specify Field dialog opens, as shown in Figure 4.6.

Select the field you want to use; you can use the pop-up menu at the top of the dialog to choose from the basic table for the layout and any related tables. You can also choose whether to automatically create a field label.

FIGURE 4.6
Select the field for
a data entry field.

The field is created using the current defaults from the Fill and Pen controls. Using the arrow pointer, you can move it around and reshape or resize it as you see fit.

For newly created fields, as well as those that already exist in layouts, you have a variety of formatting options available. They are described in the remainder of this section. Six of them are dependent on the type of data in the field (text, number, date, time, graphic, or portal); the remaining two apply to all fields and specify the format and behavior of the field.

Because FileMaker does data conversion where necessary, you can often get away with entering numbers, dates, and times into text fields. It is always best to select the exact type of field that matches the data it will store. One reason is that in doing so you can use the automatic formatting of numbers, dates, and times. If you store them in text fields, the automatic formatting features are not available.

Text

Figure 4.7 shows the Format text menu.

The first section of commands in the Format menu is also available in Browse mode when you select a text entry field.

The first commands, such as those available on the submenus for Font and Size, are standard text processing commands. The Style submenu, shown in Figure 4.8, shows the styles you can apply to selected text. (A common error in word processing is to set a style without having text selected; nothing happens, and that's as it should be. If you set a style without having text selected, it will apply to the next text that you type.)

FIGURE 4.7
Use the Format menu to format data entry fields.

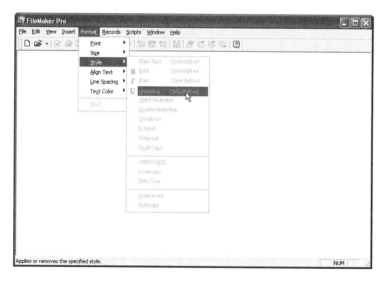

FIGURE 4.8
Use the Style sub-menu to improve readability of text.

Figure 4.9 shows the Align Text submenu.

As you can see, you can set both vertical and horizontal alignment for text. As you'll see in Hour 5, "Printing Data," if you want to automatically slide partially empty text fields up to optimize printing, the settings shown here (Left and Top) are important to set.

FIGURE 4.9
Use the Align Text
submenu to make
text consistently
aligned.

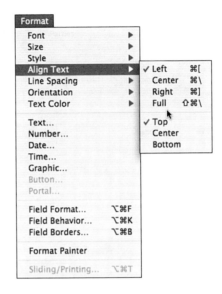

It is common to right-align labels for data entry fields and to place them to the
left of the fields themselves; it is also common to left-align labels and place them
above left-aligned fields. Sometimes you create tabular arrays of data entry fields
and place center-aligned labels at the tops of the columns.

The next three commands on the Format menu (Line Spacing, Orientation for
Asian fonts, and Text Color) are standard commands.

The next command on the Format menu is Text, which opens the dialog shown
in Figure 4.10.

FIGURE 4.10
Use the Text
Format dialog to
make settings from
a single window.

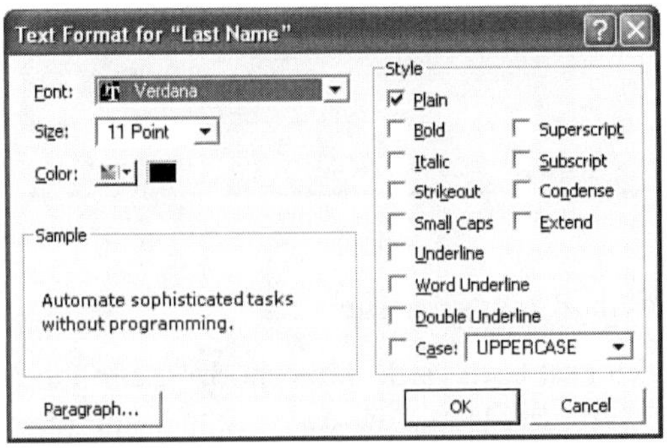

As you can see, the Text Format dialog combines many of the settings that appear in separate submenus of the Format menu. The Paragraph button opens the dialog shown in Figure 4.11.

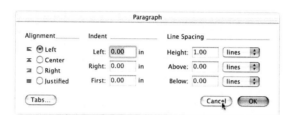

FIGURE 4.11
Use the Paragraph dialog to set margins and spacing within a paragraph.

Before leaving the area of text formatting, it is worthwhile to note that you can set a default font for each input type using the Fonts tab in FileMaker preferences, as shown in Figure 4.12. This is particularly important for non-Roman alphabets.

By the Way

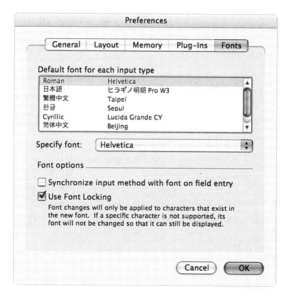

FIGURE 4.12
Use the Fonts tab in FileMaker preferences to set default fonts.

Number

When you select a field defined as a number, you can set specific numeric formatting by choosing Format, Number from the menu to open the Number Format dialog, shown in Figure 4.13.

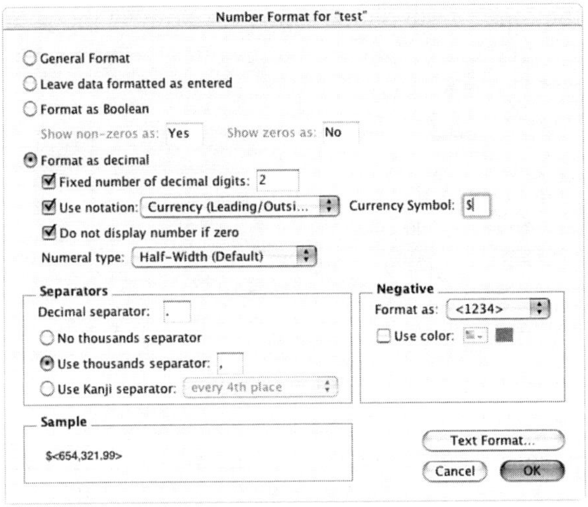

FIGURE 4.13
Format numbers
and currency.

FIGURE 4.13
Format numbers
and currency.

As you can see, it allows you to set options for automatic formatting. The key choice is to remove the default setting, Leave Data Formatted as Entered. By choosing one (or more) of the other options, you will have consistent-looking data no matter how it is entered.

Note that validation of data is covered in Hour 6, "Validating and Auto-Entering Data"; formatting takes over after the raw data has been shown to be valid.

The Text Format button at the bottom right opens the general text formatting dialog shown previously in Figure 4.10.

Date

FileMaker provides a variety of date formats in the Date Format dialog, shown in Figure 4.14. It, too, allows access to the Text Format dialog shown previously.

Time

Fields defined as containing time value can be formatted with the Time Format dialog shown in Figure 4.15. You can access this dialog by choosing Format, Time from the menu.

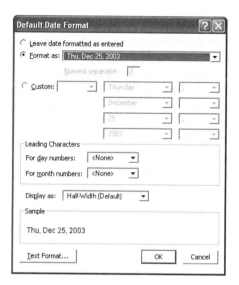

FIGURE 4.14
Automatically format dates.

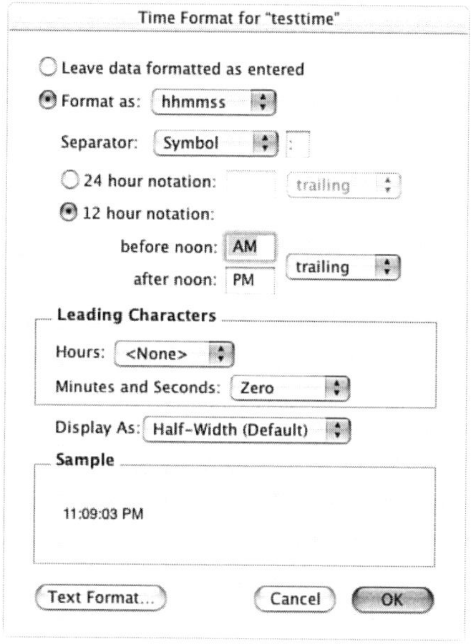

FIGURE 4.15
Automatically format time values.

Graphic

Finally, FileMaker allows you to store graphics in container fields. Many of the templates have such fields to allow you to drag and drop or paste images into them (you'll find them in the Contact Management and Asset Management templates, for example).

You can set options using the Graphic Format dialog, which is available by choosing Format, Graphic from the menu, as shown in Figure 4.16.

FIGURE 4.16
Set graphic
options.

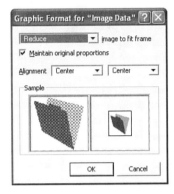

As you can see, the options determine what FileMaker should do if the graphic is not the same size as the container.

Button

You can attach script steps and scripts to interface elements using the Button command. You'll see how to do this in detail in Hour 9, "Working with Scripts."

Portal

You can format a portal by choosing Format, Portal from the menu. This is discussed in Hour 15.

Field Format

The final three commands on the Format menu relate to how the selected field(s) appear and behave regardless of the type of data it contains.

By the Way

> If you have used FileMaker in the past, you'll notice that the Field Format and Field Behavior dialogs consolidate settings that were scattered in several places in the Format menu.

The Field Format dialog box appears if you choose Format, Field Format from the menu. The default value for data entry fields is the Edit Box as shown in Figure 4.17. It enables you to type data into the field. You can use an option to include a scroll bar in the field.

FIGURE 4.17
Use the Field
Format dialog to
set up each data
entry field.

Obviously, standard edit boxes are useful, but you can leverage the power of
FileMaker with the other choices in the pop-up menu:

▶ Pop-up List

▶ Pop-up Menu

▶ Checkbox Set

▶ Radio Button Set

Each of these provides a mechanism for users to choose from predefined values
instead of typing in new text. In general, the more you can use such predefined
values, the easier it is for everyone. The user doesn't have to worry about whether
a state name should be entered as N.Y., NY, or New York. Likewise, the person
who searches the database needn't worry about searching on N.Y. and missing
those NY entries.

All these interface elements rely on a *value list* to store their entries. If you choose
one of these elements, you can then choose the value list to use with it as shown
in Figure 4.18.

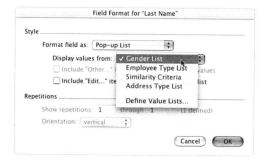

FIGURE 4.18
Associate a value
list with an inter-
face element.

Value lists are defined as part of a database file, and they can be associated with any number of interface elements. You can create a value list by choosing Define Value Lists from the pop-up menu (or from the Define submenu in the File menu). Figure 4.19 shows the Define Value Lists dialog.

FIGURE 4.19
Create and edit value lists.

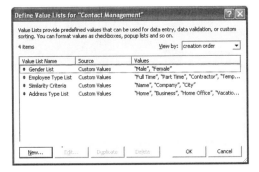

The summary shown in Figure 4.19 shows the values in each list; double-clicking a list or selecting one and clicking the Edit button opens the Edit Value List dialog, shown in Figure 4.20.

FIGURE 4.20
Work with a single value list.

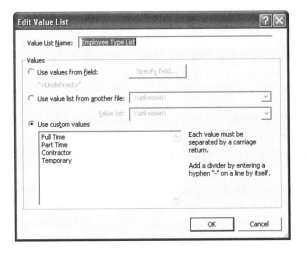

As you see, you can use values for specific fields for the value list, but on many occasions, you use custom values as is the case here. A frequent modification to the FileMaker templates is to add additional values to the value lists. Simply type the new value in the list (one value per line) in the place you want it to appear. It then appears in all pop-up menus, checkboxes, and the like that use the value list.

Even more useful is the fact that a value list can be used to sort a database or found set in custom order. In the Sort dialog (described in Hour 3, "Finding and Sorting Data"), simply select the field on which you want to sort, select Custom Order Based on Value List, and then choose the value list as shown in Figure 4.21.

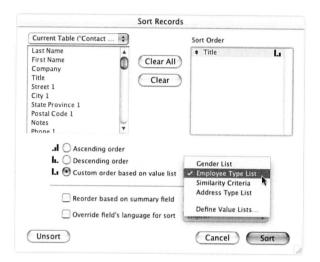

FIGURE 4.21
Use a value list for a custom sort.

The Field Format dialog also provides two additional choices for use with value lists:

▶ Other—The user can type in a value other than those in the value list.

▶ Edit—The user can edit the value list as data is being entered.

In the first case, the value list cannot be modified by the users although they can enter data that is not in the value list; in the second, it is modified as users enter data. Some FileMaker solutions start out with value lists that have only a few entries, and the users construct them as their needs require using the Edit command.

Field Behavior

Figure 4.22 shows the Field Behavior dialog. A new feature in FileMaker 7 allows you to specify whether the field can be used in Browse or Find mode. Previously, this option was unavailable, and many people made separate layouts for Browse and Find.

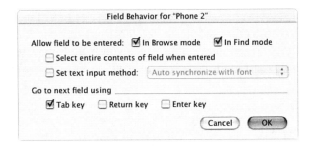

As you can see at the bottom of Figure 4.22, one of the behaviors that you can set
is how to automatically go to the next field. To do this, you need to set up a *tab
order* for the fields in the layout. The automatic layout goes from left to right and
top to bottom, but you can adjust it as you see fit. Choose Layouts, Set Tab Order
from the menu to do this. The command opens the dialog shown in Figure 4.23.

FIGURE 4.23
Set tab order.

If you choose Edit Tab Order, the layout is shown with numbered tab fields. You
can double-click in each one and supply a new number. FileMaker lets you know
if you've skipped or duplicated any numbers. Figure 4.24 shows the editable tab
order display.

If you are modifying a template by adding a field, you may want to adjust the tab
order.

Field Borders

Finally, choose Format, Field Borders to format the borders of a field. In the Field
Borders dialog, you can select which of the four borders (or a combination) to format. At the lower left of the dialog, pop-up menus let you choose the color, pattern, and width of the border. (Remember that if you're using 3D effects, a 2-point
transparent border probably works best.)

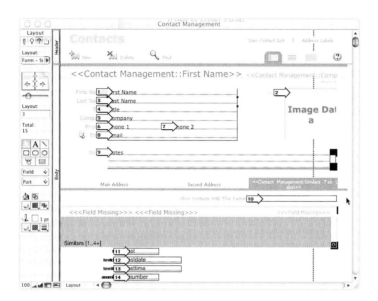

FIGURE 4.24
Customize tab order.

Figure 4.25 shows the Field Borders dialog.

FIGURE 4.25
Set field borders.

Summary

This hour showed you the basics of how layouts work, and it provided the information that you need to customize layouts and modify layouts from the templates you are using. Hour 15 shows you how to create templates from scratch.

There's only one hour left to master the basics of FileMaker; in Hour 5, you'll find out how to print your data.

Q&A

Q *How can you find out the best practices or good design tips for FileMaker layouts?*

A Watch how people, including yourself, use FileMaker. Keep an eye out for mistakes: Often mistakes are the result of faulty interface design. Train yourself to notice interfaces wherever you find them—on Web pages, in software programs, and even in the real world.

Q *Do you need separate layouts for browsing and finding?*

A No, but you may decide to create them. You can now specify whether each data entry field is modifiable in Browse or Find mode, so many cases in which separate layouts were necessary no longer require them.

Workshop

Quiz

1. Where are the 3D effects for fields drawn?

2. What is the difference between a title and a header?

3. When working with value lists, what is the difference between Edit and Other?

Quiz Answers

1. In the border area; for that reason, if you're using 3D effects, consider using a transparent 2-point border.

2. A title appears at the top of the first page of a layout; a header appears at the top of every page of a layout.

3. Edit enables you to edit the underlying value list; Other enables you to enter a value to the current field, but the value list is not modified.

Activities

Using one of the FileMaker templates, view the value lists. Modify the value list and see how the interface changes.

Using that or another template, experiment with field formats, changing borders, 3D effects, and colors.

HOUR 5

Printing Data

What You'll Learn in This Hour:

▶ About Printing—You start with a basic overview of printing.

▶ Print a Layout—Here's how to print a single layout.

▶ Print Wide and Tall Layouts—For wide or tall layouts, here's what you need to do.

▶ Prepare Layouts for Printing: Margins and Sliding—Paper is usually not the same size and shape as the computer screen. Here's how to move from one to the other.

▶ Printing Information About the Database—In addition to the data, you can print information about the database layout, scripts, and the like.

▶ Printing Envelopes and Labels—One of the most frequent tasks you may have to perform is printing envelopes and labels. It's tricky, but not difficult to master.

In this part of the book, you've received an introduction to FileMaker. You've seen how to browse and enter data, how to find data, and how to modify layouts that display data. That covers the basics of FileMaker with one exception: printing.

If you use FileMaker interactively, you can search for data and display it onscreen. You might want to print the data that you've found, and you'll find out how to do so in this hour. In other cases, you might want to enter data interactively, but rather than do ad hoc finds, you can prepare printable layouts and scripts to sort, search, and organize data for printing. These reports can be stored and distributed as needed.

You'll find the basics of printing in this hour, and you'll learn more about Preview mode. You'll also see how to merge data and how to prepare labels and envelopes.

About Printing

One pillar of the graphical user interface is WYSIWYG—What You See Is What You Get. The goal is for the display onscreen to be identical to what is printed on a page. Unfortunately, that long-ago goal has never been totally met, and, in fact, it causes some problems. These problems include the fact that the dimensions and shape of a computer screen are usually different from those of paper, color on paper (a reflective medium) appears differently than it does onscreen (a transmissive medium), and the resolution of computer screens is different from that of printers.

For all these reasons and more, FileMaker provides two mechanisms for addressing the need for printed data:

▶ You can create layouts specifically geared for printing. Their dimensions can match standard page sizes (including labels, envelopes, and postcards). In addition, they can use fonts, colors, and other features particularly appropriate for printing. Switching from one layout to another is simple using the Layout pop-up menu in Browse mode.

▶ Preview mode takes the currently selected layout and the data that it displays and performs various steps to prepare for printing. These steps include calculating page breaks (*pagination*); computing summaries; and setting headers, footers, and titles.

In addition, FileMaker provides the ability to print information about the database, including its structure, its fields, and other information.

If you want to print a single record (or find request), the simplest way is to choose File, Print from the menu (Cmd-P) [Ctrl+P]. The standard Print dialog appears, you can choose the number of copies, and you'll have your output.

Issues arise in more complex cases when you have many records to print or when they don't fit on a piece of paper. The following sections show you how to handle those issues.

By the Way

Before proceeding, look closely at the layout of the database with which you're working. Many FileMaker solutions have Print buttons on their layout that automatically switch to printable layouts and even run scripts to handle all the intermediate steps described in the following sections.

Print a Layout

You can print a layout itself in various formats. Figure 5.1 shows the FileMaker options for a standard Print dialog on Mac OS X. You'll find similar options in the Print dialog for Windows shown in Figure 5.2.

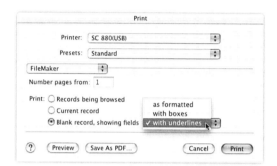

FIGURE 5.1
On Mac OS X, use the pop-up menu in the Print dialog to select FileMaker options.

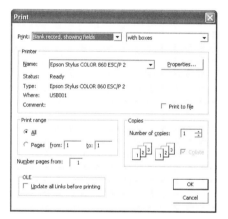

FIGURE 5.2
On Windows, the FileMaker options appear in the Print dialog.

As you can see in the figures, you can limit the output to the current record or all records being browsed (the found set).

The page range that you specify for this and other print jobs is applied after the selection is made; thus, if you specify pages 2 through 5, you print pages 2 through 5 of the current record's layout or of the found set. To print records 2 through 5, find them using one of the techniques outlined in Hour 3, "Finding and Sorting Data," and then print all the pages for those records.

The Blank Record radio button provides you with a choice of printing data as formatted, with boxes, or with lines for the data entry fields. This option is a simple way of creating data entry forms if you use either the boxes or the underlines.

Print Wide and Tall Layouts

For layouts that are too wide or too tall to print on a single piece of paper, you can employ a number of strategies.

First, if the layout is only slightly larger than the paper in one dimension, you can use the Page Setup dialog to print horizontally (landscape) or vertically (portrait). Horizontal page setups are often the answer to printing problems: It's not surprising because most screens are oriented horizontally (wider than tall), and many layouts designed for screens fit naturally in that format.

For layouts that are substantially bigger than a single sheet of paper, you can specify how the screen image is broken up. In Layout mode, choose the Printing tab in the Layout Setup dialog (choose Layouts, Layout Setup) to open the dialog shown in Figure 5.3. Here, you can select how the printing is carried out.

FIGURE 5.3
Specify printing order in the Printing tab of the Layout Setup dialog.

Prepare Layouts for Printing: Margins and Sliding

You'll see how to create layouts from scratch in Hour 15, "More About Layouts," but Hour 4, "Introducing Layouts," showed you some of the basics of working with layouts. Here are two techniques for preparing layouts for printing that you can use with existing layouts, such as those in the templates.

Margins

When you are in Layout mode, dashed lines show you the borders of the current page size. (You set the size as in other applications by choosing Print, Page Setup from the menu.)

Figure 5.4 shows that the limit of the printable area for the currently selected page size is just under 4 inches wide. (For the sake of illustration, a narrow page size—that of a vertically oriented envelope—has been used with the Contacts template.)

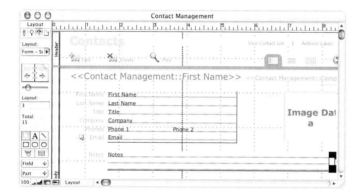

FIGURE 5.4
Dashed lines show the page boundaries in Layout mode.

With the page boundaries in mind, you can create more effective printed layouts. Note that if you want to see the actual page image (including data), you can use Preview mode as shown in Figure 5.5.

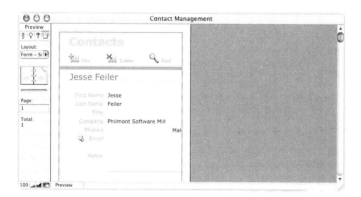

FIGURE 5.5
Preview mode shows formatted data.

Sliding

One or more fields can be set to *slide* when printing occurs. To set sliding options, use the Sliding/Printing command in the Format menu of Layout mode when you have highlighted the appropriate fields. The Set Sliding/Printing dialog opens, as shown in Figure 5.6.

FIGURE 5.6
Set sliding options
with the
Sliding/Printing
dialog.

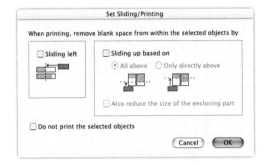

Sliding is done only in Preview mode and in printing (which relies on Preview mode). It is used to tighten up the output. For example, you can tighten up the printed text from three text fields (First, Middle, and Last Name).

Start by entering the data into the three fields in Browse mode as shown in Figure 5.7. Make sure that the alignment for the three fields is Left.

FIGURE 5.7
Enter data in
Browse mode.

Set sliding by selecting all three fields in Layout mode and opening the Sliding/Printing dialog. Click Sliding Left.

You select the fields that will actually slide, as well as the field into which the sliding fields will slide. In other words, select all three, not just the two fields on the right.

When you go into Preview mode, you'll see that the fields have slid together as shown in Figure 5.8.

FIGURE 5.8
In Preview mode, the fields slide together.

The fields still have space between them, however. That is because there is space between the fields in the layout. Butt the fields right up against one another with no (or very little) space between the fields, as shown in Figure 5.9.

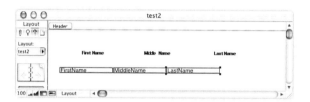

FIGURE 5.9
Butt the fields up against one another to reduce space after sliding.

Now when you go into Preview mode, you'll see that the fields are compressed within themselves, and only the minimal space you've left between them is preserved, as shown in Figure 5.10.

FIGURE 5.10
Fully compressed text is easier to read.

For horizontal sliding to work, you need to select all the sliding fields and then make sure that the following options are set:

▶ Align the tops of all the fields (see Hour 15).

▶ Set horizontal alignment to Left.

Vertical alignment is much the same, but there are two variations:

▶ With vertical alignment, you can slide a field up based on the field(s) directly above or all of the fields above it. The schematic on the Sliding/Printing dialog shows how this works.

▶ With vertical alignment, you can choose to reduce the size of the enclosing part. In most cases, you want this option to close up vertical space. (Parts are stacked one on top of the other vertically; there is never a case with two parts next to one another, so there is no comparable option for horizontal alignment.)

You need to set vertical alignment for the text in the sliding fields to Top; you do not need to align the fields as you do for horizontal sliding.

By the Way

The fields in your layout should be big enough to accommodate the largest amount of data they might be called on to handle. Fields can shrink as they slide, but they cannot grow. If your layout is designed for viewing onscreen, you can use a scroll bar in the field.

Printing Information About the Database

FileMaker allows you to print information about the database. These aspects of printing have changed with FileMaker 7, and the interface places some of the print commands in different places than they were before. (And, in some cases, you can print information that previously could not be printed.) Additional database reports are available in FileMaker Developer; they are described in Hour 20, "Creating Solutions with FileMaker Developer."

To print the database schema, choose File, Define Database from the menu. (This is described more fully in Part III, "Creating FileMaker Solutions"; for now, you may want to print descriptions of the templates and databases that you are using.)

As you can see from Figure 5.11, the Define Database dialog has three tabs. The Tables tab identifies the tables in the database. You can print information about any table by selecting it and clicking the Print button at the lower left of the dialog. By default, the fields in that table are shown with their names and field types. (You can select more than one table by Shift-clicking the names for a contiguous selection; on Mac OS X, Command-click allows you to select noncontiguous items.)

The second tab, Fields, shows you the fields for a specified table. Select one or more fields as shown in Figure 5.12 and print out information about those fields including field type, comments, validations, and the like.

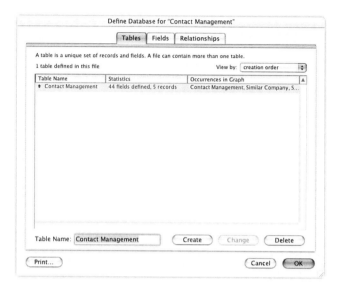

FIGURE 5.11
Print table informa-
tion.

FIGURE 5.12
Print information
for selected fields.

Finally, the Relationships tab shows you the relationships among the tables in your database (see Figure 5.13). You can print the graphical representation of those relationships (called a *graph*) with the Print button in the lower left of the window.

FIGURE 5.13
Print relationships.

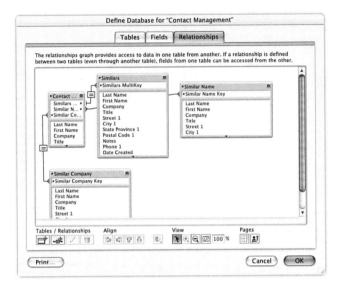

If you want to print out a script, choose Scripts, ScriptMaker from the menu; choose the script you want to print; and click the Print button at the upper right as shown in Figure 5.14.

FIGURE 5.14
Print scripts.

 Prior to FileMaker 7, scripts and field definitions were printed from the standard Print dialog.

Printing Envelopes and Labels

It's common to want to print envelopes and labels from a database. With FileMaker, it's also simple. This section shows you how to use the automated tools to set up envelope and label printing.

In both cases, the principle is the same: You create a layout for the data and then apply it as needed. You can start by finding the relevant records and sorting them if needed, or you can create a layout and keep it for whenever you need the envelopes and labels, finding and sorting the data at that point.

> If you rely on postage rates that require sorting by ZIP or postal code, remember to sort the database just before printing envelopes or labels. That way, you won't have to manually sort the addressed mail.

By the Way

Hour 15 covers more on creating layouts; however, many people find envelopes and labels so important—and so easy to do in FileMaker—that the topic is introduced here in advance of Hour 15. You can skip the section on printing envelopes and labels and wait until you read Hour 15 if you want more background on what is happening in this section.

> Whenever you are preparing to print on relatively expensive paper—envelopes, labels, photo quality paper, letterhead—print a copy on plain paper first. Hold it up to the light in front of the form you're going to use to make sure that the alignment is correct.

By the Way

Printing Envelopes

Start by opening the database containing the data you want to print. In Layout mode, choose Layout, New Layout/Report from the menu. The New Layout/Report dialog box opens, as shown in Figure 5.15.

Select the appropriate table, provide a name, and then choose Envelope from the scrolling list of layout types. Click Next to open the dialog shown in Figure 5.16.

As you double-click each field, it is added to the address area. The field names are enclosed in double angled brackets:

<<FirstName>>

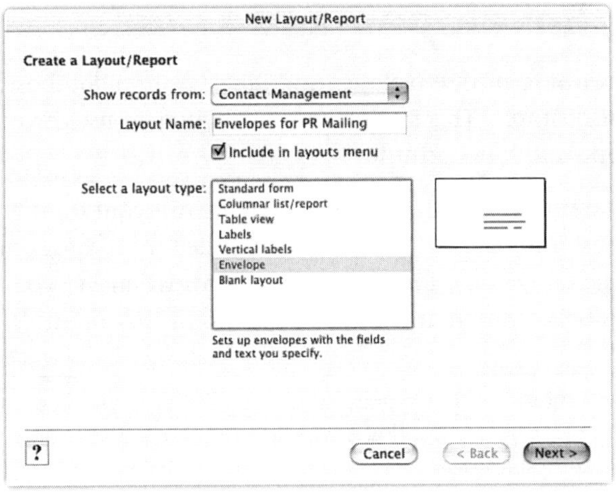

FIGURE 5.15
Create a new layout
for envelopes.

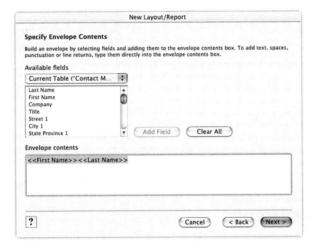

FIGURE 5.16
Double-click each
field to add it to
the address.

You can type other text into the address area. For example, a common address entry might look like this:

```
<<FirstName>> <<LastName>>
<<StreetAddress>
<<City>>, <<StateProvince>>  <<ZIPPostalCode>>>
```

In addition to the fields, note that there are spaces between them (with a double space before <<ZIPPostalCode>>. In addition, a comma is added after <<City>>.

For interoffice envelopes, you might construct an address such as this:

```
CONFIDENTIAL AND PERSONAL
TO: <<FirstName>> <<LastName>>
Mailstop: <<MailStop>>
```

The only constraint you have is the size of the address area on the envelope. (If you want to add a return address, you can modify the layout after it has been created—see Hour 15.)

Click the Next button, and you are finished, as shown in Figure 5.17. (The first option, View in Preview Mode, is the simplest to use for now.)

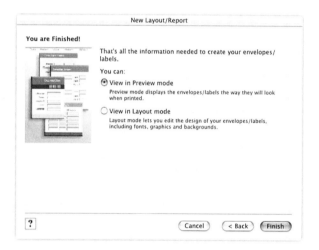

FIGURE 5.17
The envelope layout is complete.

Printing Labels

Labels work much the same way as envelopes. The primary difference is that you select either Labels or Vertical Labels from the Select a Layout Type scrolling list in the dialog shown previously in Figure 5.15.

You are next presented with a dialog that lets you select or specify a label, as shown in Figure 5.18.

If you use standard labels, you'll probably find the label you're using in the pop-up menu at the top of the dialog. If not, you can specify the label's size using the input fields in the center of the window.

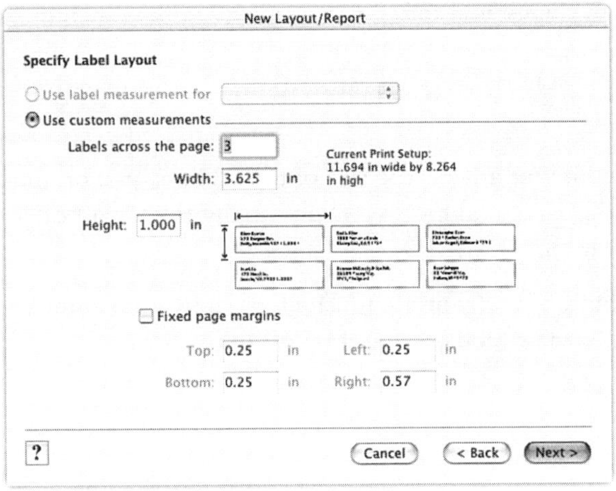

FIGURE 5.18
Select or specify
your label.

If you don't yet have the labels or the identification number of the label you'll be using, stop and obtain that information. Even if FileMaker does not support the specific label you have, the label packaging will probably provide you with the measurements you need to complete the dialog shown in Figure 5.18. In a worst case, you'll need to take a ruler and make some measurements. In any case, you need a sample of the actual label, its measurements, or its ID number.

By the Way

After you select or specify your label size, the procedure is the same as for envelopes: You double-click fields to add them to the label area, and type spaces, commas, or text before or after the symbols, as needed.

Summary

Printing is the last piece of the puzzle; you can produce reports from the database or from records that you've found; you can also produce labels and envelopes to make FileMaker a powerful mail processor.

This hour concludes the first part of the book. You've now seen the basics of working with FileMaker: entering data, retrieving it, customizing layouts, and printing data. In the next part of the book, you'll find out more about customizing the templates to make FileMaker work exactly the way you want it to.

Q&A

Q *Why do you have to use Preview mode to see how things will print?*

A WSIWYG (What You See Is What You Get) can't address issues such as different sizes and shapes of paper compared to a computer screen. If you have a printable layout and view it in Browse mode, you may see strange results—particularly with summary fields.

Q *Is it a good idea to create separate layouts for printed reports or does Preview mode do all the work?*

A It is often more important to consider the content of the report, not whether it will be printed. Use a layout with summaries in Preview mode for reports—printed or not.

Workshop

Quiz

1. How do you print information about the database itself?

2. How do you print large data fields?

3. In creating labels or envelopes, how do you add constant text, such as a comma or space after a city name?

Quiz Answers

1. Use the Print buttons on windows that display the database schema (choose File, Define Database from the menu) or scripts (choose Scripts, ScriptMaker from the menu).

2. Create the fields as large as they can possibly be and then set Sliding/Printing before viewing them in Preview mode. Remember that Sliding/Printing gets rid of unused space; there is no mechanism for automatically adding space to a field.

3. Type it in between the variables that are enclosed in << and >>.

Activities

Print data from the FileMaker template that you're working with. Print the schema and scripts (if any). Try producing a set of labels. You can use plain paper to practice on.

PART II

Modifying Templates and Databases

HOUR 6

Validating and Auto-Entering Data

What You'll Learn in This Hour:

▶ About Validation—FileMaker can edit data as it's entered.

▶ Setting Auto-Entry Options—You can let FileMaker automatically insert data, the results of calculations, information such as the current date or time, as well as unique serial numbers.

▶ Setting Validation Options—You can control the strictness with which these edits are applied.

▶ Replacing Field Values—This section explains how to do wholesale replacement of data.

Part I, "Getting Started with FileMaker—Using the Templates," provided an introduction to FileMaker. In Part II, "Modifying Templates and Databases," you'll see how you can build on the FileMaker templates to make customized solutions for yourself. Part III, "Creating FileMaker Solutions," will go further, showing you how to start from scratch to design and implement your own database solutions.

This hour focuses on the validation and auto-entering tools in FileMaker. All these tools have in common the capability to make sure that the data entered and stored adheres to rules that you provided when you set up the database. Most of the templates have minimal data editing turned on. A common customization is to add features, such as those described here, to make your data as clean as possible.

By the Way

Many people never go beyond the techniques described in Part I. Just by using them and the templates provided with FileMaker, you can use the power of FileMaker and take advantage of the design and analysis of business, educational, and general solutions.

As you move on, you will find that FileMaker has a vast array of tools and features to make your life easier—both as a user and as a developer of a custom database solution. The hours in Part II build on the templates, and some of the topics are advanced. In Part III, you'll start back with basic steps to build a database from scratch.

If you want to build your own databases, you may want to skip directly to Part III and then return here to customize your own databases with the advanced features found here.

About Validation

Validation (sometimes called *data integrity checking*) refers to the rules about the data that are enforced primarily during data entry. There are five broad types of validation rules that you can apply to data:

▶ You can specify validation rules that help to define the database table. For example, a field can be required (not empty), or its value can be unique. It can also be required to be a value that already exists in another record in the table. In each of these cases, you don't care what the value is, but you do care that the value adheres to rules such as these. (The unique value is often referred to in SQL as a *primary key*.)

▶ You can specify the format in which data is entered. For example, you can require four-digit years for dates, or you can require four decimal places to be entered (even if they are zero, as in 42.0000). You can also limit the total number of characters in a field. As with the preceding set of validation rules, you don't care about the specific values entered, only their format and characteristics. (As you saw in Hour 4, "Introducing Layouts," you can also apply formats automatically to data.)

▶ You may want to create a validation rule that requires the data entered in a field to match certain predefined values. (For example, you can limit the values in a Category field to Agriculture, Aquaculture, Horticulture, and Dairy.)

▶ You can require that a value pass a calculation test. For example, the ISBN (International Standard Book Number) for this book is 0-672-32578-0. The final digit is a *checkdigit*, calculable from the other nine digits. If you enter 1-672-32578-0, the calculation of the checkdigit will fail, and the incorrectly entered data can be rejected. FileMaker calculations allow you to check values against related tables, and they can be complex. When checking against related tables, you can implement *relational integrity*, which is integrity that checks against related fields in other tables so that your validation and integrity extend beyond the specific field and table that you're editing.

▶ A special subset of calculation tests check for the quality of the data. Calculations of this sort typically test that a data value is within a certain range of the value for a previous record (last week, for example). If sales for this week are more than 10% different from last week in either direction, you may want to notify the user, so that the data can be inspected for an extra or missing digit. These quality edits differ from the previous validation edits in that they are typically warnings or recommendations that frequently can be overridden by the user (perhaps with a notation about a snowstorm closing the business for several days).

In each of these cases, the validation rules that you establish increase the consistency of the database. That consistency can make it easier to search for data; it also can make reporting easier because data is in standard formats.

If data is invalid, it normally is not stored, although you can allow users to override validations (particularly quality edits). If you need to store the validation status of data, store that in a separate field, such as Sales Validation Status, to mirror data in a Sales field. Under no circumstances should you use special values (such as -1, 0, or 99) to indicate validation or other status of data. Data values should be just that. A large part of the billions of dollars spent finding and fixing Y2K problems was devoted to rooting out values such as these that were inserted in date fields under the assumption that "no valid year will have the value 99," and the like.

By the Way

Setting Auto-Entry Options

The simplest way to make sure that you have valid data in your database is to enter it automatically according to rules that you set up. FileMaker makes this easy. Using one of the templates, start by choosing File, Define, Database from the menu. The Define Database dialog opens, as shown in Figure 6.1.

Select the field for which you want to create auto-entry options; click Options or just double-click the field name in the list. The Options dialog opens, as shown in Figure 6.2. The Auto-Enter tab lets you set auto-entry options.

As you can see, there are seven sets of auto-entry options. Each option is described in this section. At the bottom, you will notice a checkbox in which you can determine whether users are allowed to subsequently modify the data that you have automatically entered.

FIGURE 6.1
Select the field for
auto-entry.

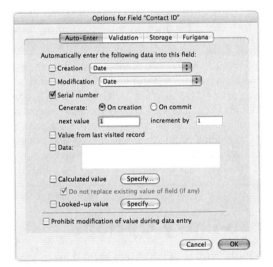

FIGURE 6.2
Set auto-entry
options.

Creation and Modification Tracking

The first two options, Creation and Modification (which are mutually exclusive), let you automatically insert data about the creation or modification date of the record. Many people routinely create creation and modification date fields in their database tables so that they can track the modifications to data. (When a record is initially created, both its creation and modification data are stored. Thus, if you don't care about preserving the information about the original creator of a record, you can store only the modification data and be confident that it will be filled in for the first modification—that is, the creation of the record.)

Depending on the type of field that you are working with, you find a variety of options in the pop-up menus. You can automatically insert any of these data elements into a text field. Dates, times, and timestamps can also be inserted into date, time, and timestamp fields, respectively.

▶ Date—The date as returned from the system clock.

▶ Time—The time as returned from the system clock.

▶ Timestamp—A combination of date and time such as 4/17/2001 9:04 AM.

▶ Name—The username set in Preferences; it may be picked up automatically from the system, or it may be entered there. It may be blank. See Hour 18, "Securing Your Solutions and Databases," for more information.

▶ Account name—The account name defined in Accounts & Privileges in the Define submenu of the File menu. It may be blank. See Hour 18 for more information.

> The timestamp field type is new in FileMaker 7. Previously, you needed to separately store the date and time of creation and modification. For most database purposes, it is sufficient to store a pair of fields for creation and modification: timestamp and name or account name. In many cases, storing only the modification values will suffice.

By the Way

If you auto-enter creation or modification data, you almost always check the checkbox at the bottom of the Options dialog to prohibit modification of the data because that would destroy the value of the data.

Serial Numbers

FileMaker can automatically create serial numbers for records. By default, they start at 1, and they are incremented by 1. However, you can provide any values that you want for start and increment.

Normally, if you ask FileMaker to create serial numbers, you can be assured that they are unique. The way in which they might not be unique is if you change the start or increment values; newly assigned serial numbers may overlap previously assigned values. Thus, you should not modify these values after you have started creating serial numbers automatically. If you do, choose a new start value that is beyond the highest serial number that has been assigned.

By the Way

> The Replace command, discussed at the end of this hour, lets your replace serial numbers in all or some records of the file using a single command. If you do this, be careful that you do not destroy links from other tables (or from this one) that are based on the old serial numbers.

There will normally be gaps in serial numbers as records are deleted. Don't worry about this.

In FileMaker 7, you can choose when serial numbers are assigned:

▶ On Creation—This behavior existed before FileMaker 7; serial numbers are assigned as soon as you choose New Record or otherwise create a record.

▶ On Commit—This is new behavior for FileMaker 7. The serial number is assigned as part of the record commit process—the process by which the data you have entered into a layout is stored in the database.

The practical difference between these two options is that if a record is not committed in the first case (possibly because the user chooses Records, Revert Record from the menu), the serial number assigned will not be reused even though the record wasn't stored.

In most cases, if you auto-enter serial numbers, you do not allow users to change the data, so you click the checkbox at the bottom of the Options dialog as shown in Figure 6.2.

By the Way

> If you are converting data from another application, you frequently will enter serial numbers from the old data. After you finish converting data and want to enter new data into FileMaker, you can turn on serial number auto-entry, choosing a starting value larger than the previously assigned maximum.

"Sticky" Values

The option to auto-enter a value from the last visited record can speed up data entry. If people are entering data into your database in any kind of ordered batches, you might want to automatically enter certain fields. For example, if you are entering purchase orders or invoices, the date of the purchase order or invoice might be carried forward. This might be the current date, but it also might be a different date as people pre- or post-date their entries. (Sometimes these are called *sticky values*.)

If you use sticky values, you frequently do allow people to modify the values that you have auto-entered.

Data Values

You can choose to auto-enter a specific value into a field. If you do, you type that value into the auto-enter dialog. The value might be something like "missing data," so you can distinguish between a blank field that represents a blank or zero value, and one that has not yet been entered.

The data value that is auto-entered is a constant; that is, you specify one value that is always used. Other examples of data values are values that are usually the same for all records. For example, Canada might be auto-entered for a Country field in a database of a Canadian company.

If you use data values, you often do allow people to modify the values. In the example here, a Canadian company might have almost all clients in Canada, but for the handful that are not in Canada, the auto-entered value could be changed.

> If you auto-enter a data value and do not allow people to modify it, all the records in the table will have the same value for that field. If this is really what you want, you would use a global field rather than an individual field in each record. See Hour 13, "Creating a FileMaker Database," for more on globals.

By the Way

Calculated Results

Whereas a data value is a constant, you can create a calculation that dynamically calculates a value to be auto-entered. Hour 7, "Working with Calculations, Formulas, Functions, and Repeating Fields," shows you how to do this.

If you use a calculated value, you might not want to allow it to be modified. Note that a calculation for auto-entry is different from a calculation field. In the case of calculations for auto-entry, if you allow subsequent data entry, the calculated value may be changed. In the case of a calculation field, it always has the calculated value.

Looked-up Values

Finally, you can enter looked-up values into a field automatically. Looked-up values are determined by relationships. When you click the Looked-Up Value option in the Options dialog, the Lookup for Field dialog, shown in Figure 6.3, opens.

For a looked-up value to be used, you must first have defined a relationship for the table. Many templates already have relationships; the Contact Management template in Figure 6.3 has three. (Relationships are described at length in Hour 14, "Working with Relationships.")

FIGURE 6.3
Specify looked-up values for auto-entry.

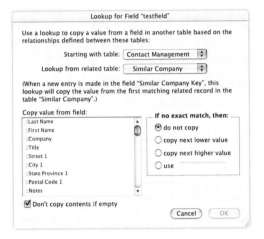

Next, the match field must have been entered. In other words, if the relationship matches a field in your table called Manager with a field in another table called Supervisor, you must have entered data in Manager (the field in your own table) for the relationship to be active.

After that happens, the looked-up value is auto-entered according to the options that you set in the lower right of the Lookup for Field dialog:

▶ If there is no match for the relationship, you can specify that no data value be auto-entered.

▶ If there is no match, you can use the match for the next lower or upper value of the match field.

▶ If there is no match, you can auto-enter a value that you type into the Lookup for Field dialog.

If there is more than one matching record, the first one supplies the value.

If you specify a relationship, you do not need to auto-enter values from the related table; those values are available through the relationship. There are two reasons for auto-entering looked-up values from relationships:

▶ If the related table is available at the time of data entry but may not be available during later processing (perhaps because it is on a network server that is not always available), you may want to cache the related data in your own table. This situation also applies to databases that are interacting with PDAs or cell phones using FileMaker Mobile. In this case, you normally do not allow users to modify the looked-up value because the related data can get out of sync.

▶ If you want the looked-up value to be a starting point for users, you allow modification to the looked-up value. It will get out of sync with the related value, but that may be what you want. For example, the related data might be the shipping address for a customer's previous order. That's a good guess for the shipping address for a new order, but you might want to change it.

Setting Validation Options

You can use the Validation tab of the Options dialog to set validation options, as shown in Figure 6.4.

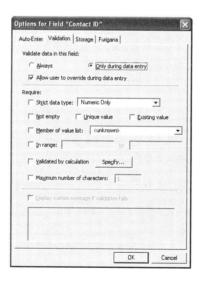

FIGURE 6.4
Set validation options.

This dialog has three sections. Samples of the settings are provided in the next few figures.

▶ At the top, you can specify whether the edits are applied only during manual data entry, or whether they should also be performed during data entry and manipulation performed by the Set Field script step, ODBC, imports, and Apple events. You also can specify whether the user can override the edit. The combination of always and not allowing users to override means that you can rely on the validation being successful for every record stored in the database (unless you have changed the validation rule after some invalid data has been entered).

▶ The middle of the dialog lets you specify any of the six types of edits described later in this section.

▶ Finally, you can specify a custom message to be displayed.

Figure 6.5 shows an example of a standard FileMaker error message that catches poorly formed dates if you selected the edit that requires a four-digit year to be entered.

FIGURE 6.5
Standard FileMaker error message.

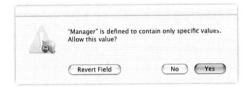

Figure 6.6 provides an example of a customized error message. You can choose to simplify the default error message or to provide customized information (such as the person in the organization to contact for further information).

FIGURE 6.6
Custom error messages can provide simpler information for users.

By the Way

Whether to allow overrides of edits is a thorny issue. If you do not allow overrides, people may enter data and then reach a point beyond which they cannot continue. Anyone who has entered a lot of data knows ways to get around this (the simplest is to enter some valid but incorrect data). If you customize the error messages, you can provide people with the tools that they need to find the correct data and minimize this problem.

The six types of validation edits available in the Options dialog are described in the following sections.

Strict Data Types

You can require that a field contain only numbers, that it have a valid time of day, or that it have a four-digit year (if it is a date). This edit interacts with the Field Format options that allow people to enter dates not in the specified format. You usually use one or the other.

Not Empty/Unique/Existing

This edit requires a field to have an entry, for it to be unique, or for it to already exist in another record in the table. If you require unique data, you may want to auto-enter a unique serial number.

Member of Value List/Specific Values

To validate against a specific set of values, you specify a value list that contains those values. Because a value list can consist either of the list itself or of the values in a field in a table that you specify, you can use this edit to require that data being entered in the table exists elsewhere. This can be a useful way to enforce a relationship because you require the match value to exist in the other file.

Range

You can perform range checks by supplying the lower and upper bounds for valid data. Range checks can apply to number, date, time, and text fields. In the case of text fields, the data entered is compared to the strings for the range bounds. If the range bounds are "cat" and "dog," the value "cathouse" is allowed, but "doghouse" is not.

Calculation Edit

You can create a calculation that returns a Boolean value (0 or 1) to determine whether the edit has succeeded. Anything that you can express in a calculation (see Hour 7) can be done at this point. This can be done to implement quality edits where a value must be within a certain range from another value; it can also be done to implement complex edits with multiple branches in an if statement.

Maximum Number of Characters

You can limit the number of characters entered in a text field. This edit particularly comes in handy if you will be printing highly formatted reports or labels.

Replacing Field Values

FileMaker provides the Replace Field Contents command in the Records menu to let you easily replace values in a given field for a selection of records. The records can be all records in the file or the current found set.

Start by finding the records on which you want to act. Then select the field by clicking in it. The Replace Field Contents dialog opens, as shown in Figure 6.7.

FIGURE 6.7
Replace field values for a group of records.

The first option lets you replace the field contents in the found set with the value from the current record. Other options let you insert new serial numbers or the results of a calculation.

This command is useful if you've made a consistent error. It's also useful if you have to change a name (perhaps there's a new employee and all tasks formerly done by Gail need to be done by Susan, or perhaps someone has gotten married or divorced and changed the name). It also is useful in preparing test data from real data: You can replace actual credit card numbers with fake numbers and do other data hiding replacements so that confidential data is not revealed.

Summary

In this hour, you saw how to use FileMaker's validation and auto-enter features, along with its wholesale field replacement command. All these have in common the capability to take part of the data process out of the hands of the user and into the automated world of FileMaker.

Further automation comes when you use FileMaker's built-in calculations and functions. You can calculate derived data automatically, saving time and ensuring consistency and accuracy. That is the topic of Hour 7.

Q&A

Q *Is there a way to provide some kind of expert mode for validation?*

A Validation rules are set in the Define Database dialog and apply to all users, so the basic answer is "no." However, as with so many aspects of FileMaker, there's a relatively simple way of implementing this. You can create pairs of fields. Assign the validation rules to fields that you place in a layout for most people to use. In the companion field, use the auto-enter features to copy the value from the other field into the companion. If the validation rule fails (and the user cannot override it), there is no way of entering invalid data and thereby overriding the validation.

However, if you use the companion field on a layout only available to advanced users, they can modify the auto-entered value (if any). Because you don't place a validation rule on the companion field (which is the one you use in calculations and reports), people with access to the layout that allows entry into those fields—advanced users—can effectively override the validation rules that mere mortals cannot escape.

This architecture is common. You'll frequently find it useful to have both as-entered and as-used fields. Sometimes you use the reverse structure, allowing anything to be entered (without validations) and using a calculation to reformat or modify the raw data into the data that you will use.

Q *What is the best way to test validation settings?*

A Try entering some actual data with the settings. Particularly if you are using validation settings that don't allow overrides, make sure that you can enter all possible data. Look also at legacy data that needs to be converted or imported to make sure that it can pass the validation rules. You can bypass those rules, but remember that you can't rely on the data being valid.

Workshop

Quiz

1. Can you allow users to enter data in a serial number field that is automatically filled?

2. Does Replace Field Contents act on the entire file?

3. Can you apply date and time validations to dates and times stored in text fields?

Quiz Answers

1. Yes, so be careful to set your options carefully so that your unique serial numbers remain unique.

2. It acts on the current found set, which may be the complete file.

3. No. This is yet another reason why you should use the date, time, and time-stamp field types rather than the generic text type.

Activities

Most of the templates ship with only minimal validations (if any). One of the most powerful ways of customizing them to your needs is to add your own validations. Select one or more of the templates and add validations to it. Then practice entering some actual (not made-up) data to see whether your validations help or hinder your data entry process.

HOUR 7

Working with Calculations, Formulas, Functions, and Repeating Fields

What You'll Learn in This Hour:

▶ About Calculations, Formulas, and Functions—This section provides the basic definitions used throughout the hour.

▶ Calculations In Use: The Expense Report Template—This real-life example can make the Expense Report template more useful to you.

▶ Setting Calculation Storage—Setting calculation storage options can significantly impact the performance of a database.

▶ Working with Repeating Fields—FileMaker can store arrays of values in repeating fields. This section shows you how this works and why you may want to use the technique. You'll see how repeating fields can be integrated with calculations.

▶ Creating a Calculation—Finally, here's how you create a calculation from scratch.

Hour 6, "Validating and Auto-Entering Data," showed you how to use FileMaker's automated tools to enter data and to validate data entered by users. This hour and Hour 8, "More on Calculations and Functions," explore such tools further by focusing on calculations, formulas, and functions. You use them to compute data from the data already stored in your database; the results of these computations can be used in further computations, as tests for validations and If statements in scripts, and to compute the auto-entered values that you can use in database fields.

These hours show you some of the ways in which you can use calculations, formulas, and functions. You'll see how they are used in a FileMaker template, and you'll see how you can modify other templates with your own calculations. Along the way, you'll find out about some of the other power features of FileMaker, such as repeating fields.

About Calculations, Formulas, and Functions

Calculations, formulas, and functions are related concepts. These three terms have specific meanings that you need to understand to get started. Each will be described more fully throughout the hour.

- *Formulas* are operations performed on data that can be stored in the database or entered as part of the formula. A formula can consist of one or more *expressions*; each expression yields a resulting value. Formulas frequently combine *constants* (values entered into the formula) and *field references* (contents of a specified field in the current record). 2+2 is both an expression and a formula; it contains two constants. 2*mileage is an expression and formula containing one constant and one field reference (assuming your table has a field named "mileage"). (2+2)/(2*mileage) is a single formula composed of two expressions.

- *Functions* are formulas that return a result from one or more *arguments*, which are placed in parentheses. For example, Sum(merchandise; salestax; shipping) is a formula that computes the total for an invoice. FileMaker defines a number of built-in functions such as this one. Some take an unlimited number of parameters (such as Sum); others take specific parameters in a specific order (such as Sqrt, which takes a single number from which a square root is calculated and returned). Still other functions have no arguments—Pi returns the geometric constant, and Random returns a single random number. A function can be an expression, which in turn can be a formula or part of a formula.

- *Calculation fields* are database fields that contain formulas (and, by extension, expressions and functions).

Formula is the most general term, and it is used in this hour except where the specific meaning of *function* or *calculation* is needed.

The examples given in this section involve numbers, but FileMaker provides a host of functions for strings, dates, and other purposes; you can write formulas using any of these data types. In addition, FileMaker provides a number of conversion functions that convert dates to strings, and so forth. Appendix B, "FileMaker Functions," provides a complete list of FileMaker functions.

By the Way

Calculations in Use: The Expense Report Template

Here is an example of the use of calculation fields from the Expense Report template. Figure 7.1 shows the template as it is when you first open it and add one record.

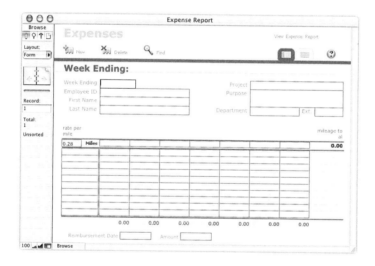

FIGURE 7.1
Start with a blank record in the Expense Report template.

As soon as you enter a date in the Week Ending field, the window changes, as you see in Figure 7.2. The days and dates for each day of the week are filled in automatically.

Examining a Calculation

You can see how this works by looking at the Fields tab in the Define Database dialog (choose File, Define, Database). Figure 7.3 shows the Define Database dialog.

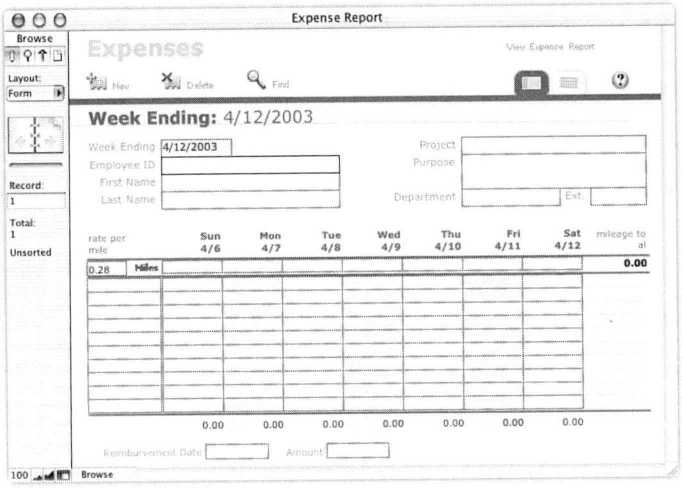

FIGURE 7.2
Calculations popu-
late the database.

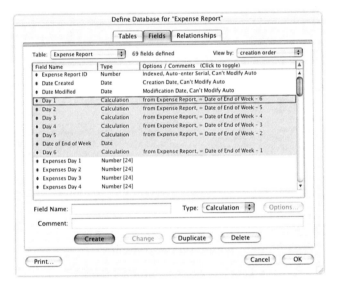

FIGURE 7.3
The Fields tab
shows field types
and names.

In the highlighted section, you can see one date field—Date of End of Week—and
six calculation fields (Day 1, Day 2...). If you double-click one of the calculation
fields, you'll see the Specify Calculation dialog shown in Figure 7.4.

This is the same Specify Calculation dialog that you see when you define a calculation field, when you specify a calculation for a conditional statement in a
script, or when you specify a calculation for auto-entering or validating a field.
You can use the scrolling list at the top left of the window to double-click field

names to enter them into the calculation; you can single-click operators to add them to the calculation; and you can double-click functions from the function list at the top right. You need never type anything (or you can type everything). In addition, the *context* in which the function should execute is specified at the top of the dialog. Contexts are discussed in Hour 14, "Working with Relationships." For now, pay attention to the lower part of the dialog where the actual calculation is specified.

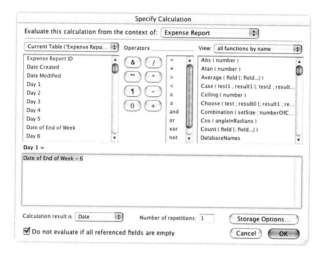

FIGURE 7.4
Specify calculations.

The large data entry field at the bottom of the dialog lets you type the calculation. In this case, it's

Date of End of Week - 6

That subtracts six days from the ending date and gives you the date of the first day. Just above the data entry field, the text Day 1 = appears to indicate what will happen to the result of the calculation. It is placed in the Day 1 field.

Beneath the data entry field, you can specify the type of the result; in this case, it's a date.

Displaying the Calculation

If you go into Layout mode, you see the names of the fields displayed in each field on the layout. Note that the fields Day 1...Day 6 appear twice. Select the top Day 1 field, choose Format, Date from the menu, and you see the settings for this field's date formatting, as shown in Figure 7.5.

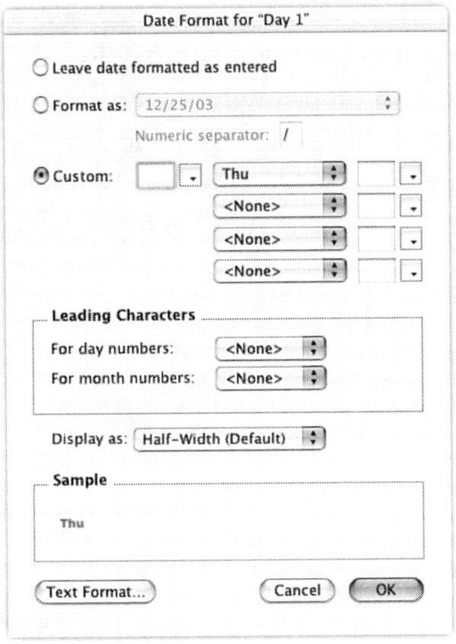

FIGURE 7.5
Specify a day for-
mat for a date.

This is an example of a custom date format. You can use the pop-up menus to select the components for the format; you can also specify separators. In this case, only one component is specified: the day of the week (Thu). It appears in the sample at the bottom of the dialog.

In Figure 7.6, you see how the second row of Day 1...Day 6 is formatted. Another custom date format is used, and it includes only the month and day (12/25).

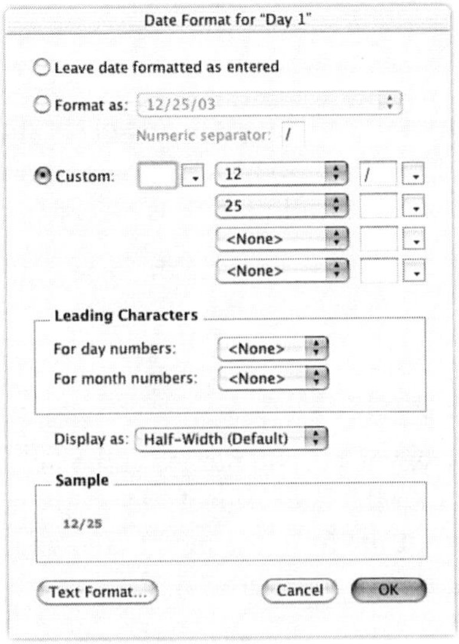

FIGURE 7.6
Specify a
month/day format.

Thus, you have the output shown previously in the column heads in the expense report in Figure 7.2. When you enter one field—Date of End of Week—all the date fields on the layout are filled appropriately.

> Not only does this demonstrate how to use custom date formats, but it illustrates the fact that you can display the same data field more than once in a layout using the same or different formatting.

By the Way

Formatting Calculations

FileMaker calculations are formatted just as formulas and calculations are in most programming languages (including spreadsheets). They are evaluated from left to right, except that parenthesized expressions are evaluated first. You can use parentheses not only to change the sequence of evaluation but also to make the calculation easier to read.

Line spacing doesn't matter in calculations (except within quotation marks). Thus, if you have a complex calculation, you can split it over several lines with each line containing a logical component. You can also parenthesize the components if you want.

Like other programming languages, FileMaker determines the priorities in which operators are executed. You can change this sequence, too, by parenthesizing expressions within the calculation. Many people find that it's safer to use parentheses than to rely on the order of evaluation because, in the future, someone could modify your code and not notice that it relies on the order of evaluation.

Setting Calculation Storage

In the Specify Calculation dialog, the Storage Options button below the calculation entry field at the right opens the Storage Options dialog, where you specify whether to store the result of the calculation. Part of the power of calculations is that they need not be stored but can be calculated automatically by FileMaker when they're needed. This saves space in the database file at the expense of more processing time (depending on the complexity of the calculation, it may be faster to retrieve data from the database than to recalculate it).

Your choice with regard to storing the calculation depends on what it is, what it's used for, and how often it's accessed. The Expense Report template used in this hour provides two sets of examples.

In Figure 7.7, you see the storage options for the Day 1 field. You enter the storage choice for the calculation in the Indexing area of the dialog.

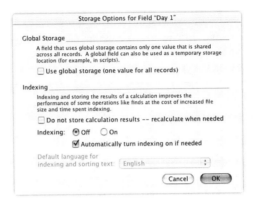

You'll find more on setting storage options in Part III, "Creating FileMaker Solutions," of this book.

Working with Repeating Fields

FileMaker provides the concept of *repeating fields*—fields that can contain more than one entry. The issue is germane at this point because a calculation can be a repeating field, and it can use a repeating field as one or more of its operands.

In the Specify Calculation dialog, shown previously in Figure 7.4, the number of repetitions can be specified in the center just below the calculation entry field. For fields that are not calculations, the repetitions are specified in the Options dialog, which you open from the Fields tab in the Define Database dialog. Figure 7.8 shows the Options dialog (note that the Field Options dialog shown in Figure 7.8 is similar to the Storage Options dialog shown in Figure 7.7).

Repeating fields can be used in a variety of ways. There are two basic paradigms for their use, and it's important to be able to identify those paradigms and to know when to use repeating fields and when not to.

How Repeating Fields Work

Most database fields contain a single value. A repeating field contains multiple values—you specify the number. You can enter each of the values in a layout; you can also use functions to retrieve specific values.

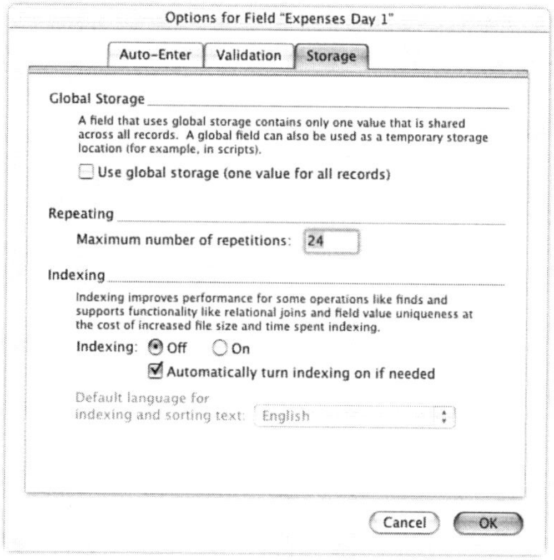

FIGURE 7.8
Specify repetitions for a field.

Operations on repeating fields may affect all the values at once or only some of them.

▶ If you perform operations on two repeating fields, the operation is carried out on each pair of repetitions. Adding a repeating field with five repetitions to a repeating field with three repetitions adds the first three repetitions of each field together and stores them in a repeating field (if that's what the destination is). If a repeating field for student test scores has the results of five tests and another repeating field for student essays has the scores from three essays, adding the fields together adds the first three test results to the three essay scores with the simple expression `TestScore + EssayScore`.

▶ If you perform operations on a repeating field and a nonrepeating field, you can use the `Extend` function to extend the nonrepeating field to appear to be the same length as the repeating field. Multiplying a repeating field with five repetitions by a nonrepeating field that is called `singleValue` and specified as `Extend (singleValue)` multiplies each of the five repetitions by the value of `singleValue`. (Without the `Extend` function, only the first value would be multiplied.)

For example, to multiply a discount rate (a nonrepeating field) by a repeating field of several prices, you could write `Extend(discount) * prices`. FileMaker extends the nonrepeating field as necessary to multiply it by as many repeated values of prices as you need.

▶ Certain functions such as Sum can take a repeating field as an argument; the function then operates on all the repeating values. Thus, Sum (aRepeatingField) provides the sum of all the repetitions of aRepeatingField.

▶ To access a single value of a repeating field, you can use the GetRepetition function. To get the first price in a repeating fieldof that name, use GetRepetition (price, 1). A special function returns the last nonblank repetition: Last (price).

When to Use Repeating Fields

A repeating field works well in two particular cases:

▶ If you have a data value that consists of multiple values (numeric or otherwise), repeating fields are perfect. Colors, for example, can be specified as a trio of numbers specifying values for red, green, and blue (*RGB colors*); they also can be specified as a quartet of numbers specifying values for cyan, yellow, magenta, and black (*CYMK colors*). If you want to store colors, repeating fields with three (RGB) or four (CYMK) repetitions are just what you need. Other types of data for which repeating fields might work are start/end dates, high/low values, and so forth.

▶ If you have multiple values for a data field, you can use repeating fields even if the number of repetitions is not fixed, as it is for start/end dates or RGB colors. The danger here is that if you define a repeating field of, for example, 10 repetitions, you have immediately limited the number of data values to 10. If you use a relationship, the number of related values is unlimited. These types of internal limits are responsible for many bugs as systems grow. (Who would have thought that your little boutique would ever have more than 10 items on a single sales slip?)

When Not to Use Repeating Fields

Using repeating fields cuts down on the total number of fields in your database; they also help to organize closely related data. The normal way of displaying the repetitions of repeating fields is either horizontally or vertically; it is possible to split individual repetitions out and display them in different places in a layout, but that is an uncommon use and usually indicates that you're using repeating fields incorrectly.

Repeating fields are generally not indicated in the following two cases:

▶ If the data is not closely related (and this may be demonstrated by the fact that you want to separate the repetitions on your layout and even provide separate labels for different repetitions), repeating fields are a poor choice.

▶ If you have several repeating fields with matched data, you probably want a relationship and a portal (see Part III). An example of this would be a pair of fields such as Invoice Number and Invoice Amount. Each might be a repeating field with the *n*th Invoice Number repetition matching the *n*th Invoice Amount. This is a relationship masquerading as repetitions, and it will be much easier in the long run if you just create a relationship.

Some FileMaker templates do use repeating fields in the manner just described. It works, but if you begin to extend the templates, you'll see that you're wandering into a degree of complexity that would not happen if you used relationships.

Creating a Calculation

You've seen how calculations work, and what the Specify Calculation dialog looks like (refer to Figure 7.4). Now it's time to actually create a calculation. This is a step-by-step walkthrough; in Hour 8, you'll find more details on the specific types of functions available to you.

The Expense Report template has a database field called Rate per Mile. It is used to calculate the reimbursement for an employee's use of a car based on a rate of 28 cents a mile. If you enter the number of miles driven, the database calculates the appropriate reimbursement. The field is defined as an auto-enter field; you can modify it for any record in the table if you want to use a different value.

In this section, you'll see how to use a calculation to automatically calculate the mileage reimbursement based on the year in which the expense takes place. Many organizations base their reimbursement rates on the rates allowed by the tax authorities for reimbursement of automobile use for business purposes. Thus, the individual organization's rates change as the tax authorities change their rates. In the United States, the mileage reimbursement for 2003 was 36 cents, and for 2004 it was 37.5 cents. Here's what you'll need to do:

1. Change the Rate per Mile field from a Number field to a Calculation field.

2. Enter the Calculation. First, you need a test to find out whether the year of the last date of the expense report record is 2004.

3. If it is 2004, use 37.5 cents; otherwise, use 36 cents. (Note that this is an oversimplification. In reality, you should check for 2003, 2004, and other years that might be entered.)

4. Modify the layout to display three digits to the right of the decimal point. The default template only displays two digits.

Change the Field to a Calculation

Open the Define Database dialog and click the Fields tab as you saw previously in Figure 7.3. Select the Rate per Mile field, and using the pop-up menu below the list of field names, change Number to Calculation. (You may have to scroll down to find the Rate per Mile field.)

The Change button now becomes highlighted. Before you continue, click Change to complete the change of field type. You are warned that you may lose data, but click OK and continue. Unless, of course, you have used the Expense Report template to enter lots of real data!

Create an If Test

You now have the Specify Calculation dialog available. You can type in your calculation, but FileMaker provides a variety of tools that let you just double-click the components of the calculation that you want.

First, you need an If test. If is a function, and all the functions are shown in a scrolling list on the right side of the dialog. Scroll down until you see If. (If you don't see it, check that the pop-up menu above that list shows either All Functions or Logical Functions.) Double-click the If function, and it appears in the central editing field as shown in Figure 7.9.

Each function has placeholders for the arguments that it needs. In the case of an If test, you have a test and two values—the first value is used if the result of the test is true, and the second value is used if the result of the test is false.

```
If ( test; resultOne; resultTwo )
```

Double-click the placeholder test: What you type (or double-click) replaces it as the actual test. You want to test whether the year of Date of End of Week is 2004. The Year function extracts the year from a given date. (Hour 8 provides more details on the specific types of functions available.)

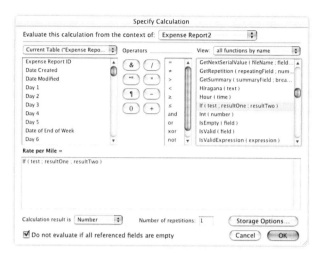

FIGURE 7.9
Double-click a function to place it in the editing field.

With the placeholder `test` highlighted, scroll down the list of functions to the Year function; double-click it, and `test` is replaced with the Year function. When the Year function is inserted, you see that it also has a placeholder—this time for the date to be evaluated. Follow the same procedure: Double-click the `date` placeholder and then replace it with the field Date of End of Week. You could type it in, but you can also use the scrolling list of fields at the upper left of this dialog to select it. With the `date` placeholder highlighted, just scroll and double-click Date of End of Week.

The test is almost complete. It should now read as follows:

```
If ( Year ( Date of End of Week )
```

You extracted the year from the date; now you need to test whether it's 2004. You can simply type in the test as shown here:

```
If ( Year ( Date of End of Week ) =2004 ; resultOne; resultTwo)
```

Set Values in the If Test

The last step is to replace the `resultOne` and `resultTwo` placeholders with the values you want: .375 and .36. (These values are in dollars.) Type them in and you're finished with the calculation. Click OK to exit the calculation, and click OK again to get out of the Database Design dialog.

Modify the Layout

You can now run the template and see your handiwork—sort of. The default template displays two decimal points, so you see values of .36 and .38. Using the layout tools described in Hour 4, "Introducing Layouts," select that field in Layout mode and then use Format Number to change the number of decimal places to 3, not 2.

By the
Way

This is typical of the type of minor modification you may need to make to databases from time to time. It's not difficult with FileMaker, and you shouldn't hesitate to add or customize calculations. If you do make changes, though, remember two important points. First, always make a backup copy of the database in case your changes are less than perfect. Second, as in this case, check to see where the results of calculations are used so that you can see whether any layout format changes are needed. This example also demonstrates the importance of using correct data types. The Year function works because Date of End of Week is a date, not a text string. You can get away with using the default type—text—for data fields, but if you want to start exploiting any of the real power of FileMaker, using correct data types makes life much easier for you.

Summary

In this hour, you saw the basics of calculations in FileMaker. They can be used not just for standard arithmetic calculations but also can be combined with logical functions to return results that vary based on data conditions.

Q&A

Q *Why aren't there more calculations in the templates?*

A As you saw in this hour, you can customize templates with calculations that match the way you use a specific template. The basic templates are jumping-off places for such customization.

Q *Do calculations slow down FileMaker?*

A Calculations that are stored cost you only when they are calculated. Thereafter, they are retrieved like any other data field. Calculations that are unstored need to be recalculated each time they are accessed. If a calculation involves data located across a network, there may be a noticeable delay in accessing it and then performing the calculation. The delay is not so much in the calculation, but in the data access across the network.

Workshop

Quiz

1. Does an If function need to return a value in all cases?

2. Can you label the repetitions in a repeating field (as in "Home," "School," or "Office")?

3. Is there a limit to the length or complexity of a calculation?

Quiz Answers

1. Yes. Often the final value is an empty value (""), but something does need to be returned.

2. No. If they are different, they should be in different fields.

3. The practical limit—comprehensibility—is much lower than any FileMaker limits.

Activities

The example of changing the mileage rate provides a calculation for each record. You can enter the same calculation as an auto-enter calculation using the techniques described in Hour 6. If you do so, the calculated result will be put in the field, but users will be able to override it by entering another value. Try doing this. Also consider when it would be appropriate to do it as an auto-entered and overrideable value and when the field should simply be a calculation.

More on Calculations and Functions

What You'll Learn in This Hour:

▶ Overview of Functions—Here's the high-level overview.

▶ Logical Functions—These logic and control functions let you make choices within a calculation.

▶ Calculations in the Time Cards Template—Here is an in-depth look at the calculations that make time cards work.

In Hour 7, "Working with Calculations, Formulas, Functions, and Repeating Fields," you saw the basics of calculations—how to use them and how to create a relatively powerful calculation.

In this hour, you'll find out more about functions. One of the most important aspects of FileMaker functions is the ability to use logical functions to vary results based on conditions. This is true programming, and this hour focuses on the logical functions.

Then, you'll see how the Time Cards template uses calculations to manipulate its data: Each of the calculations in that template is described so that you'll be able to modify them and to use similar calculations in your own work.

Appendix B, "FileMaker Functions," provides a complete list of the functions in FileMaker 7.

By the Way

Overview of Functions

Functions perform an operation on zero or more *parameters* or *arguments* and return a *result*. Each function has its own defined parameters, the order of which matters. For example, the RGB function takes three parameters, which together define a color using values for red, green, and blue; those three parameters must be specified in that order. The Get function takes a single parameter, which is a predefined value (*a constant*); Get (UserName) returns the name of the current user. The functions DatabaseNames, WindowNames, Pi, and Random take no parameters, but they do return results.

You use functions in calculations. You can combine them as much as you want: A function can be used to calculate a result, which in turn is used as a parameter. To set the color of a short text string to red, you can use the RGB function to specify that color:

```
TextColor ("text string", RGB (255, 0, 0)
```

The result of the function is the string set to the color red.

Logical Functions

These functions have been significantly expanded in FileMaker 7 to allow more sophisticated handling of conditional operations as well as more complex processing. Many of these functions allow you to write code that returns different results based on data conditions. They move you well on the way to actually programming FileMaker as you would in a standard programming language. Because they are so important and in some cases unique to FileMaker, each of the logical functions is described here.

The logical functions fall into three sets:

- ▶ The first set lets you return different results after evaluating some choice that you create in the function. They are If, Case, and Choose. (You saw the If statement in Hour 7.)

- ▶ The second set lets you check attributes and values of fields such as whether they are empty, whether they are valid, and the like. They are Evaluate, Quote, EvaluationError, GetField, IsEmpty, IsValid, and IsValidExpression.

- ▶ The final set allows you to program mini-subroutines and to otherwise act on one or more fields. They are Let, Lookup, and LookupNext.

If

This function lets you specify a test followed by two values. If the test succeeds, the first value is returned; otherwise, the second is returned. Consider the case of two fields: `firstName` and `lastName`. If both are present, you might want to display them in common library style: `lastName, firstName`. If, however, `firstName` is missing, you want to display only `lastName`. You can assemble the components of this name by including this calculation:

```
If (Length(firstName)>0; ", "; "")
```

If the length of `firstName` is greater than 0, the calculation returns the comma and space that follow `lastName`. Otherwise, it returns nothing (the empty string). You would use this code within a calculation to generate the characters placed between the two names. Another way of achieving the same result is to use an `If` statement in a script.

Case

`If` functions are used to choose between two values. If you have more than two, you need the `Case` function. Here is a case function to calculate a letter grade from a numeric score where A is 90-100, B is 80-90, C is 70-80, D is 60-70, and Fail is below 60. (The function is shown on several lines for the sake of legibility. You can enter it on a single line if you want.)

```
Case (
numericgrade ≥ 90 ; "A" ;
numericgrade ≥ 80 and numericgrade < 90 ; "B" ;
numericgrade ≥ 70 and numericgrade < 80 ; "C" ;
numericgrade ≥ 60 and numericgrade < 70 ; "D" ;
"Fail")
```

Note that the final value has no test associated with it: It is the default value used if none of the other tests pass.

Choose

The `Choose` function lets you select from a list of values based on a calculated index. Whereas the `Case` function lets you perform different tests for every element, the `Choose` function simply provides a number as in the following:

```
Choose (taxTier; .1, .15, 0)
```

You can set a field, taxTier, to 0, 1, or 2 to indicate whether merchandise should be taxed at 10% (perhaps foodstuffs), 15% (perhaps clothing), or not at all. In an inventory database, you can enter a taxTier for each item; if and when tax rates change, you only need to change the calculation that contains the Choose function. This makes maintenance of the database much easier than if you coded the actual current tax rate for each inventory item.

Evaluate

This function lets you introduce a level of dynamism to FileMaker and its calculations. You can let a user enter a calculation into a text field and then evaluate that calculation with Evaluate. For example, if a text field called Formula contains the string "4 + 3", the result of

```
Evaluate (Formula)
```

is 7.

You can supply one or more field names following the name of the field to evaluate. Those field names are treated as triggers: If any of them changes, the Evaluate function is reevaluated. Thus, changes to either firstName or lastName would cause the following calculation to be reevaluated:

```
Evaluate (Formula; firstName; lastName)
```

You can also enter the actual expression to be evaluated into the Evaluate function, but its most common use is with a field name.

Quote

In view of the fact that anything can be entered into a text field that is passed to the Evaluate function, you need to be careful not to open security holes. In addition to a numerical operation, any valid FileMaker calculation can be entered. This can compromise the security of your database.

The Quote function can be used with the Evaluate function to place quotes around the contents of a field, thereby ensuring that the field contents are treated as text. Applying Quote to the example in the preceding section gives a different result. If a formula contains the string "4 + 3", the result of

```
Evaluate (Quote(Formula))
```

is the string "4 + 3".

EvaluationError

You can check to see whether an expression can be successfully evaluated. A common use of this function is to check to see whether the `Evaluate` function will succeed. Given a field named Formula, you can evaluate it with `Evaluate`, but you run the risk of an error occurring if the field contains an invalid function. The following script tests to see whether an error occurs, and, if not, then proceeds to evaluate the field:

```
If [EvaluationError (Evaluate(Formula))] = 0
  Set Field (Result; Evaluate (Formula))
End If
```

You can also incorporate the function in a calculation field as follows:

```
If ( EvaluationError(Evaluate(Formula))=0 ; Evaluate(Formula) ; 0 )
```

> EvaluationError returns the error code that results from the evaluation of the expression. Every evaluation results in an error code, although most result in 0—the code for no error. Other functions discussed in this section return a Boolean result in which 0 is false and 1 is true.

By the Way

GetField

This function is replaced by the `Evaluate` function in FileMaker 7 although it still remains part of the software.

IsEmpty

This function checks to see whether a field is empty.

IsValid

This function checks to see whether a field is valid. The most common reasons for a field being invalid are invalid characters, such as a date field that contains the word "strawberry" or a missing related table.

IsValidExpression

This function takes as its parameter an expression rather than a field. It checks to see that the expression is valid (that is, well-formed with matching parentheses and correctly spelled function names).

Let

This function allows you to create variables for use in an expression. It can save you from needing to create intermediate fields to store calculation results. Here is a calculation that incorporates the test presented previously for creating a last name-comma-first name string.

```
Let (
[ first = firstName ; spacer = If (Length(firstName)>0; ", "; "")] ;
lastName & spacer & first)
```

Within the square brackets, you can declare any number of variables. In this case, the local variable first is set to the value of the firstName field. A second local variable, spacer, is set either to ", " (comma followed by a space) or to an empty string depending on whether the firstName field has any data in it.

The expression itself concatenates the lastName field, the spacer variable (which might be empty), and the firstName field (which also might be empty). (Note that it is not necessary to create a local variable for a copy of the firstName field; it is done simply to show you how to create more than one local variable.)

Lookup **and** LookupNext

These are covered in Hour 14, "Working with Relationships."

Calculations in the Time Cards Template

The Time Cards template lets you enter data for up to two weeks at a time. Figure 8.1 shows the basic layout.

This is a sophisticated template that uses a wide variety of FileMaker features. One of the most interesting is a self-join. It allows you to enter an employee's name and ID and thereafter look up the name automatically from the ID. Self-joins and other relationships are described in Hour 14. The relationship is shown in Figure 8.2.

The Time Cards template lets you type in the date on which the week begins. When you do so, the individual lines of data toward the bottom of the layout are filled in with the appropriate dates and days of the week. Thus, the template automatically adjusts for weeks beginning on Monday, Friday, Thursday, or any other day.

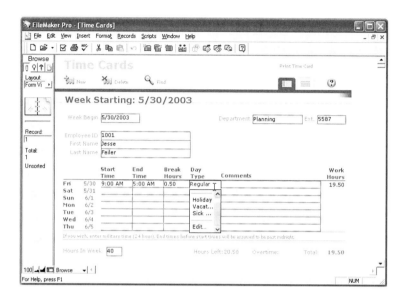

FIGURE 8.1
Use the Time Cards template to record time.

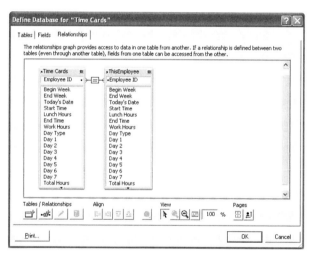

FIGURE 8.2
A self-join relationship lets you look up names from ID numbers.

Also, there is logic based on a calculation that lets you enter work periods that span a day. As shown in Figure 8.1, 9:00 a.m. to 5:00 a.m. is entered. The template correctly calculates this as being 20 hours.

By the
Way

> If you type in 9 and 5 for start and end times, FileMaker assumes that they are 9:00 and 5:00 a.m. If you mean 9:00 a.m. and 5:00 p.m., a different sort of calculation is needed than the one shown here. But what happens if you type in 9 and 5 and you might mean 9:00 a.m. to 5:00 p.m. or 9:00 a.m. to 5:00 a.m. the next day? Can you think of a way to handle this? A common method is to have a field into which you enter data and from which an assumption is made in a calculation that appears in a changeable field. That is, the calculation is used as an auto-enter calculation for the modifiable field.
>
> In that way, you can write a calculation that adjusts 5:00 a.m. to 5:00 p.m. based on certain criteria (such as the length of the work day, perhaps). Because the calculation is auto-entered into a modifiable field, the user can indeed come along and change it if the other choice is wanted. Some FileMaker solutions have nearly total duplicates of data entry fields and derived fields that make assumptions—modifiable—about what the user might mean.

Many of the calculation fields in the template are described in the following sections so that you can see how different types of calculations are used.

The Time Cards template also demonstrates another useful feature of FileMaker. In addition to standard layouts for forms and list views, there is also a Timecard Form layout. It is designed to be printed as a form to be filled in. You'll see spaces for employee and manager signatures.

Unstored Calculations for Today

A series of unstored calculations are used to manipulate the current date and day name. Today's Date is an unstored calculation defined as

```
Get (CurrentDate)
```

Today's Name, also unstored, is defined as

```
DayName (Today's Date)
```

This set of two calculated and unstored fields is common in FileMaker solutions that manipulate dates.

Converting a Date to a Week Number

The Begin Week field is the date field in which you enter the starting date of the week for which time is being recorded. Current Week is a calculation that converts that date to a week number using the built-in function in FileMaker:

```
WeekOfYear (Begin Week)
```

Computing Hours Worked—The Work Hours Field

The heart of the template is this calculation, shown in Figure 8.3.

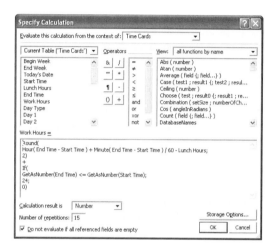

FIGURE 8.3
Calculate the hours worked.

Like many calculations, it has a certain degree of complexity. Some of that is eased by its spacing in the calculation dialog. As you type in calculations, feel free to space them out as you see here to improve readability.

To read a complex calculation, first look at its overall structure and then work from the inside out. In this case, the calculation consists basically of the addition of two terms. Simplified, it looks like this:

```
Round() + If ()
```

Remember that parentheses determine the sequence of operation. Match them up, and you'll see the structure of the calculation.

Look at the first part of the calculation—the calculation that is rounded. Again, split it into its basic structure:

```
Round (...;2)
```

The terms represented by the ellipsis (...) are calculated and then rounded to two digits of precision.

Once again, go down another level. This time, look at the terms that will be rounded. The calculation represented by the ellipsis is

```
Hour () + Minute () - LunchHours
```

Now it's easy to look at the heart of the calculation. It assembles the number of hours between the start and end times, the number of minutes, and then subtracts the lunch hour (which is entered in hours):

```
Hour (end time - start time) + Minute (end time - start time) / 60 - LunchHours
```

You may wonder why you just can't subtract start time from end time. The reason is that the default conversion of a time to a number in FileMaker converts it to seconds. Thus, if start time is 9:00 a.m. and end time is 5:00 p.m., the previous calculation results in 8 hours (if there is no lunch hour); simply subtracting start time from end time gives 28800 (the number of seconds in 8 hours).

The second part of the overall calculation handles the case in which the end time appears earlier than the start time and thus should be considered to be a day later. The If function is used to test this case:

```
If (
  GetAsNumber(end time) ≤ GetAsNumber (start time);
  24;
  0)
```

This adds 24 to the result of the previous calculation. (In the case of 9:00 a.m. to 5:00 a.m., the first part of the calculation gave the result of –4, so adding 24 to it results in the correct answer—20.)

By the Way

> If you used versions of FileMaker prior to FileMaker 7, you may not be used to the GetAsNumber function. You need to use it to convert the times to numbers so that the less-than-or-equal comparison (which is numeric) can be made.

Summarizing a Repeating Field: Total Hours

The Time Cards template uses repeating fields for the start and end times; the calculation of Hours Worked just described is also a repeating field. Total Hours uses the Sum function to automatically sum all the repetitions. If you look at the calculation, you'll see it consists of the following:

```
Round (Sum (Work Hours); 2)
```

Remember to work from the inside out in reading this function; it consists of two parts. The outer part is

```
Round (...; 2)
```

The inner part is

```
Sum (Work Hours)
```

By the Way

In performing calculations, it is frequently desirable to round at every step of the process and to store the rounded data. The reason is that it is possible for FileMaker to correctly calculate data from unrounded data that has many digits of precision.

When the data is rounded for display, the underlying data remains much more precise. Adding (or performing other arithmetic operations) on the unrounded data can result in slightly different results than working with the rounded data, which is exactly what the user sees. This situation is not unique to FileMaker. You probably have seen footnotes in tables to the effect that "Numbers may not add due to rounding errors."

Summary

With this hour and Hour 7, you saw the range of functions and calculations available within FileMaker. You can use calculations to create values for fields or to dynamically create tests for If and Case functions.

All these functions ultimately are a single line of code (albeit perhaps a long and complex line of code). Hour 9, "Working with Scripts," and Hour 10, "More on Working with Scripts," explore scripting: the ability to combine multiple lines of code into scripts that control FileMaker (and that may, in places, include calculations).

Q&A

Q *What is the context of a calculation in FileMaker 7?*

A Before FileMaker 7, only one table per file was allowed, and relationships were simple. Today, relationships can be complex, and, in fact, a single table may appear in several relationships within the same database. The context helps FileMaker keep things straight. Fortunately, for most cases, you don't have to worry about this: The default value is fine (and, in fact, for most simple databases, there is no possibility of using anything except the default value).

Q *Can I rely on functions being updated as needed?*

A FileMaker takes care of dependencies among functions and the fields that they reference. As a result, not only can you rely on their being updated, but you also need to be aware that those updates happen in the background. If your functions and calculations reference fields in databases located across a network, this can impact performance.

Workshop

Quiz

1. What is the difference between If, Choose, and Case?

2. Why can the Evaluate function be a security risk?

3. How do you continue a calculation from one line to another?

4. Why can't you just subtract starting and ending times to calculate the duration of an event?

Quiz Answers

1. If is a simple two-way logical test. Case is a series of logical tests of any length. Choose lets you choose results by number from a list of values.

2. The text passed to the function is evaluated at runtime. If that text can be entered by a user, it could contain valid FileMaker commands that might do things you do not want to be done.

3. Keep typing. Return characters are ignored. To enter a return character in a text string, use the ¶ symbol.

4. By default, the calculation returns seconds, not hours and minutes.

Activities

In Hour 7, you added a calculation to compute the mileage rate for expenses based on different annual values. In that case, the year was embedded in the calculation. Revisit that example and remove the data from the calculation. Here's how to start:

Create global repeating fields in your database—one for year and one for rate. Now, using logical and repetition functions, revise the calculation to use the data from the database.

For a complex but real-life test of your abilities, change the units used in calculating time. Some people use a decimal representation of time as in the Time Cards template; others use hours and minutes. In a decimal representation of time, 1.25 means one hour and one quarter (15 minutes). The alternative representation would be read as 1 hour and 25 minutes. Can you change the calculations to use this alternative method of working with time?

HOUR 9

Working with Scripts

What You'll Learn in This Hour:

▶ About Scripts—This section explains the basic concepts and terminology.

▶ Using ScriptMaker—FileMaker's built-in scripting tool, ScriptMaker, provides a simple point-and-click way of creating scripts without having to understand all the syntax and type detailed commands.

▶ Create a New Script—Here's how to start from scratch with a new script.

▶ Look at a Simple Script—Here's how to read a script.

▶ Script Step Categories—ScriptMaker organizes script steps into categories; they are summarized here.

▶ Script Steps and the Web—More script steps than ever are available to users accessing FileMaker databases with browsers.

▶ Use Comments in a Complex Script—Comments keep your scripts useful long after you've forgotten what you did, why you did it, or how you figured out the solution to a problem.

▶ Attaching Scripts to Layout Elements—Anything can be a button if you attach a script to it.

▶ Handling Errors in Scripts—One of the most powerful features of scripts is that you can intercept and handle errors before they come to a user's attention.

▶ Running Scripts Automatically When Files Are Opened or Closed—See how to clean up databases before and after you and other users have "improved" them.

By writing FileMaker scripts, you can greatly extend the usefulness of FileMaker and your solutions. For frequently repeated tasks, automation can mean that a single mouse click replaces a multitude of clicks, typing, and other interface actions. For complex tasks, the single mouse click that starts the script can replace lengthy documentation that tells people how to perform the task. Scripts can now be integrated with Web-based FileMaker solutions. As a result, they are available in all the environments in which FileMaker databases are available (single user, FileMaker network, and Web).

This hour introduces you to FileMaker scripts. You'll see what they can do, how to use the built-in script editor, and how to attach scripts to layout elements, as well as how to have them run automatically when files are opened or closed. Hour 10, "More on Working with Scripts," shows you how to write scripts to perform common tasks, such as finding data. You'll also see how to use dialogs to communicate with the user as a script is running.

Later, in Part III, Hour 16, "Advanced FileMaker Scripting: Design Issues, Script Parameters, and Working with Related Records," explores script parameters, importing, exporting, and sharing scripts.

About Scripts

Scripts are stored in database files along with one or more tables. They can access data in the tables in the file, as well as in related tables that may be in other database files.

FileMaker scripts use their own programming language; however, they can be integrated both with ActiveX on Windows and AppleScript on the Macintosh.

Scripts handle repetitive tasks as well as complex tasks. In many cases, scripts embody domain-specific logic or business rules—sometimes more clearly and fully than in policy and procedure documents.

You can create sophisticated scripts that run on their own; you can also combine scripts into complex processes because scripts can run other scripts.

Using ScriptMaker

You create and edit scripts with ScriptMaker. This section introduces you to the basics of ScriptMaker. You'll see how to

- ▶ Open ScriptMaker
- ▶ Create a new script
- ▶ Look at a simple script
- ▶ Use comments in a complex script

The scripts in this section are from the Recipes template.

Open ScriptMaker

To open ScriptMaker, choose Scripts, ScriptMaker from the menu. When you first open ScriptMaker, you see the Define Scripts dialog, shown in Figure 9.1.

FIGURE 9.1
Open ScriptMaker to define scripts.

The scripts in your database file are listed. You can change their order by dragging the small double-arrow icon to the left of the script name up or down. The most common reason for reordering the scripts is that you can display them in the Scripts menu, and, by reordering the scripts, you reorder the Scripts menu. (It matches the order in this dialog.)

Not all scripts are visible in the Scripts menu: To make a script visible, use the checkbox at the left of each script's entry. The first nine scripts are automatically assigned command-key equivalents using the numerals 1 through 9.

In Figure 9.1, some scripts are named "-". These are empty scripts that have been created simply to organize the Scripts menu in which they will appear. Dividing lines appear in the Scripts menu in place of these scripts.

You use the buttons to perform a script; create new ones; and import, delete, or duplicate scripts. You can also print scripts. (Importing is discussed in Hour 16.)

Create a New Script

In the Define Scripts dialog, click the New button to create a new script. The Edit Script dialog opens, as shown in Figure 9.2.

FIGURE 9.2
Create a new script.

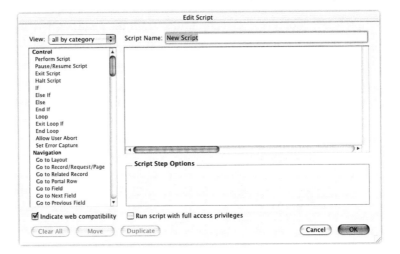

If you've been using FileMaker in versions prior to FileMaker 7, you'll notice some minor changes in these dialogs. Most significantly, the field in which you edit a script's name appears on the Edit Script dialog shown in Figure 9.2 rather than in the Define Scripts dialog shown in Figure 9.1.

The Edit Script dialog has three basic areas:

▶ At the left, a scrolling list of script steps appears. They are organized by category, and you can use the pop-up menu at the top to select only one category if you want. To insert a script step into the script, double-click it or select it and click the Move button at the bottom.

▶ At the top right, your script appears in the large area. You cannot type directly into this area (as you can in the similar area in the Specify Calculation dialog). The only way to enter script steps into the script is by either double-clicking or selecting the step and then clicking the Move button.

▶ Below the script area is the Script Step Options area. Here, you can control options for those script steps that support them. For example, the Go to Layout script step requires you to choose a layout to go to.

The script step syntax is generated as you move script steps into the script area and as you choose script step options. Each script step appears on one line. In this book, some script step lines appear on more than one line because of page layout limitations. If a script step spans more than one line, the second line is slightly indented. (This is in addition to some automatic indenting that ScriptMaker does for `If` statements and the like.)

By the Way

Look at a Simple Script

Figure 9.3 shows a simple script from the Recipes template.

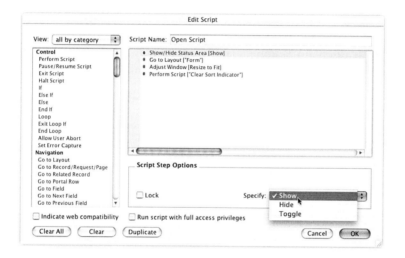

FIGURE 9.3
Recipes uses a script when the database is opened.

This is a common type of script, and its four lines of code introduce you to common forms of syntax. This script runs automatically when the database file is opened. (You'll see how to do that later in this hour.) The purpose of the script is to start with a specific layout displayed and with the window in a known state, which the user can then modify.

First, the status area is shown. The `Show/Hide Status Area` script step takes one option, which is either Show, Hide, or Toggle. Options are displayed in square brackets, as you can see in the first line of code:

```
Show/Hide Status Area [Show]
```

The Script Step Options area changes with each selected script step, allowing you to enter the appropriate options. If there is a single Specify button, you can double-click the script step in the script itself to open a dialog that lets you specify values for the script step. If there's more than one button, you need to click the button you want.

The second script step goes to a specified layout (Form), which is set in the option for that script step:

```
Go to Layout ["Form"]
```

Next, the window is resized for the layout with this code:

```
Adjust Window [Resize to Fit]
```

Finally, another script is run. As you browse the data, you can modify it in various ways; you also can manipulate it by sorting it. A script that runs automatically when the database file is opened normally doesn't touch the data itself, but it commonly will modify status fields, such as an indicator in the layout showing how the file is sorted. That's what the script performed here does.

```
Perform Script["Clear Sort Indicator"]
```

Thus, when the file is opened, it will be in a known state, ready for the user to work with it.

Script Step Categories

The script steps are divided into a dozen categories, as shown in Figure 9.4.

FIGURE 9.4
Script steps are divided into categories.

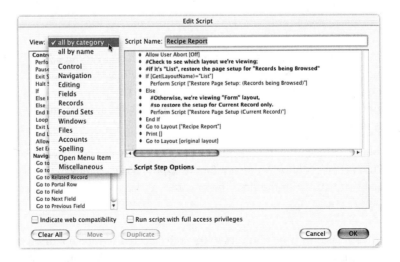

Each of those categories is briefly described here. The individual script steps are fully described in the online help.

Control

You've already seen one of the Control script steps: `Perform Script`. These script steps control script processing itself. They include steps to stop a script, as well as looping constructs. If your script is more than a few lines long, you probably will use one or more of these.

Navigation

The Navigation script steps let you control the mode you're in, as well as layouts to use for display. They also let you go to fields and records that you can specify in a variety of ways (next/previous, first/last, or using a calculation).

Editing

The Editing script steps handle cut/copy/paste commands, as well as selection commands, undo, and performing finds on text.

Fields

The Fields script steps operate on fields. They let you insert data into fields. The data can be any of the normal FileMaker types, such as text or graphics; it can also be specific values, such as the current date or time. In addition, it can be the result of a calculation that you specify in the script. You can insert data into fields in Browse mode; you can also insert data into fields in a Find request to construct a specific search.

Records

The Records script steps allow you to work on records (in Browse mode) and requests (in Find mode). You can delete, duplicate, and open them.

In addition, you'll find a script step that is not available as a command when you're working interactively with FileMaker: `commit`. Records are committed (their data is saved) when you finish working with them. If you're working interactively, FileMaker knows that you're finished with a record when you start to work with another. When you're running a script, sometimes you need to let FileMaker know when to commit the data. This matters particularly in multiuser solutions.

Found Sets

Before FileMaker 7, most of these script steps were in a category called Sort/Find/Print. The Print script step is now located in the new Files category. The script steps here, as expected, enable you to control sorts and finds.

Windows

The Windows script steps operate on windows and their components—for example, the Show/Hide Status Area script step is located here. (This step and Show/Hide Text Rules were called Toggle script steps before FileMaker 7.)

Files

The Files script steps enable you to open and close files, convert XML and ODBC data, and manage multiuser settings.

Accounts

With Accounts steps, you manage security. Accounts are discussed in Hour 18, "Securing Your Solutions and Databases."

Spelling

The Spelling script steps enable you to automate the spelling interface described previously in Hour 2, "Using FileMaker and Its Basic Templates."

Open Menu Item

The Open Menu Item script steps implement the various commands that open FileMaker dialogs. Using them, you can open such varied dialogs as Define Database, Find/Replace, and even ScriptMaker (Define Scripts).

Miscellaneous

This category includes the rest of the script steps not collected elsewhere. You've already seen the Comment script step. Other steps let you send email from FileMaker, display a custom dialog (and retrieve data from it), and use AppleScript.

Script Steps and the Web

Finally, you can use the Indicate Web Compatibility checkbox in the lower left of the dialog to gray out those script steps not applicable for scripts running on the Web. Figure 9.5 shows the result.

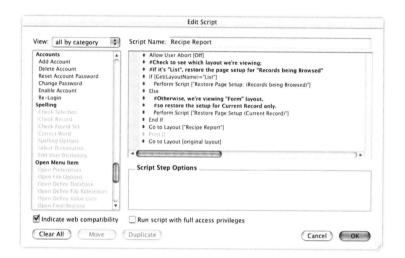

In general, script steps that apply to the database will work; those that apply to the interface (which does not appear on the Web) do not.

Use Comments in a Complex Script

Scripts quickly grow in length and complexity. You can make them easier to understand in two ways. One way is to split up scripts into two or more scripts, each of which does one or two clearly defined things. The other way is to use comments. (And nothing prevents you from doing both; a comment can explain how one script relates to another.)

In Figure 9.6, you can see a script's comments displayed in boldface type. To enter a comment, use the Comment script step in the Miscellaneous category. In the Script Step Options portion of the dialog, a Specify button lets you enter the comment.

FIGURE 9.6
Comments make a script more readable.

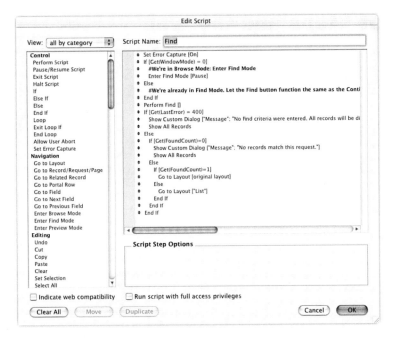

Attaching Scripts to Layout Elements

An interface element to which a script is attached is called a *button*. It's a button in the sense that a click on it causes something to happen. The button can be a graphic image that you have drawn, it can be a FileMaker button that you draw in Layout mode, or it can be text. Figure 9.7 shows the pointer changing to a hand as it passes over the Print This Recipe button.

The New, Delete, and Find icons are buttons, as are the tabs on the tab view and the help (question mark) icon.

To attach a script to a layout element, select it in Layout mode. Then choose Format, Button from the menu to open the Specify Button dialog, shown in Figure 9.8.

Use the Specify Button dialog to choose from the scripts in the database file. You also can select scripts from other files if you want.

As you can see from the figure, you can select specific script steps to perform from a button: One of them just happens to be Perform Script. Many FileMaker solution authors automatically attach scripts, rather than specific script steps, to buttons. The script that's attached may start out as a single script step, but if you need to modify the behavior, it's much easier if you've got a script attached to a button than if you have to stop what you're doing and go back to create a script.

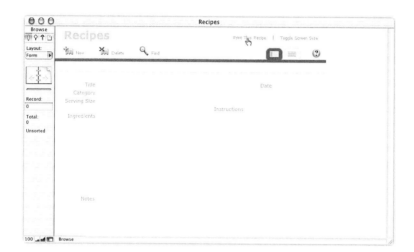

FIGURE 9.7
"Print This Recipe" is a button.

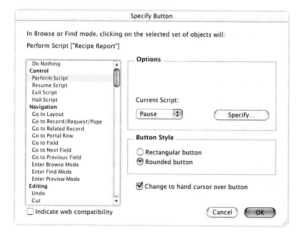

FIGURE 9.8
Attach a script to a button.

Menu commands can accomplish what the New, Delete, and Find items do. If you examine the Recipes template, you'll see that New and Delete use the basic script steps, but Find performs a script (called "Find").

Handling Errors in Scripts

The Find script from the Recipes template, shown previously in Figure 9.6, provides an example of custom error handling—one of the reasons for using a script rather than the basic FileMaker script step.

To handle errors yourself in a script, you use Set Error Capture to tell FileMaker that you do not want it to display an error message. The first line of this script does that:

```
Set Error Capture [On]
```

After a script step that might trigger an error (such as the Find script step), you can check for errors using the Get function with the LastError constant. The list of FileMaker error numbers is available through online help in the documentation for the Get(LastError) function. You can search on LastError in FileMaker Pro Help to find that documentation.

Thus, you can write the following script steps as shown in Figure 9.6:

```
If (Get(LastError))=400
  Show Custom Dialog ["Message",
    "No find criteria were entered. All records will be displayed"]
  Show All Records
Else
```

This catches error 400—no find criteria—and, instead of returning only an error message, does what makes most sense in this case—displays all records. (The Show Custom Dialog script step is discussed in Hour 10.)

> How do you enter an If test? Move the script step into your script by double-clicking or selecting it and clicking the Move button. Click the Specify button, and you are presented with the same Specify Calculation dialog that you saw in Hours 7, "Working with Calculations, Formulas, Functions, and Repeating Fields," and 8, "More on Calculations and Functions." The result automatically is set to Boolean, and you can create any type of calculation you want.

In many cases, setting error capture on and checking for common errors allows you to customize and even eliminate error messages. Normally, you turn Set Error Capture on after you have finished the processing for which you do your error checking and when you want to revert to standard FileMaker error capture.

Running Scripts Automatically When Files Are Opened or Closed

In addition to attaching scripts to buttons or running them from the Scripts menu, you can set them to run automatically when files are opened or closed. To attach a script to a file in this way, choose File, File Options from the menu to open the File Options dialog shown in Figure 9.9.

FIGURE 9.9
Attach a script to the opening of a file.

Summary

This hour provided an introduction to FileMaker scripting. In Hour 10, you'll see how to create a script to find data.

Scripting one area in which FileMaker provides functionality beyond that of a simple data manager. Together with layouts, scripts let you create full-fledged solutions with FileMaker.

Q&A

Q *Are there guidelines for writing good FileMaker scripts?*

A Two guidelines apply to all programming tools, including ScriptMaker. First, document your work with comments in the script. Don't rely on your memory—or on written documentation separate from the script. Second, make each script as self-contained as possible and have it do one logical operation. By focusing each script on one task, you may be able to reuse the script in other contexts. A master script can then perform several tasks simply by calling Perform script steps.

You can further refine your script architecture by separating interface steps, such as dialogs, from noninteractive processing. A common method is to write a script that gathers parameters and information from a user and then passes control to a second script that performs the work. You'll see how to use parameters to implement this structure in Hour 16.

If you do this, adopt a consistent naming convention for your scripts. One such naming convention uses pairs of names. A script called Enter Budget Amount might be the interactive script, one that queries the user for the data using a dialog. It could then call a script called Do Enter Budget Amount, which is not interactive but does the database update. Alternatively (or in addition), you can flag scripts that are interactive by using names such as Enter Budget Amount Interactive or Enter Budget Amount HI (for human interface). Knowing which scripts require user intervention helps to prevent cases in which you reuse a script that winds up stalling at 2:00 a.m. because no one is there to click a button.

And finally, remember that any script that can generate an error message in a dialog—custom dialog or standard FileMaker dialog—is potentially interactive. If you capture all potential errors and dispose of them without a dialog, your script is truly noninteractive and safe to run unattended.

Q *If you attach scripts to text buttons (such as Print This Report), how do people know that they are buttons to click?*

A You can specify that the pointer changes to a pointing hand when it moves over the button, but that requires the user to know to move the pointer over it. In the templates, the area at the top of the layout is devoted to buttons. In this way, users come to know that this is a control area, not a data area. You can use any technique that you want to isolate a control area, but being consistent helps your users divine what is data and what is a button.

Workshop

Quiz

1. Can you copy and paste scripts?

2. How do you add scripts to the Scripts menu?

3. What is Set Error Capture for?

Quiz Answers

1. No. Because scripts aren't stored as text, you have to move script steps into the editing area. You can import scripts from the Define Scripts dialog, but you can't copy and paste.

2. Use the checkboxes in the Define Scripts dialog.

3. Set it to On if you want to check for errors using Get (LastError).

Activities

Explore the scripts in the templates. Frequently, you'll find scripts that perform other scripts as recommended in this hour. Now might be a good time to experiment with modifying layouts. Frequently, the top right of a layout contains text attached to a script using the Button command in the Format menu when in Layout mode. Try your hand at creating a graphic object to attach the script to. (When you do this, you'll soon discover how difficult it can be to convey a complex thought such as "find incomplete tasks" graphically.)

Review the script steps in the scrolling list at the left of the Edit Script dialog to see exactly what you can do with scripts. Now sit down with your favorite FileMaker template and decide what routine or complex task you want to implement. Deciding what to script can be almost as difficult as deciding how to script it. At the end of Hour 10, you can try your hand at implementing the script.

HOUR 10

More on Working with Scripts

What You'll Learn in This Hour:

▶ Writing a Find Script—A Find script is one of the most common types of FileMaker scripts. You can use this script over and over in other contexts.

▶ Implementing the Cancel Button with an If Script Step—Allow users to stop a script by clicking the Cancel button in a dialog.

▶ Specifying Find Requests— Find requests can be complex. Here's additional information to complement what was presented in Part I, "Getting Started with FileMaker—Using the Templates."

▶ Debugging Scripts—The Script debugger helps you find out where your scripts are misbehaving.

▶ Sharing Scripts—Sharing scripts can save time, whether your own or someone else's.

You've seen the basics of ScriptMaker and FileMaker scripts; now it's time to start from scratch to create a script. You'll start out this hour doing just that. Then you'll see how to debug it with FileMaker Developer, and finally how to share scripts among solutions and with other people.

Writing a Find Script

Once again, the Recipes template will be used as the base. As you saw in Hour 9, "Working with Scripts," a Find script is attached to the Find icon on the layout. It takes you into Find mode and intercepts error messages.

But what if the user doesn't know about Find mode? When you click the Find button, you get a blank data entry window just like the one in which you enter data.

What is this? (In fact, this is an aspect of FileMaker that briefly confuses many new users.) In this hour, you'll create a customized find script that puts up the dialog shown in Figure 10.1.

FIGURE 10.1
Use a dialog to
customize your
find.

The dialog customizes the instruction to the user by adding the user's name to the end of the instruction, as you can see in the figure.

The script you will write consists of the following actions:

1. Enter Find mode.

2. Create a new find request.

3. Display the dialog. When the user types in the ingredient to search for, the script continues.

4. Set the field Ingredients in the find request to the text from the dialog.

5. Perform the Find.

6. Return to Browse mode.

Before you start, create a record in the Recipes database with an ingredient for which you can search. The tuna casserole shown in Figure 10.2 is one possibility.

By the Way

Create another recipe with different ingredients. That way you can test the positive case—that the find does indeed find what it should—and the negative case—that it does not find what it should not. Failing to test negative cases is a common cause of bugs.

Begin by creating a script as described in Hour 9. Choose Script, ScriptMaker from the menu, and then click New to open the Edit Script dialog. Enter the name of the script at the top of the dialog. You can call this "Custom Find" or any other descriptive name that you want to use.

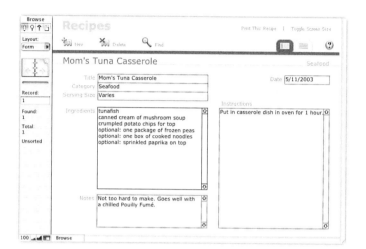

FIGURE 10.2
Tuna casserole is
made easier than
ever with FileMaker.

Entering Find Mode and Creating the Find Request

The first script step you need to execute is `Enter Find Mode`. It's in the Navigation category. Select it and click the Move button or double-click it to add it to the script. At this point, your script looks like this:

```
Enter Find Mode [Pause]
```

The square brackets indicate that there is an option you can set, and at the bottom of the editing dialog is a button you can use to specify the option. In this case, the option is to pause the script at this point. You don't want to do that, so uncheck the checkbox in the lower left of the editing dialog.

There are two ways to script finding data. In the first, you prepare a find request and attach it to the script. You do that with the Specify button. The second method—which you use here—is to create a find request in the script. If you know what you're searching for—perhaps all invoices marked "Ready to Bill"—you can prepare the find request and the user need never know what the find criteria are. However, if you need to let the user specify the criteria, you'll need to create the find request.

Displaying the Dialog and Getting User Input

The `Show Custom Dialog` script step from the Miscellaneous category lets you communicate with the user. Add it to your script.

```
Show Custom Dialog []
```

When you click the Specify button, the dialog shown in Figure 10.3 appears.

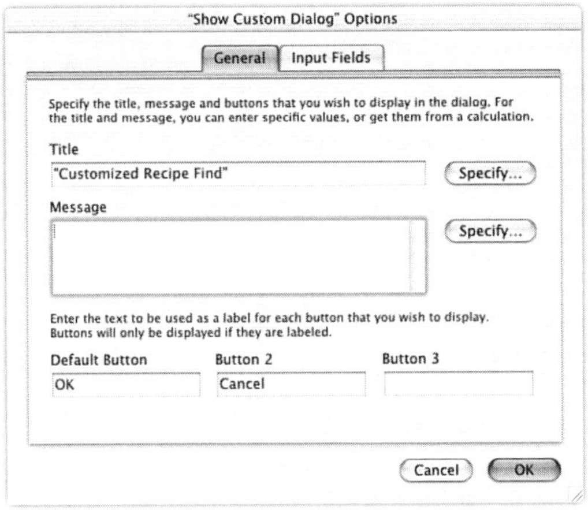

FIGURE 10.3
Specify custom dialog parameters.

You can type a title for the dialog as shown in Figure 10.3. Rather than type the title directly as shown in Figure 10.3, you can use the Specify buttons to create a calculation that returns a text value for either the title or the message text.

In this case, you want to append the user's name to the question in the dialog. That requires a calculation, so click the Specify button to open the Specify Calculation dialog as shown in Figure 10.4.

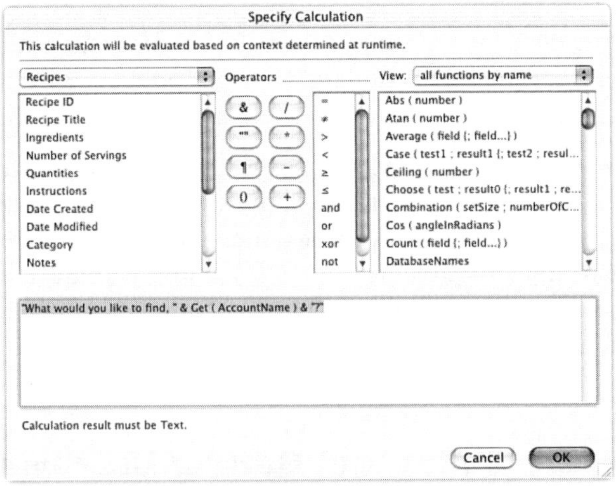

FIGURE 10.4
Create a calculation for dynamic text.

The calculation uses the Get function to find the account name associated with the current user of the database. When you close the calculation dialog, you'll see that the account name has been entered into the dialog as shown in Figure 10.5.

At this point, you can rename the buttons if you want. You can even remove one of the buttons. In this case, you may want to temporarily remove the Cancel button (just erase the text), because it won't be implemented until after the first pass at creating the script.

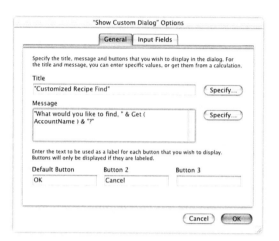

FIGURE 10.5
Complete the dialog.

The Input Fields tab (see Figure 10.6) lets you collect data from the dialog and place it in fields in the current database record (Browse mode) or request (Find mode). For each input field, use the first Specify button to select the database field into which the data should be placed. Next, create a label for the input field—either by typing directly or by using the Specify button to create a calculation as you saw previously.

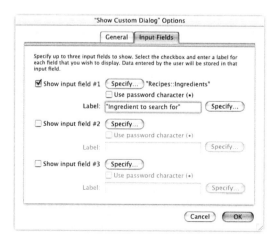

FIGURE 10.6
Specify input fields.

Performing the Find and Returning to Browse Mode

The dialog sets up the find request that you created when you entered Find mode. Now all that's left is to perform the find and return to Browse mode. Here are the lines of code:

```
Perform Find []
Enter Browse Mode []
```

Both steps can take options, but you won't use them. `Perform Find` allows you to specify a find request—you are creating your own find request, so you don't need to specify one. `Enter Browse Mode` lets you pause the script, but when you go into Browse mode, you're ready to let the user take over.

You want to pause a script if the user is to do something and then click the Continue button so that the script can continue with whatever the user has changed. A script with a `Pause` script step in it is shown in Figure 10.7. Note the Continue and Cancel buttons in the status area. (Figure 10.7 is for illustration only; you don't want to pause the script that you are writing in this section.)

FIGURE 10.7
A Pause script step lets the user take over and then continue or cancel the script.

Attaching the Script to the Button

Click OK twice to finish editing the script and then to leave ScriptMaker. Then, following the same steps you used in Hour 9, you can attach your script to the Find button.

First, go into Layout mode and select the Find button. Choose Format, Button from the menu to open the Specify Button dialog shown in Figure 10.8.

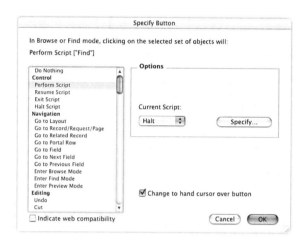

FIGURE 10.8
Connect the script
to the button.

As you can see at the top left of the dialog, the button in the template is attached
to the script Find. Click Specify to open the "Specify Script" Options dialog shown
in Figure 10.9, which lets you substitute your script.

FIGURE 10.9
Use your Custom
Find script.

That's it. Leave Layout mode and go into Browse mode to test your handiwork.

Because this is a basic script, test it with a basic test. Try to find data that you
know exists. If you try to find data that doesn't exist (either because you typed
something wrong or you actually searched for nonexistent data), FileMaker tells you
that "No records match this set of find requests," and it invites you to modify the
find request. That's fine, but if you're not used to using the find request, you may get
lost at this point. So confine your testing to known data.

Implementing the Cancel Button with an If **Script Step**

The script as shown here does what it's supposed to do, but you can easily improve it in several ways. One way is to use the `Set Error Capture` script step to capture errors so that you can provide your own error handling. (This was described in Hour 9.)

Another enhancement is to implement the Cancel button. As it stands, the script works. But if you have removed the Cancel button from the dialog, when you run the script, if you decide you don't want to search the database, you have to keep going, perform some meaningless search or other, and then get control of your database yourself.

It's easy to test to see which button is clicked. You saw an `If` statement in Hour 9 that was used to test for error codes. Here's how you start from scratch to create an `If` statement to test which button was clicked (or any other test that you want to use).

Start by selecting the script step after which you want the `If` to appear. (You can put the script step anywhere you want and then drag it to its correct place with the double-arrow icon, but it's easier to put it in the right place to begin with.) Because the `If` test tests which button in the dialog has been clicked, it goes after the `Show Custom Dialog` script step. Highlight that script step and then add the `If` script step.

By the Way

> As noted previously, you add a script step either by double-clicking it in the scrolling list at the left or by selecting it and clicking the Move button. From now on, these details will be omitted.

When you move the `If` script step into your script, you'll see that the `End If` script step is moved with it. That's because every `If` needs its matching `End If`.

With the `If` step selected, click the Specify button to enter the calculation that returns the Boolean result determining whether the test succeeds.

As you saw previously in Figure 10.5, the buttons in the dialog are numbered. The default button is in the lower-left corner and is number 1. (The default button is always present.) You can specify two additional buttons. To check which button has been clicked in FileMaker 7, you use the `Get` function with the `LastMessageChoice` parameter. Thus, you specify the calculation in the `If` step as

`Get(LastMessageChoice)=1`

The result is true if the OK button has been clicked; false if the Cancel button has been clicked.

> One difference between FileMaker 7 and previous versions is the removal of the Status function and its replacement by the Get function in most cases. Before FileMaker 7, you would have written Status(CurrentMessageChoice) instead of Get(LastMessageChoice). If you open an earlier database in FileMaker 7, this conversion is done for you automatically.

At this point your script looks like this:

```
If [Get(LastMessageChoice=1)]
End If
Perform Find []
```

Drag the Perform Find step up so that it moves between the If and End If steps. It automatically is indented for you:

```
If [Get(LastMessageChoice=1)]
  Perform Find []
End If
```

> Many people follow exactly these steps in developing scripts. Start by implementing the basic functionality to make sure that it works. Then, go back and add in the features such as Cancel buttons. Just make sure that you do this, or you and your scripts will get a reputation for sloppiness.

Specifying Find Requests

You didn't need to specify a find request in this case because you ask the user for the search criteria. However, in cases where you know the search criteria (and the user may not know), you'll need to specify a find request.

> Being able to specify a find request is new in FileMaker 7. In the past, you needed to perform a specific find and then write a script that would pick up that find and store it with the script. Now you can specify the find request directly. Many FileMaker users have waited a long time for this particular enhancement.

Clicking the Specify button in Enter Find Mode or Perform Find opens the dialog shown in Figure 10.10. It shows find requests that you have specified; it also shows the last find request that you executed interactively. You can use it as a find request or create a new one. (Depending on what experiments you have done with the Recipes template, you may have other find requests—or none.)

FIGURE 10.10
Find requests can
be managed using
the Specify Find
Requests dialog.

Both the New and Edit buttons open the Edit Find Request dialog shown in Figure 10.11.

FIGURE 10.11
Edit find requests.

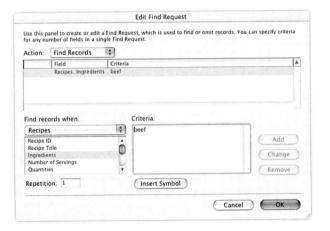

Select a field from the list at the left and then type the search criteria in the field at the right. Basic searching just searches for text. Just as with an interactive find, you can insert symbols that modify the search. Clicking the Insert Symbol button opens the list shown in Figure 10.12. You can double-click the symbols or type them into the Criteria field.

FIGURE 10.12
Insert symbols to
refine searches.

You can construct complex searches that use several fields. Simply select the field in question, click Add, and then enter the criteria for that field as shown in Figure 10.13. As the display reminds you, multiple fields with their criteria all must succeed; this is a logical AND. As with an interactive find, you use OR with separate find requests. The rule is: Within one request, everything is ANDed; across requests, everything is ORed.

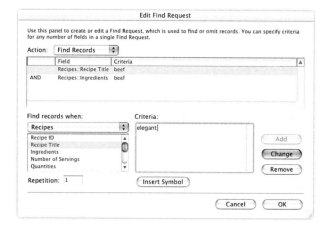

FIGURE 10.13
A single request
can have multiple
components.

Debugging Scripts

In FileMaker Developer, the Scripts menu includes a Debug Scripts command, which can help you develop scripts. (If you are doing significant amounts of scripting, consider using FileMaker Developer. Not only does it provide the debugger, but also its other developer tools will likely come in handy. If you use a lot of scripting, you probably have the complexity in your databases that will benefit from FileMaker Developer and its diagnostic and documentation tools.)

When you choose Scripts, Debug Scripts, the Script Debugger window shown in Figure 10.14 is displayed whenever you run a script.

FIGURE 10.14
Use the script debugger to troubleshoot your scripts.

The script is shown in the center of the window. You use the buttons across the top of the window to control how it operates.

Stepping Through Scripts

Most commonly, you use the first button at the upper left to step through the script one line at a time. You can watch to see how the script executes; not just what it does, but how control passes through If steps and the like. The line that is about to be executed is identified by a small blue arrow to its left. In Figure 10.14, the arrow points to the Show/Hide Status Area script step.

The next two buttons, Step Into and Step Out, let you work with scripts performed by a script. When a Perform Script step is encountered, the Step button steps to the next step in the script; that is, it performs the script and then stops at the next step in the original script. On the other hand, if you click Step Into, it starts to perform the script and stops at the first step. You can then use Step to step through the performed script. If you want to short-circuit the process, you can use Step Out to finish performing the embedded script and stop at the next step of the original script.

Using ScriptMaker

The last icon on the right at the top (the note pad) takes you into ScriptMaker, where you can modify the script.

Using Breakpoints

Rather than stepping through the script, you can set *breakpoints*—points within the script steps at which you want the script to stop. There are two ways of setting breakpoints. In the Script Debugger window, you can click to the left of any script steps; a red square appears to the left of the `Adjust Window` script step, as you can see in Figure 10.14. You can remove a breakpoint by clicking on the red square; it disappears.

You use breakpoints by clicking the Run to Breakpoint button—the fourth from the left in the row at the top of the window. The script runs until it hits the next breakpoint that you selected.

You can use the various control buttons together. For example, you may want to set a breakpoint at an `If` statement. Run the script to that breakpoint and then go step-by-step with the Step button. When you're finished, you can use the Stop Execution button to leave the script. Alternatively, use Run to Breakpoint to run to the end of the script (if there are no intervening breakpoints).

You can set breakpoints in the Edit Script dialog as shown in Figure 10.15. Just click in the gray area to the left of the steps. To remove a breakpoint, click on its rectangle. This can be convenient when you're creating a script. Place a breakpoint at a point that may have a problem and then place a comment in the script to remind yourself what you want to check.

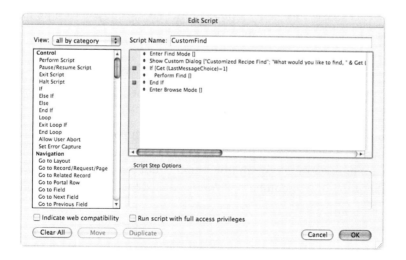

FIGURE 10.15
You can set breakpoints in ScriptMaker.

Sharing Scripts

When you've gone to the trouble of creating scripts, it's nice to be able to share them with other FileMaker solutions and other users. Because scripts are not text-based, you can't just copy and paste. Instead, you can import a script from a database file to which you have access. From the Define Scripts dialog, click Import to open a standard file dialog. Navigate to the database file from which you want a script. Open that file, and you see the Import Scripts dialog shown in Figure 10.16.

FIGURE 10.16
Import scripts from other database files.

Check the checkboxes next to the names of the scripts that you want to import; then click OK. The scripts are imported.

However, before you use them, open each one and review it carefully. Because scripts may have references to fields, layouts, or tables that do not exist in your database file, sometimes those references are undefined. You have to specify the elements in your own database file to which they should refer.

If you want to import the script with its references still pointing to the other database file, you may be better off using the Perform Script step. That step lets you set the script to perform as a script from another database file. When it is executed, it is executing in that database file and is linked to the data in that file.

Summary

This hour showed you how to start from scratch to write a script, debug it, run it, and share it with others. These are the basic tools you need to use ScriptMaker and the script steps described in Hour 9.

Scripts encapsulate logic at a different layer than the raw data encapsulated in the database. With scripts added to the data, you can literally define the operations of a business or other organization. You've seen how to share scripts, so it's not far-fetched to proceed to sharing data in Hour 11, "Importing and Exporting Data."

Q&A

Q *Is there anything in Hour 9 that bears repeating?*

A Comment your scripts and focus them on performing a single task. Those two items cannot be stressed enough.

Q *How do you handle cases in which you need more buttons or data fields than a custom dialog can handle?*

A One way of doing this is to use multiple dialogs, but that can get tedious both for users and for the person writing the dialog. A more efficient way is to create a new layout that is used as a dialog. If you need to collect data for four fields (one more than a custom dialog can handle), just place those four fields on the layout. Add instructions as well as OK and Cancel buttons. Remember to restore the original layout as part of the script's processing. (And remember that data collected either in a dialog or through a layout might properly go to global fields rather than individual record fields. This is the correct implementation if the data is used simply to carry out a command and doesn't need to be stored with separate values in each record.)

Q *Can you debug scripts with FileMaker Pro (rather than FileMaker Developer)?*

A One common way of debugging scripts with FileMaker Pro is to insert Pause script steps. The script pauses at that step, and you can see what the values of data fields are and how the script is operating. It's somewhat less sophisticated than using FileMaker Developer's debugger, but it can get the job done, albeit in a bit more time.

Workshop

Quiz

1. How do you turn on the script debugger?

2. How do you implement AND and OR functionality using FileMaker?

3. How do you determine which button in a custom dialog has been clicked?

Quiz Answers

1. Choose Scripts, Debug Script from the menu in FileMaker Developer.

2. All the values shown in a single find request are ANDed together. All the find requests are ORed.

3. Use `Get (LastMessageChoice)` to test for the *number* (not name) of the button. The numbers are shown in the General tab of the "Show Custom Dialog" Options dialog.

Activities

In this hour, you saw how to create your own Find dialog and to carry out a find request. Using one of the templates, create a different type of customized find that searches for all records with specific data values. Hint: The To Do List template has scripts that search for today's items and incomplete items. That shows you one way of doing this using an existing find request. Can you implement the scripts again dynamically creating a find request as described in this hour?

At the end of Hour 9, you decided on a script that you want to add to one of the FileMaker templates. Can you implement it now? If not, perhaps you'll be able to later in this book. Or maybe you should revisit your design and scale it back so that you can do it now. Either way, start with a brand-new script and see how it goes.

HOUR 11

Importing and Exporting Data

What You'll Learn in This Hour:

▶ About Data Sharing—This section explains the basics about data sharing, including tips for not letting your data be held hostage by applications that can't export it.

▶ File Formats—FileMaker supports a wide variety of file formats in addition to its own. This section describes each one.

▶ Importing Data into FileMaker—Here is a step-by-step guide to importing data (in this case, loading contact information into the Contact Manager template).

▶ Replacing and Updating Data with Match Fields—FileMaker allows you to import data and integrate it with existing data.

▶ Converting Excel Spreadsheets to FileMaker Databases—FileMaker can open Excel spreadsheets and convert them automatically to databases.

▶ Exporting Data from FileMaker—When you export data, you can control what data is exported as well as how it is formatted.

▶ Importing from a Folder—You can use FileMaker to import several files from a single folder with one command.

In this hour, you'll see how to move data into and out of FileMaker. By using the tools described in this hour, you'll easily be able to populate many of the FileMaker templates with your own data gleaned from other sources. In this hour, for example, you'll see how to use the Contact Manager template to organize data that you have entered in products such as the address books in email programs or PDAs.

About Data Sharing

The ability to share data among applications, across networks, and with various people is critical to individuals as well as organizations large and small. Databases serve as repositories of data, but they also normally come with features and software that let them import and export data on a grand scale. FileMaker is no exception.

You can share FileMaker databases over networks using both FileMaker software and standard Web browsers. Those topics are the subject of Part IV, "Sharing FileMaker Solutions," of this book. You can also use the industry standard Open Database Connectivity (ODBC) API, which is the topic of Hour 12, "Working with ODBC and JDBC." Also, on the Macintosh, you can import images directly from a digital camera. (That is described in the user documentation.)

This hour shows you how to import and export data with FileMaker. The techniques involve creating a file in a standard format which can be read by another application. FileMaker supports a wide variety of file formats, and you can use them to share data with many other applications.

By the Way

> Not all applications share data with others. Some, notoriously address books and contact managers, read a variety of formats so that you can convert your data to their format. However, after your data is converted (and you may have added hundreds or even thousands of addresses or appointments), you may discover that data conversion was a one-way trip. The only way to move your data to another application may be to print it out and retype it. When shopping for hardware and software that stores data for you, make sure that it can export the data that you will be putting into it. It's your data, after all.

FileMaker lets you export selected records from a database; it even lets you export summary data. You can export the raw data, or you can export it as it is formatted in the current layout complete with currency symbol, decimal points, and the like.

Finally, don't think that importing and exporting data must involve another application. You can import data into FileMaker that you previously exported from another FileMaker database. You can also export selected data from a FileMaker database, delete records from the database, and then import the selected data into the now-empty database. In yet another variation, you can export selected data (such as last year's appointments) to a standard file format and simply store it on the off-chance that it might need to be loaded later.

Why store it as exported data rather than as a FileMaker database? If you don't know what the future use might be or even who might need the data, a generic file format might be easier to manipulate. For safety's sake, many people keep such archival data both in the FileMaker database format as well as in an exported file.

> When data is exported from a database into a file, that file can easily be read by other people. Be careful that your import and export files are safeguarded, both physically and with passwords or encryption if possible.

By the Way

File Formats

FileMaker reads and writes a number of common file formats used to share data. The file formats are listed in this section along with brief descriptions. Because these formats are used to transfer data between possibly incompatible applications and systems, and also because many of them date to the earliest days of personal computers, many of them are based only on text. If you have italicized some of your data, such formatting will generally be lost in data transfer using these formats. Furthermore, if your data contains movies, images, or other non-text data, you may not be able to transfer those data elements with these formats.

The formats differ in several ways:

▶ Some are binary, and some are plain text. Often there are pairs of formats. (SYLK is a text-based spreadsheet format; WKS is a binary counterpart.)

▶ Some explicitly import and export field names; in others, field names (if present) are represented by the values in the first record.

These are the major common file formats:

▶ Tab-separated text—One of the most basic formats, this separates each field in a record with a tab character; records are separated with return characters. Almost all word processors, spreadsheets, and database applications support this format as do many address books, contact managers, and even basic accounting products. The filenames normally have an extension of .tab.

▶ Comma-separated text—The fields are enclosed in quotation marks and separated by commas. The file extension is usually .csv (comma-separated values) or .txt. Because the fields are enclosed in quotation marks, if the data can contain quotation marks as data, it is usually preferable to use tab-delimited text. Many applications that support tab-separated text also support comma-separated text.

▶ DBF—Originally designed for dBase (an early data manager), this file format supports related products such as Clipper, FoxBase, FoxPro, and FlagShip. Because this format was designed for a database, it includes the concepts of fields with specific types. Thus, numeric fields are differentiated from text fields. It supports dates and times, but not graphics. Unlike the previous formats, which are plain text, this format is specified in bytes.

▶ DIF—Data Interchange Format (DIF) is designed for tables consisting of rows and columns (or, in database parlance, records and fields). It is text-based.

▶ BASIC—This is another binary format (like DBF). It was designed for the BASIC programming language; its files usually have the extension .bas.

▶ HTML Table—The HTML TABLE tag with its associated data row and data element tags can represent two-dimensional data. This format is text-based, and the common extensions are .html and .htm. If you need to publish FileMaker data on the Web, you may be able to export it using the HTML Table format and simply paste the resulting code into a Web page. (Note that this is for static data only; to use a FileMaker database interactively on the Web, see Part IV.)

▶ Merge—With an extension of .mer, this format was designed for use with mail merge programs in word processing.

▶ SYLK—Symbolic Link Format (SYLK) files are used primarily for spreadsheet data. They are text-based, and represent the tabular data along with the calculations found in spreadsheets. The usual extension is .slk.

▶ Lotus 1-2-3—The Worksheet File Format (WKS, WK1) was developed by Lotus. It stores data similar to that in a SYLK file, but the data is stored in binary form rather than as text.

The formats designed for spreadsheets and databases are likely to have more information in them that FileMaker can process than the strictly text-based formats such as tab- and comma-delimited files. Perhaps the most common example of such data is names and formats of data fields in addition to the raw data.

In addition to these formats, FileMaker can read Excel spreadsheets directly. You'll see how to do this later in this hour.

By the Way

Whenever you are exporting data from one application to be used in another one, it may be worthwhile to export it several times in several different formats (if the application supports multiple export formats). That way, if you have trouble importing one file, you can try another one.

Also, remember that your data transfer might turn into a several-stage process. For example, you might need to export address data from an address book into a spreadsheet to get it into one of the FileMaker formats.

Importing Data into FileMaker

Start by exporting data from an address book, PDA, or other data source using one of the formats described in the preceding section. If you don't have such a data source, create a spreadsheet or a table within a word processing application, enter some dummy data (perhaps three fields: name, address, and telephone number), and export the data from the spreadsheet or word processor.

Launch FileMaker, and use the Contact Manager template to create a new database. Choose File, Import from the menu, and in the submenu, select File. You'll be prompted to select the file you have prepared. When you open it, you'll see the dialog shown in Figure 11.1.

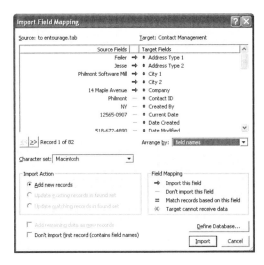

FIGURE 11.1
Control importing with the Import Field Mapping dialog.

The heart of this dialog is the mapping of fields from the imported file to your database. (Importing works for a single table in a database: It's the table on which the current layout is based. You cannot import into two tables at the same time.)

At the right, you'll see the names of the fields in the table to which you'll import data. At the left, you may see field names or data depending on the file format. Use the double-arrow icons below the main section of the dialog to browse forward and back in the file that you're importing.

It's a good idea to browse the data in this way. Often you'll spot exporting or data quality errors. For example, errant characters may show up, and you may find addresses split up or combined. Also, in deciding what imported data fields map to what FileMaker fields, reviewing the data can help. (Field names may not be descriptive; over time, they may have been used for other purposes than they were originally intended.)

You cannot rearrange the order of the data in an imported file. However, you can rearrange the order of the fields in your FileMaker database using the double-arrow icons in the center of the dialog. Drag the fields up and down until the field names on the right-hand side match the data and/or field names on the left.

Use the field mapping symbols identified at the lower right of the dialog to control what happens to the mapped data. You can import data or choose to skip a field in the imported data. You also can select a match field for replacing and updating data. That topic is described in the following section.

Once again, browse several records when you think your work is done to see whether the data looks reasonable. Compare Figure 11.2 with Figure 11.1 to see what the correct mapping looks like when you examine data.

FIGURE 11.2
You can browse data from the Import Field Mapping dialog.

As you set up the field mappings, you may discover that you need to modify the database. You can do so with the Define Database button in this dialog.

The most basic import task is to add new records. After you set up the mapping, choose the Add New Records radio button from the Import Action area in the lower left, and click Import.

You are presented with the Import Options dialog shown in Figure 11.3, which lets you choose whether to perform various auto-enter functions such as storing creation dates. If you are importing data that contains such information, do not perform the auto-enter functions, or you will lose the original creation dates. However, if your imported data does not contain that information, you can use the auto-enter features to time stamp all the newly imported records with the current date.

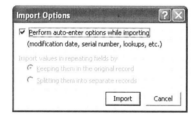

FIGURE 11.3
Choose auto-enter options.

When finished, you'll have moved your contact information from its original source into your Contact Manager FileMaker database.

Whenever you convert data, you may have to do some cleaning up. Not only are there errors that may have been there for years, but two different database structures may require slightly different approaches to data. Each person has different ways of handling this. Some people clean up the data before exporting it and then again when it's imported. Others ignore possibly bad data and do a (possibly bigger) cleanup after importing. Whatever you do, make sure that you review and clean up the data after it's imported. If you haven't used Find mode extensively, this might be a good time to practice with it as you search for problems.

For example, over the years, a mailing list may have been modified to put post office box numbers in the Country field (if all customers are in one country, that field is more or less a spare). As you've entered data, perhaps you've changed your mind about how to handle hyphenated names. And, there are also many cases in which data has been updated incompletely. Postal codes may no longer match addresses; in the United States, recent changes to telephone area codes mean that many long-distance phone numbers are out of date.

Replacing and Updating Data with Match Fields

The direct importing of data described in the preceding section is the most basic and straightforward. You can also use the Import command to replace and update data in FileMaker.

To replace data in your FileMaker database, use the Replace Import action rather than the Add action. The number of records in the imported file should match the number of records in the found set. For each record, the data that you have mapped will be placed in the FileMaker record; existing data in that record will be untouched.

For replacement to work properly, the records in the imported file must be in the same order as they are in the FileMaker database. Many people find that replacing data works best as part of a scripted workflow that can guarantee this.

A related and safer method of updating data is to use match fields. To do so, you need to designate one or more fields as *match fields*. These are fields in your FileMaker database that match fields in your imported data. For example, if you designate First Name and Last Name as match fields, imported records that match existing records with these two fields will be mapped onto the existing records; the data from the imported records will overlay the data in the matched records in the table regardless of their order.

To use matching, select the matching option at the lower left of the Import Field Mapping dialog (in the Import Actions section). Then for the match field, use the match option in the Field Mapping section at the lower right of the dialog.

Converting Excel Spreadsheets to FileMaker Databases

FileMaker can read Excel spreadsheets directly. If you drag an Excel worksheet onto the FileMaker application icon, it automatically is converted to a FileMaker database and opens in Browse mode and Table view, looking remarkably like a spreadsheet.

For most simple spreadsheets created in the way in which most people use spreadsheets, this conversion works seamlessly.

Exporting Data from FileMaker

Exporting data from FileMaker is the reverse side of the coin, and it's equally easy. Start by choosing File, Export from the menu. This opens the Export Records to File dialog shown in Figure 11.4, where you can specify the name and location of the file as well as the format.

Next, you select the data to be exported (see Figure 11.5). By default, all the fields in the current table are shown. You can clear some of them (or all of them) and then move other fields into the scrolling list in the lower right of the dialog. You can also rearrange the order of the exported fields using the same double-arrow icons you used in the Import Field Mapping dialog.

You can also group the data if it is sorted. Depending on where the data is going, you may have a choice when it comes to mapping it. Because FileMaker can rearrange and map data both on import and export, you may prefer to always export all data without any rearranging and then map it on import—or vice versa, or whatever suits you at the time.

Finally, note that a checkbox in the lower-left corner lets you apply the current layout's formatting to the data. If, for example, a data value is 17, but it is formatted by the layout as $17.00, using the layout exports $17.00 rather than 17.

The importing software must be able to read the formatted value (which normally is a string, not a number). You may have to do some experimentation with both ends of the data conversion process to get your options set up properly.

FIGURE 11.5
Select and order
exported fields.

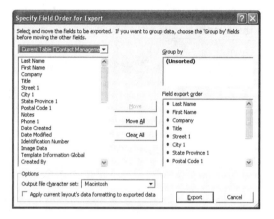

Importing from a Folder

You can import all the text, image, or movie files in a folder into a database by choosing File, Import Records, Folders from the menu. The Folder of Files Import Options dialog shown in Figure 11.6 opens.

FIGURE 11.6
You can import
files from within a
folder.

For images and movies, you can choose a container field in the database into which to import the data—either the actual data or a reference to it. For text files, you choose a text field.

In both cases, the name of the file is imported as a field; you can place it in any field you want in the database.

An example of this feature can be created using the Asset Management template and a digital camera. Take photos of the assets you want to track. (They might be office equipment, home furnishings, or even plants in your garden.) Download the photos to a folder on your computer and name them appropriately. (Their default names may be less than meaningful—something like `DSC00432.tiff`.)

In a blank Asset Management database, choose File, Import Records, Folders from the menu. Map the image to the Picture field, and map the filename to the Item field. All the images and their names are imported into the database. At your leisure, you can enter the other data such as cost and serial number. If you're looking for a record of your assets, this is a quick way of creating it.

Summary

Importing and exporting data is easy with FileMaker. Many of the templates can be put to work right away if you load them with data that you've collected in organizers, spreadsheets, and other documents.

This hour showed you how to move data in batches. In Hour 12, you'll see how to use ODBC technology to perform live updates of data.

Q&A

Q *If I'm moving data from another contact manager to the FileMaker template and the data fields don't match, what's the best way of handling the problem?*

A You can modify the FileMaker Contact Management template to add other data fields. However, you have to also modify the layouts to display those fields—and possibly not use the fields that the template has. Review the situation on both sides to decide whether to modify the database or to reinterpret the data. By now, you have tools that you can use to massage the data after it's imported. (Those tools include scripts and calculations.) You can even take a middle road. For example, the Contact Management database declares two telephone fields—phone 1 and phone 2. If your other contact management tool stores home phone and work phone, you can map home phone into phone 1 and change the name of the phone 1 field.

But what if your other data manager stores phone 1, phone 2, and so forth along with tags such as home phone 1 label (which might be "home")? In this case, why not modify your FileMaker database structure to accommodate the more sophisticated data in the other contact manager.

Q *Given that FileMaker can convert Excel spreadsheets to databases, and Excel can do the reverse, can I share data back and forth with someone and just convert it this way?*

A Yes and no. Depending on the databases and what you're doing with them, you might wind up losing data at some point. This conversion isn't meant for ongoing back-and-forth operation. Instead, consider ODBC as described in Hour 12.

Workshop

Quiz

1. Do fields have to be in the same order when you import them from another data source?

2. How do you remove fields from the Import Field Mapping dialog?

3. How do you format data for export?

Quiz Answers

1. No. You can drag them up and down with the double-arrow icons.

2. Click the icon at the left of the field name to indicate that it should not be imported or exported. (For the sake of clarity, you might want to drag all the fields you won't be using to the bottom of the list.)

3. You can use the checkbox in the lower left of the dialog to apply the formatting from the current layout. You may want to create a special layout used just to format output.

Activities

Take a template and convert data from another application into the template.

Working with ODBC and JDBC

What You'll Learn in This Hour:

▶ What is ODBC?—First, you will find out what ODBC is all about.

▶ Very Basic SQL—Next, there is an introduction to the SQL terminology that you need to know to deal with ODBC.

▶ The FileMaker ODBC Example—The example that ships with FileMaker is used as the basis for the hands-on tutorial in this hour.

▶ Setting Up a Data Source—You will see how to set up a data source on both Windows and Mac OS X.

▶ Importing Data from a Data Source with FileMaker—The actual import of ODBC data is done from FileMaker. You will see how to do that.

In Hour 11, "Importing and Exporting Data," you saw how to import and export data; you can use those techniques to share data between FileMaker databases as well as between FileMaker databases and other applications. This hour introduces you to a much more powerful technology that lets you share data with other database management systems (including the largest ones on mainframe computers).

If you are in an environment that has databases other than FileMaker, ODBC is the most likely way to access data on Oracle, DB2, SQL Server, or other products. It is also the most likely way in which you may export data from your FileMaker databases to those databases. (ODBC export is a feature of FileMaker Server; only ODBC import is described in this book.)

One of the most important features of FileMaker is that it makes database management easy for people without a background in the sometimes arcane world of data management. Interacting with major database management systems using ODBC is relatively painless: Just a few setup steps, and you will be on your way using the familiar FileMaker interface and its elegant but powerful approach to data management.

What Is ODBC?

In 1991, Microsoft developed its Open Database Connectivity interface (ODBC). It was designed to address the problem of communicating between database management systems from different vendors. Despite the fact that most database management systems are based on SQL, they were often unable to easily communicate with one another. In 1991, trying to increase its presence in the corporate world, Microsoft saw an opportunity to provide this connectivity, thereby adding value to its desktop systems.

Later, Sun added Java Database Connectivity (JDBC) to the mix. It relies on the same architecture as ODBC, but it makes that architecture available to people writing in Java.

By the Way

> ODBC and JDBC are based on the same architecture; sometimes they are referred to as xDBC. In this hour, they are referred to as ODBC.

ODBC is implemented in different ways on different platforms. On Windows, it is implemented as part of the operating system itself; on Mac OS X, it is implemented both in the operating system as well as in additional software distributed with FileMaker. You use the FileMaker files in that case. Both sets of interfaces are shown in this hour.

In Hour 11, you saw how to import and export data to and from other applications using standard files with delimiters such as commas or tabs. That process requires you to export data from the sending application and then import it using the receiving application.

The chief difference between that structure and ODBC is that with ODBC, after the initial setup is done, you control both the sending database and the receiving database through the ODBC interface. In other words, if you are importing ODBC data into FileMaker, FileMaker requests the data from the external database. You do not have to go into that database to generate a file that will be imported into FileMaker.

You need to know two aspects of using ODBC:

▶ You must set up a data source that identifies the database from which you will be extracting data. This is done using ODBC software.

▶ In FileMaker, you import data from an ODBC data source; at that time, you specify what data is to be extracted.

Very Basic SQL

ODBC is designed to work with SQL, the standard for relational databases. All databases use SQL in one way or another. FileMaker does not use SQL internally for its own data storage, but it can import SQL data through ODBC, and (with FileMaker Server) it can export SQL data through ODBC. Before addressing the mechanics of ODBC, a brief description of SQL is provided because you need to know some terminology. This section introduces that terminology and provides a summary of the basic SQL data retrieval statement: the *query* statement.

Terminology in SQL and FileMaker

SQL uses some terminology that is different from FileMaker terminology. However, the basic database structures are much the same even though FileMaker implements them differently from SQL-based data management systems.

Data is stored in *tables*; one or more tables can be stored in a *database*. (In FileMaker 7, this terminology matches that of SQL; previously, FileMaker did not use the concept of tables, and a FileMaker database was equivalent to an SQL table. In FileMaker 7, a database may contain only one table, even though it often contains more than one, but the two concepts—table and database—are distinct.)

FileMaker refers to *fields* within a table; SQL uses *columns* within a table. The concepts are the same.

FileMaker stores data in *records*; in SQL, the data is stored in *rows* of a table.

When you set up your data sources and when you specify queries, you use this terminology. (But do not worry: The graphical user interfaces display the appropriate terms, and you can focus on the data that you are working with.)

Constructing Queries in SQL

SQL was originally an acronym for Structured Query Language. (It is no longer considered an acronym.) The core of SQL is the capability to manipulate relational data, and that is done with a `select` statement that constitutes a query. A `select` statement often appears to be a natural language statement such as

```
select address, phonenumber from employees where employeename = "Brown"
```

An SQL query has three major components:

- ▶ What—After the word `select`, you specify what you want to retrieve.
- ▶ From—After the word `from`, you specify the table from which you want to retrieve the data.
- ▶ Where—After the word `where`, you specify the condition(s) to use in selecting data.

In addition to `what`/`from`/`where`, several components may appear in `select` statements: Group by, having, and order by let you aggregate data and sort it.

The Basic SQL Rule

SQL can be summed up in a simple sentence: Everything is a table. A single data value is a table—a table consisting of one row and one column.

You can combine two tables with SQL; the result is another table. The most common type of combination is a *join*—a table with columns from one table and columns from another table. In most cases, a join uses a common key (such as a unique identifier) to match up data from one table to another.

In this way, an SQL join is like (but not identical to) the relationships you create in FileMaker. A primary difference between the two architectures is that with FileMaker, your joins and queries are specified as relationships before you start using the database and its table. In SQL, you define your database and tables, and you then create joins or queries as you need them.

The FileMaker ODBC Example

FileMaker comes with an ODBC example that serves as the jumping-off point for this hour. The sample consists of a database and two text files. The text files are comma-delimited files; you could import them into the database using the techniques you learned in Hour 11. However, the FileMaker example shows you how to import that data using ODBC.

One advantage of using ODBC is that after the data source is set up, you do not have to worry about the external database (or flat file, in this case). Converting an import command in FileMaker from a comma-delimited file to one that accesses a database is simply a matter of changing the data source.

In this hour, FileMaker will be expanded; you will see how to import only certain data from the example files. The example uses data from a text file. To use one of the other ODBC drivers, you need not only the driver but also the database (Oracle, SQL Server, Microsoft Access, and so forth). The text example is used because everyone can process text. Although setting up the data source for text differs from setups for database tables, the actual use of the data source in retrieving data for FileMaker is the same whether you are going from a text file or from the largest mainframe database management system.

The ODBC example is installed automatically with FileMaker. It is located inside the FileMaker folder in English Extras/Examples.

Setting Up a Data Source on Windows

Your data source identifies where you get the data from. You set it up with ODBC software outside FileMaker. In some cases, you may not need to set it up at all; in an organization's database environment, the data sources may have been prepared for you by the database management team. Data sources are used by FileMaker, but there is nothing specific to FileMaker about them. Thus, a data source that identifies data in a personnel database can be used for ODBC data by FileMaker, Oracle, or any other ODBC application.

The steps involved in setting up a data source on Windows are

1. Run ODBC Data Source Administrator.
2. Create a new data source.
3. Select the driver.
4. Set up the driver.
5. Define the data.

Run ODBC Data Source Administrator

Start by running ODBC Data Source Administrator, located inside My Computer/Control Panels/Administrative Tools as shown in Figure 12.1.

The data sources you have configured are listed as shown in Figure 12.2. (DSN stands for Data Source Name.)

The first three tabs display lists of three types of data sources—User, System, and File. (The data sources listed vary from computer to computer; Figure 12.2 shows the common data sources that you will find installed before you create your own.)

FIGURE 12.1
Run data sources
(ODBC).

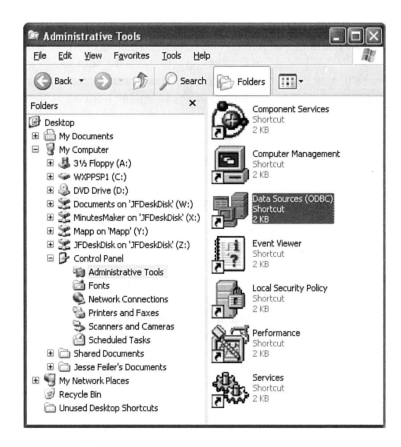

FIGURE 12.2
ODBC Data Source
Administrator lists
existing data
sources.

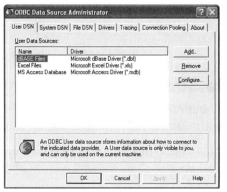

The three types of data sources are

▶ User DSN—A data source for your own use.

▶ System DSN—A data source available to all users who have access to your computer.

▶ File DSN—A file with the extension .dsn that describes a data source. The advantage of using a file to describe a data source is that it can be copied to another computer.

Create a New Data Source

Choose whether to create a User, System, or File DSN, and then click Add to start the process. If your data source is just for your own use, User or System is fine. If you want it to be available to others, System or File is the best choice. (Use File to be able to copy the .dsn file to another computer.)

Select the Driver

You next see the dialog shown in Figure 12.3. Select the driver that you want to use. The driver needs to match the file or database that you will be accessing: an Oracle driver for an Oracle database, a text driver for a text file, and so forth.

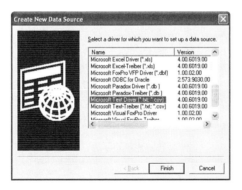

FIGURE 12.3
Select a driver.

The process described here sets up a text data source; each type of driver has its own setup, but they all more or less follow this outline.

By the Way

Set Up the Driver

After you select a driver, the setup dialog shown in Figure 12.4 appears. (Note that this is the setup dialog for the text driver; other drivers have different settings.)

FIGURE 12.4
Set up the driver.

Name and describe the data source at the top of the dialog. For the text driver, you need to specify the directory in which the data source will be found. (If you click the Use Current Directory checkbox, you do not need to specify the directory further.)

Having done that, click Options to enlarge the dialog as shown in Figure 12.5.

FIGURE 12.5
Set the options.

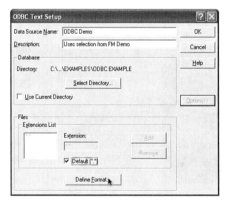

Define the Data

Click Define Format to complete the setup of your data source as shown in Figure 12.6. In the Define Text Format dialog, you can specify whether the text file is tab- or comma-delimited. More important, you select the specific file or database table that will be used; you also select the columns you will access as shown in Figure 12.6.

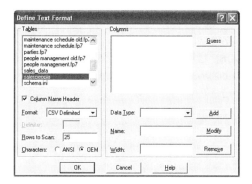

FIGURE 12.6
Select tables and
columns for the
data source.

Your data source is now set up and is ready to be used by any ODBC-compliant
application (such as FileMaker).

Setting Up a Data Source on Mac OS X

The process of setting up a data source on Mac OS X is comparable to the process
on Windows, but its details are different. Perhaps the most important difference is
that you use the drivers and administration software distributed with FileMaker
rather than the operating system ODBC setup tool located in the Applications
folder.

Inside the FileMaker folder you will find a folder called ODBC Import Drivers.
Inside it is an installer for the drivers; run it to install the drivers.

> The ODBC drivers are from a third-party developer. They are installed for free use for
> 30 days. The drivers—which may change over time—include drivers for Oracle, SQL
> Server, and plain text files.

By the
Way

As with Windows, the steps are

1. Run ODBC Data Source Administrator.

2. Create a new data source.

3. Select the driver.

4. Set up the driver.

5. Define the data.

Run ODBC Configure

The installer creates a folder called DataDirect ODBC Folder inside your Applications folder. ODBC Configure is located inside it; run it to configure your ODBC data source. When you first launch it, you see the Configuration Manager dialog shown in Figure 12.7.

FIGURE 12.7
Run ODBC
Configure to set up
your data sources.

Create a New Data Source

Like the ODBC configuration program on Windows, ODBC Configure lets you create and manage your data sources. The interface is similar because the technology is basically the same on both platforms. (One difference you will notice is that you cannot create System DSNs on Mac OS X.)

Any data sources you have already set up are shown in the list. (There may be none.) To add a new one, click Add.

Select the Driver

Just as on Windows, you now need to select your driver. Three drivers are automatically installed with FileMaker when you install the ODBC software as described previously (Oracle, SQL Server, and text). For this example, select the text driver as shown in Figure 12.8.

Set Up the Driver

Set up the driver as shown in Figure 12.9. Provide a meaningful name and a description; then, select the directory in which your text files will be located. (As with Windows, each different driver has its own setup needs; for databases, you do not locate the directory.)

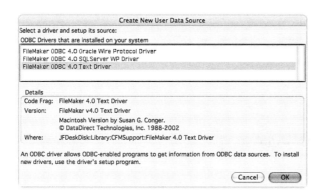

FIGURE 12.8
Select the driver.

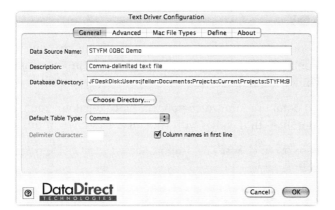

FIGURE 12.9
Set up the driver.

Define the Data

As shown in Figure 12.10, you next click the Define tab to select from the files in the directory you have chosen (or from the tables in the database you have chosen if you are using the Oracle or SQL Server driver).

The software automatically uses the settings you have provided with regard to type of delimiter (tab- or comma-delimited text) and whether the first line has column names in it to display the appropriate columns (fields) for the selected file (table).

FIGURE 12.10
Define the data.

Importing Data from a Data Source with FileMaker

After your data source is set up (and remember that you only have to do that once), you can import data from it using FileMaker. The process from now on is the same on Windows and Mac OS X.

Open or create a database into which you will place the data. You can use the ODBC sample database that comes with FileMaker as shown in this section.

With the database open, choose File, Import Records, ODBC Data Source from the menu as shown in Figure 12.11.

FIGURE 12.11
Import ODBC data
into FileMaker.

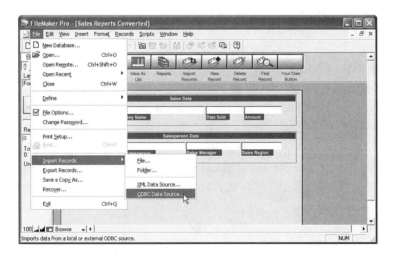

Select the data source you have created as shown in Figure 12.12.

FIGURE 12.12
Select the data source.

You now start to build your query. The next dialog that appears shows you the tables in the data source you have selected. Select the one you want to use, and its columns appear at the upper right of the dialog as shown in Figure 12.13.

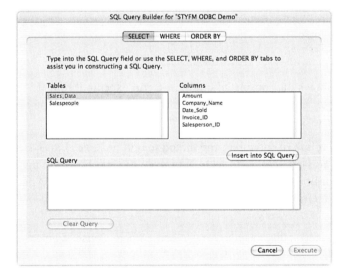

FIGURE 12.13
Select your data source table.

One by one, select each column that you want to use and click Insert into SQL Query to automatically add it to the query. The query can be built with mouse clicks: You do not have to type any SQL (or remember its syntax). However, if you want to just type the SQL query yourself, you can do so.

Figure 12.14 shows the first part of the query.

FIGURE 12.14
Add columns to
your SQL query.

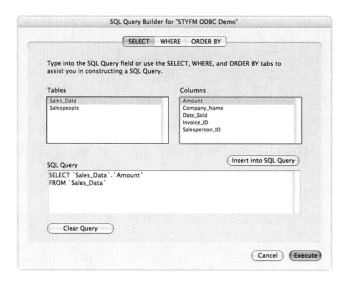

In the sample query presented earlier in this hour, you saw unqualified column
names. Now, you see qualified column names: They are preceded by the name of
the database table. This is important for cases in which you may be mixing data
from two tables.

Figure 12.15 shows the completed query. You can execute it now if you want to
import the data, but in the following section, you see how to refine it before actually running the query.

Click the Where tab at the top of the dialog to add a where clause as shown in
Figure 12.16. You can choose to include or exclude data based on a value (as
shown here) or based on the relationship between two columns. When you click
Insert into SQL Query, the appropriate code is added.

It is always faster—often much faster—to use a where clause to select data from
the external data source rather than importing everything and then removing data
from your FileMaker database.

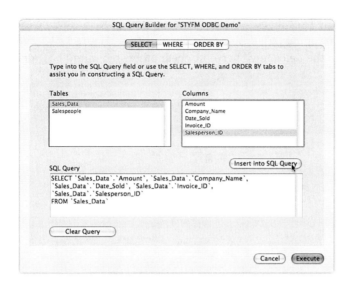

FIGURE 12.15
Complete the
query.

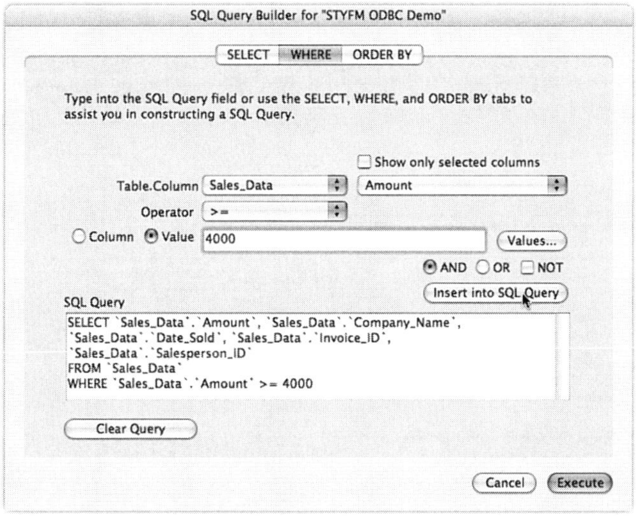

FIGURE 12.16
Add a where
clause.

You can also sort the data in the SQL query using the Order By tab as shown in
Figure 12.17.

Finally, click the Execute button to start the import process. You see the familiar Import Field Mapping dialog shown in Figure 12.18. (Figure 12.18 shows the dialog as some of the fields have been mapped; others remain to be properly mapped.)

FIGURE 12.17
Sort the data if
necessary.

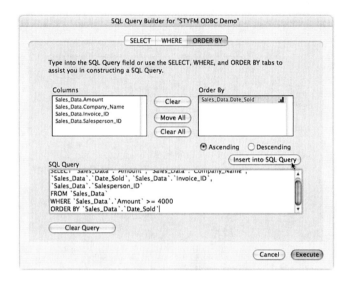

FIGURE 12.18
Map the imported
fields.

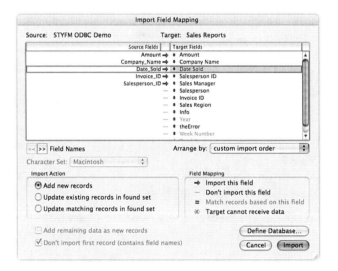

Summary

In this hour, you saw how to use ODBC to import data into FileMaker databases. ODBC allows you to directly control another database instead of using the two-stage export/import process described previously. Because FileMaker ships with drivers for SQL Server and Oracle (two of the most widely used databases in the corporate world), you can interact with many large-scale databases in your organization while preserving your ability to quickly implement FileMaker solutions.

The process of using ODBC is simple: You set up data sources (once), and then you import records into FileMaker dynamically selecting the data and conditions you want to apply to the data.

So far, you have seen how to use FileMaker, and how to work with the templates that come with it. In this hour and in Hour 11, you saw how to import and export data from and to other applications (both FileMaker and other databases).

The next part of the book tackles the truly daunting task: starting from scratch with a blank database.

Q&A

Q *In view of the fact that it is possible to do calculations in SQL queries, is there a rule of thumb about whether it is better to do necessary calculations in queries or after data is imported into FileMaker?*

A There is no hard-and-fast answer to this, but some guidelines may be useful. First, if the calculation is already created in the external database, you might as well use it (unless it is also created in your FileMaker database). Second, databases running on large database management systems may be faster than FileMaker. However, you may also want to get in, get your data, and then get back to FileMaker so as not to add a burden to the external database.

There definitely is a significant advantage to selecting data on the external database so that you extract as little as possible, thereby minimizing processing and data transfer needs.

Q *Where can I get more drivers?*

A You need an ODBC driver for a specific database and the platform on which it is to run. The first stop should be the database vendor itself (or, if you are in a large organization, your internal IT department or data management area).

Workshop

Quiz

1. Do you need a new data source each time you do an extract?

2. How much SQL do you need to know to use ODBC?

3. How does ODBC differ from the import/export mechanism described in Hour 11?

Quiz Answers

1. No, you set up the data source once.

2. Little if any. You can point and click your way through creation of a query.

3. With ODBC, you actually pass a query to the database. With the import/export mechanism, you need direct access to the external database to produce a file that can then be imported into FileMaker.

Activities

Experiment with the ODBC example to implement a join. The Sales_Data file contains a SalespersonID field; so does the Salesperson file. Salesperson also contains a name for each salesperson. To pick up the name, you need to join the two tables so that the SalespersonID field in each one matches the SalespersonID in the other one. When it does, you can then access the name.

If you have access to a database and ODBC drivers, experiment with extracting data into FileMaker. If you are planning to do this in an organization with a database support staff, start now because you may need to complete some paperwork and get administrative approval to access the external database.

PART III

Creating FileMaker Solutions

HOUR 13

Creating a FileMaker Database

What You'll Learn in This Hour:

▶ Database Programming—You'll find out more about the concepts of database programming in this section.

▶ Creating a Database—You start by creating a database as described here.

▶ Working with Field Types and Repeating Fields—This section shows you how to use FileMaker's field types such as numbers, dates, and text.

▶ Exploring the Define Database Dialog—The heart of your database design is this dialog, which lets you define fields, tables, and relationships.

▶ Value Lists—These lists let you store selected values for data entry as well as provide a customized sort order. You'll see how to create value lists for a new database.

▶ File Options—Finally, you'll see how to set up spelling options as well as scripts to automatically run when a file is opened or closed.

In this part of the book, you'll see how to create your own FileMaker solutions. In Parts I and II, the emphasis was on using FileMaker and making changes to the templates. Now, you'll confront that most daunting of all dialogs: an empty database design dialog. You'll see how to start by creating a simple database (in this hour), and in Hour 14, "Working with Relationships," you'll move on to relationships. Later, you'll find out more about layouts and scripts, and you'll learn about security as well as techniques for testing, maintaining, and verifying your databases and solutions.

First, in this hour, you'll create a database. It's a simple database in which you can store information about parties—menus, dates, budgets, and so forth. There's even room for a photo of the event.

But what's a party without guests? In Hour 14, you'll see how to relate a file of people to your parties. You won't have to enter information about people for each party because if one person is invited to two parties, that person's data can be related to both parties.

Database Programming

Computer programming evolved from manual procedures codified for machine use. Just as you can tell someone to carry out a series of steps, you can tell a computer to do so. You can specify tests to perform at various junctures; depending on their results, you will continue with one set of steps or another set (or stop entirely). This type of programming is called *procedural programming*.

In the late 1970s and early 1980s, a variety of programming techniques evolved that were not procedural. Rather than a do this–do that approach, they defined conditions or states that existed or that were to be achieved. Various approaches to nonprocedural programming were developed; they range from object-oriented programming to functional and declarative programming. Rather than wander off into discussions of programming theory, this book uses *database programming* to describe the type of nonprocedural programming you do with databases such as FileMaker.

Take the simple task of printing statements for a company's accounts. One procedural way of doing this is to examine each account in turn. If there was no activity this month and there is no balance due or owing, you do nothing. If there were transactions, you print them. If there is a balance due or owing, you need to print a reminder. The procedure involves looping through each account, examining its status, and then acting accordingly.

Using a database, you can simplify the logic as follows. Retrieve all accounts with transactions; for each account, print the transactions. Next, retrieve all accounts with no transactions but with balances; print those using a different format. And don't retrieve accounts with no balance or transactions.

The distinction is that the logic of what to do with each account is part of the repetitive loop in the procedural case. In the database case, that logic is pushed up into the criteria for retrieval: You retrieve all records that fulfill certain criteria, and then you do the same thing to each of them. The processing, which in this case requires little decision making, is more straightforward than the procedural scenario, in which each condition must be checked for each record.

If you're not used to database programming, it might take you a while to start thinking in nonprocedural terms. Just remind yourself to set up your FileMaker solutions so that you can get all the records that fulfill certain criteria and then do the same thing to each of those records. It might seem that you're doing more work by retrieving different sets of records, but, in fact, the simpler processing (the same thing for each record retrieved in each batch) makes implementation, debugging, and maintenance of your FileMaker solutions easy.

Creating a Database

Before you sit down with FileMaker, start by planning your project. Make sure that you understand its scope and the nature of the data. At this stage, it's wise to collect some samples of real data: Experienced database designers know that real data holds keys to the exceptions and special cases you'll need to deal with.

In addition to finding exceptions and special cases, try to identify and keep track of limits and assumptions to be built into the system. A customer name will never be more than 35 characters long? Document it. If you're working with other people, they might assume that you know their data as well as they do. Don't be afraid to ask simple questions—repeatedly, if necessary.

> Some people worry that they might appear naive or stupid if they ask basic questions. Have no fear: Most people who ask someone to design a database for them will gladly talk at length about their data and the work that they do.

By the Way

When you have a sense for the scope of the project, it's time to design the database. Traditionally, great pains were taken to get the design right before any implementation work was done. That tradition remains in many places, but with a tool such as FileMaker, the tradition may have outlived its usefulness.

It is so easy to create databases with FileMaker and then to modify them that it may be easier to actually start creating databases much sooner than you would with a corporate mainframe system. Create a database that does what you think needs doing. By yourself or with others, test it: Can you enter that particularly nasty transaction from last summer? Don't test whether it can handle your made-up data—use the real thing to see whether it works.

You can easily modify your first database or even scrap it altogether. Going through several complete iterations of database designs with FileMaker may well be faster and easier than going through traditional design review procedures.

Another tip is not to let people simplify the database design for you. Particularly if you are working with people unfamiliar with FileMaker, you might find that they edit their specifications and requests to avoid what they consider difficult database design issues. Often, such design issues are simple or even trivial. Encourage people to actually give you all their wildest dreams so that you can be the one to tell them what will work easily and what won't.

Armed with whatever information you have collected, it's time to start building the database. The steps that you will follow in this section are

1. Create the database.
2. Define a field.
3. Set field options.

Creating the Database

As noted at the start of this hour, the database will contain party data. Choose File, New Database from the menu, and, in the standard New File dialog, name the database Parties. (It is frequently a good idea to create a new folder for the database. You can collect additional information, including your research, in the same folder.) When you have created the database, the Define Database dialog opens, as shown in Figure 13.1.

FIGURE 13.1
Create a new database.

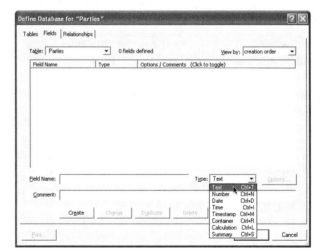

This dialog has tabs at the top to let you define tables, fields, and relationships. Tables and relationships are dealt with in Hour 14. The initial setting is the Fields tab, shown in Figure 13.1.

Defining Fields

As you can see from the Type pop-up menu in the lower right of the Define Database dialog in Figure 13.1, you can create eight different types of fields. However, for all types, certain basics apply. They are described in this section, and you'll find information about specific field types in the following section.

Start by entering a name for the field at the bottom in the Field Name entry field. The names should be simple and descriptive. They can be up to 60 characters in length, and they can contain any character or string except the following:

> , + - * / ^ & = ≠ < > ( ) " ; : :: AND OR XOR NOT

Spaces can appear in field names, but they can cause problems in Web publishing, ODBC, and exporting data to other applications. In general, it is easier to avoid spaces in field names. You can use the underscore character instead, but sometimes it's difficult to notice, particularly if the field name is itself underlined in documentation or other contexts. A more reliable method is to elide the multiple words and capitalize them:

`BalanceDue`

After entering the field name and choosing the type for the field, use the Comment feature (new in FileMaker 7) to identify the field further. Figure 13.2 shows data entered for the first field.

Using the Type pop-up menu, select a type for the field.

Click the Create button in the lower left of the dialog to store the data. (The OK button in the lower right closes the entire dialog. You usually want to create more than one field, so don't close the dialog yet.)

Setting Field Options

After you click the Create button, the field is added to the list of fields in the center of the dialog. Use the title of the Options/Comments column to toggle its display as shown in Figure 13.3.

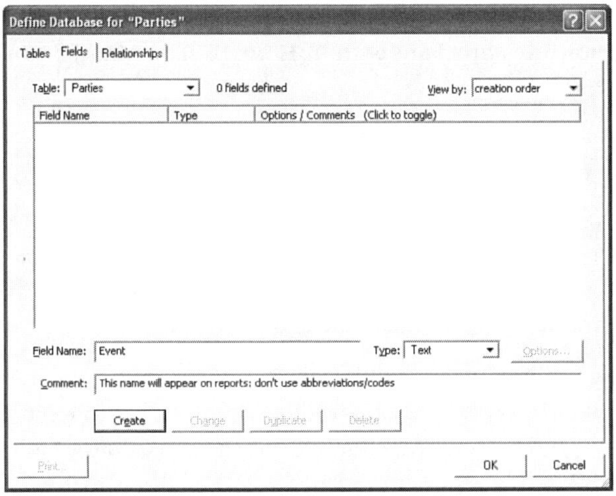

FIGURE 13.2
Enter name, type, and comments for a new field.

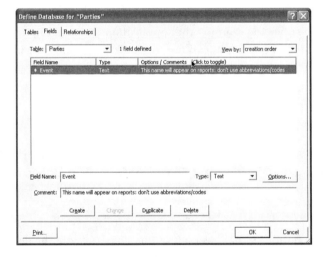

FIGURE 13.3
Toggle between options and comments.

You can set options by selecting a field in the list at the center of the dialog and clicking the Options button in the lower right, which opens the Options dialog.

Setting Storage Options

You might want to click the Storage tab now to set additional options as shown in Figure 13.4.

The Storage options let you specify global storage, repeating fields, and indexing.

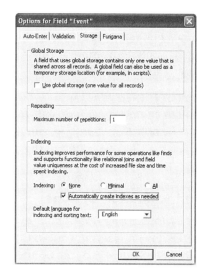

FIGURE 13.4
Set storage
options.

Using Global Storage

Storing a global value stores a single value for all records in the database. One of the most common uses of a global value is for information needed while a script is running. The script can store data (once) into a global variable, and the script or another script can then retrieve it. If you allow users to set options for reports, for example, those options can be stored in global values and picked up by the script that creates the report.

Using Repeating Fields

In the center of the dialog, you can set repetitions. You'll see more about repetitions in the following section "Working with Field Types and Repeating Fields."

Setting Up Indexing

At the bottom of the dialog, you'll see options for indexing a field. Many people find the default setting, which lets FileMaker create the index if necessary, to be best. A field that is indexed can be accessed more quickly using a Find command. However, an indexed field takes more space on disk (the index needs to be stored), and it takes slightly longer to update (because the index also needs to be updated). You can experiment by changing indexing settings to see whether the change has any performance effects.

FileMaker can create two types of indexes: value indexes and word indexes. Minimal indexing lets FileMaker create just the indexes it needs and is usually the most efficient. Value indexes are used for joins and value lists; they also are used when you do a Find based on a literal string (enclosed in quotation marks). A word index is used for Finds not based on a literal string. Thus the Find for "Now time" (a literal string) matches only that string. A Find for Now time (not a literal string) matches the text that reads "Now is the time."

The one setting that you might need to adjust is the language to be used in sorting text. This correctly handles characters with accents as well as upper- and lowercase letters. If you want to be able to sort data so that upper- and lowercase characters sort separately, use the Unicode option at the bottom of the pop-up menu.

Setting Auto-Enter and Validation Options

In Hour 6, "Validating and Auto-Entering Data," you saw how to set auto-enter and validation options. Make any entries you want in the Auto-Enter and Validation tabs. As you can see in Figure 13.5, the Event field is limited to 35 characters, and the user can override the validation.

FIGURE 13.5
Create auto-enter and validation settings.

After you have set the options you want, click OK to close the Options dialog, and then click OK to close the Define Database dialog. You'll see that a layout has been created for you (see Figure 13.6). FileMaker uses the current layout settings for labels and fields; you can change them later if you want.

If you type more than 35 characters in the field, you get an overrideable error as shown in Figure 13.7.

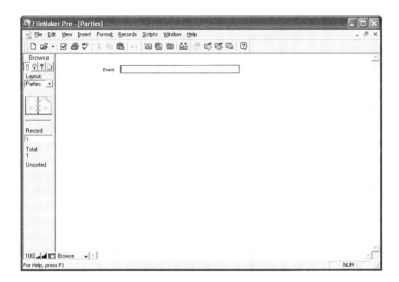

FIGURE 13.6
FileMaker creates
the first layout for
you.

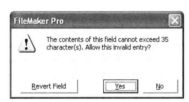

FIGURE 13.7
FileMaker enforces
your validation
rules.

Working with Field Types and Repeating Fields

FileMaker provides eight types of fields. After completing the steps outlined in the previous section to create a field, you need to identify the field type. Each of the FileMaker field types is discussed in this section as the Parties database is built. The field types are as follows:

- Text
- Repeating
- Date
- Time
- Number

- Calculation
- Container
- Timestamp
- Summary

The fields that will be added to the database were chosen to demonstrate the various field types. In addition to Event, they are

- Menu—A repeating field with 20 occurrences that lists each menu item.
- Date—The date of the party.
- Start Time and End Time—The time for the party.
- Budget—The amount to be spent.
- Number of Guests—How many people are invited.
- Budget Per Guest—Calculated automatically from the two preceding fields.
- Photo—A photo of the party.
- Last Modified—An automatically entered timestamp.
- Budget Summary—An automatically calculated total of all the party budgets.

You specify field types in the Define Database dialog described in the previous section and shown in Figure 13.1.

Text Fields

The text field is the most common field type and, not surprisingly, consists of text. The text can represent numbers, dates, or times, but if they are specified as text, the special formatting available for numbers, dates, or times is not available.

In the Parties database, the first field to be added is Event: the name of the event as shown previously. Unlike some other databases, FileMaker doesn't limit the length of a text field unless you specify a maximum length in the Options dialog. You can use a layout to limit the number of characters a user can enter, but that doesn't limit the actual size of the field. FileMaker is good at optimizing storage, so only the amount of space needed for the currently stored data is used.

Repeating Fields

The next field to be added contains the menu to be served. It, too, is a text field. However, it contains 20 repetitions. Each repetition contains the name of one of the menu items.

To set repetitions, choose Options at the lower right in the Fields pane of the Define Database dialog and enter the number of repetitions as shown in Figure 13.8.

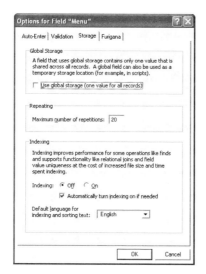

FIGURE 13.8
Set repetitions.

This means that you can enter up to 20 menu items; you don't need to use all the repetitions. Although Menu is a text field, you can set repetitions for any type of field. Using a repeating field is more efficient than creating separate fields such as Menu Item 1, Menu Item 2, and so forth. In Hour 14, you will see how to be even more efficient by using related tables.

Date Fields

Each party has a date field associated with it that stores the date of the event.

Time Fields

Start Time and End Time are time fields.

Number Fields

The budget for every party is a number field. The Number of People is also a number field.

Calculation Fields

The calculation field Budget per Person is calculated from the Budget and Number of People fields. When you select a calculation file type and click Create, the Specify Calculation dialog automatically opens, as shown in Figure 13.9. You can enter the calculation as shown in Figure 13.9. Note that the field type is calculation; the type of the result (Number) is specified at the bottom left of the Specify Calculation dialog. (Calculations were covered in Hour 7, "Working with Calculations, Formulas, Functions, and Repeating Fields," and Hour 8, "More on Calculations and Functions.")

FIGURE 13.9
Create a calculation field.

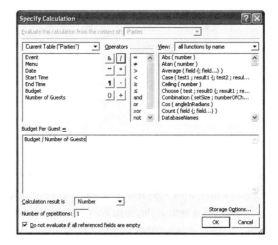

Use the Storage Options button to set storage options for a calculation. For many cases, stored calculations that are indexed if FileMaker needs to do so are the best choice. That is the default setting as shown in Figure 13.10.

FIGURE 13.10
Set storage options for the calculation.

Container Fields

A container field can contain an image, movie, or any kind of file. In the Parties database, a field called Photo is created as a container so that you can store a photo of the party.

Users place files into containers using the Insert menu. You can insert pictures, QuickTime movies, sounds, or files of any sort using the commands in the Insert menu. The specific command that you use can affect how the container's contents appear. For example, a PDF file inserted as a file shows the file icon. A PDF file inserted as a QuickTime file shows the PDF contents.

Timestamp Fields

A timestamp field contains both a date and time. You can use the auto-enter option to automatically set it to the creation or modification timestamp. The Last Modified field is an auto-enter field that contains the last modification timestamp. You can modify the layout so that users cannot enter this data as shown in Figure 13.11.

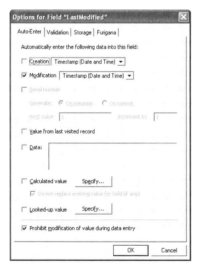

FIGURE 13.11
Use a timestamp field to track modifications to a table.

This is a common feature of many FileMaker solutions. An auto-enter timestamp, date, or time for modification is automatically updated with each modification.

By the Way

Summary Fields

You can create summary fields that contain summaries of data for all the records in a found set or for all the records in a sorted section of a report. To create a summary field, choose Summary as the field type. The Options dialog shown in Figure 13.12 opens so that you can specify the type of summary and what field it summarizes. You'll find more about summary fields in Hour 17, "Working with Summaries and Layout Parts."

FIGURE 13.12
Specify the type of summary.

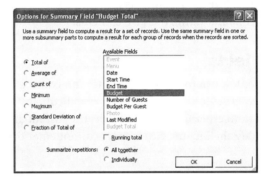

Exploring the Define Database Dialog

When you create a database, the Define Database dialog opens automatically to the Fields tab, which is what you've been working with so far. The two other tabs are particularly relevant when you work with relationships, as you'll see in Hour 14. However, even for a single table they contain useful information.

Tables Tab

The Tables tab, shown in Figure 13.13, lists all the tables in your database. In the example shown in Figure 13.13, there is only one table in the database, but you can have more. (Remember that before version 7, a FileMaker database was a single table.)

Relationships Tab

The Relationships tab portrays the tables in your database in what is called a *graph*. Each table is shown with its fields, as you can see in Figure 13.14.

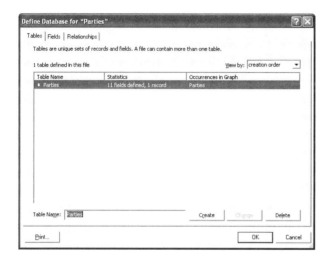

FIGURE 13.13
Use the Tables tab to add or rename tables in a database.

FIGURE 13.14
The database graph shows all the tables in the database.

You can drag tables around by dragging the top part of the table. You shorten or lengthen the table's display by dragging the bottom of the table up or down. In the center of the bottom of a table that is not fully displayed, a small arrow lets you scroll up and down in the list of fields.

In the top right of the box for each table, a minimize icon lets you reduce the table to its title. In the top left, a small arrow icon lets you display information about a table.(You don't need to click the small arrow icon; when you hover the pointer over it, the information appears.) Figure 13.15 shows a minimized table with the information shown.

FIGURE 13.15
View information about a table.

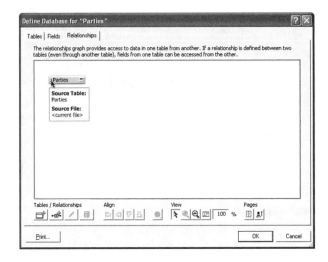

When you click OK to close the Define Database dialog, you'll see that a default layout has been created for you, as shown in Figure 13.16.

FIGURE 13.16
FileMaker creates a default layout when you define a database.

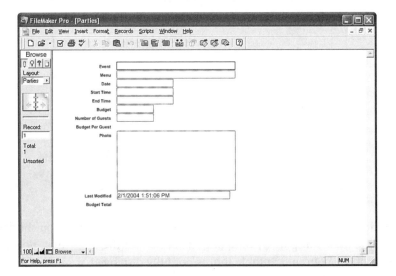

Value Lists

As you have seen, databases contain tables, fields, and relationships. In one way or another all these are present in most data management systems. FileMaker also allows you to create *value lists*—lists of values either from fields or that you explicitly enter. These value lists can be used in validations (to check that an entered value is in the value list), in layouts (to populate pop-up menus, radio buttons, and the like), and to create custom sort orders (when you sort on a value list, the order of the items in the list is the order used to sort).

In this section, you'll see how to create two common types of value lists. Start by choosing File, Define Value Lists from the menu to open the Define Value Lists dialog, as shown in Figure 13.17.

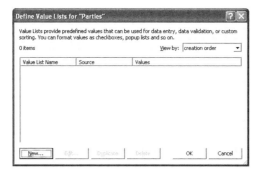

FIGURE 13.17
Define value lists.

Click New in the bottom left to create your first value list.

The first value list you'll create is one of the most common value lists used to support the interface. It's a list of two elements—Yes and No—that can populate radio buttons.

> For two items, radio buttons are always preferable to pop-up menus or lists because the radio buttons display all choices even before a mouse is clicked over them.

By the Way

In the Use Custom Values option, simply type in the values for your value list. Remember to name the list at the top of the dialog as shown in Figure 13.18.

That's all there is to it.

The next value list consists of the values in a field in the database. In this case, the value list contains the names of all the events in the Parties database. You can use it to populate a pop-up menu.

Select the first option (Use Values from Field); when you click the Specify Field button, the dialog shown in Figure 13.19 opens.

First you need to select the table that contains the field, as shown in Figure 13.19.

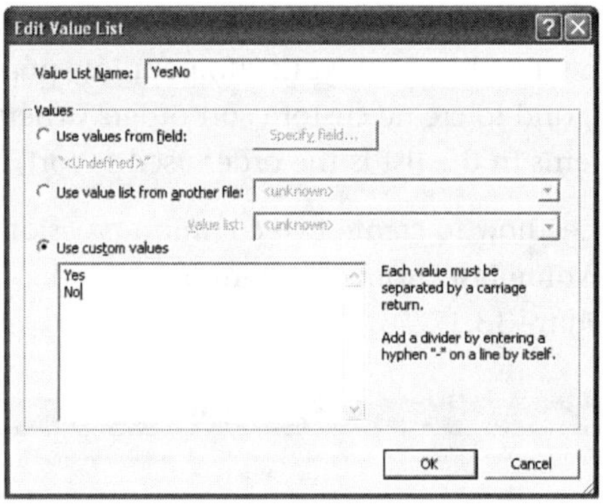

FIGURE 13.18
Create a Yes/No
value list for radio
buttons.

FIGURE 13.19
Select the table
that contains the
field.

Next, select the field you want—Event in this case. (The checkboxes below the field names let you use only related values or all values. Relationships and related values are discussed in Hour 14, and value lists will be revisited there from that point of view.) You can see the field selection dialog in Figure 13.20.

When you close the field selection dialog, the value lists are now shown in the Define Value Lists dialog, as you can see in Figure 13.21.

FIGURE 13.20
Select the field.

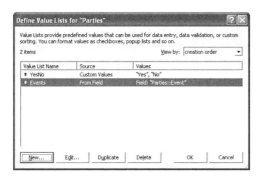

FIGURE 13.21
View completed
value lists.

File Options

At this point, you may want to choose File, File Options from the menu to select additional options for your database file. These features implement security and automatic running of scripts when you open or close files, spelling, and text services. For many people (particularly where security is not an issue and where the Roman alphabet is used), default file options are fine.

Set Open/Close Options

If you followed the example in this hour, you have no scripts and only one layout, so the only option you can set has to do with users and security. There's more on security in Hour 18, "Securing Your Solutions and Databases," but the Open/Close tab of the File Options dialog is shown here for reference in Figure 13.22.

FIGURE 13.22
Set Open/Close
options.

Set Spelling Options

The Spelling tab lets you set spelling options as shown in Figure 13.23. If you're going to use FileMaker's spelling checker, it's a good idea to use it from the beginning so that all the data that's entered gets checked.

FIGURE 13.23
Set Spelling
options.

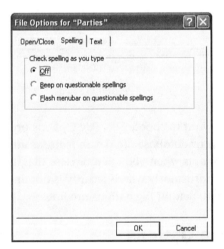

Set Text Options

Finally, the Text tab, shown in Figure 13.24, lets you set Roman/Asian text handling, smart quotes, and localized date and time settings.

FIGURE 13.24
Set text settings.

Summary

This hour showed you how to start a brand-new database file and create your own database with a single table. You saw the array of field options that you can set. However, to move beyond the simplest one-table database, you need to understand how to create and use relationships. That is the topic of Hour 14.

Q&A

Q *Given that storing calculations and indexing fields both affect performance, are there any rules for determining the best choices?*

A There is one simple rule for optimizing performance: test. You can understand the conceptual difference in storing or calculating a value, but until you actually attempt to use the database file (over a network if necessary), you will not understand the performance impact. Typically, people identify performance "problems" that turn out not to be actual problems when databases are deployed. Use your understanding of issues that may affect performance to guide your stress testing of a database, but in most cases, do your optimization after determining that a problem exists or will soon exist. And always remember that performance issues tend to become visible only after significant amounts of data are stored in the database.

Q *Are there guidelines for naming fields?*

A "Meaningful" is the first guideline, and it's amazing how frequently it is ignored or misinterpreted. Wherever possible, use the terminology that users of the system will use; they frequently will see field names as they modify layouts and databases. An apparently small issue such as the description of people served by a social service agency ("patients," "clients," "residents," "users," and so forth) actually can be a significant issue. Beyond that, try for concise field names without undue abbreviations ("PatientNURM" is rather murky). And, if you're ever going to use ODBC or the Web, try running words together rather than using spaces in field names. And always use the new Comments area in the Fields tab of the Define Database dialog to provide information about your fields.

Workshop

Quiz

1. Given that FileMaker can do data conversions at will, is it OK to use text fields for everything?

2. How do you create Yes/No radio buttons?

3. Where are summary fields stored?

Quiz Answers

1. No, because layout formatting for numbers, dates, and times requires that the fields be declared as those field types.

2. Create a value list with Yes and No and attach it to the radio buttons.

3. If they are stored, they are stored in the database table just like other filelds. If they are not stored (either by your choice or because they contain related fields, summary fields, global values, or a reference to another unstored calculation), they are calculated each time they are used.

Activities

How would you add people to your Parties table? One way is to use a repeating field as you did for Menu. Think through what that would entail and how you might implement it. What are the problems with that type of implementation? (Do you want an easier way than repeating fields? If so, Hour 14 is for you!)

Working with Relationships

What You'll Learn in This Hour:

▶ Introducing the Relational Model—Used by most databases today, the relational model lets you combine data from a number of tables for efficient use.

▶ Normalizing a Database—These techniques optimize performance and logical storage. They apply to all relational databases.

▶ Add Tables to a Database—To create relationships in FileMaker, you first need to add tables to your database.

▶ Create Relationships—This section shows you how to create the relationships between tables.

▶ Relationships to Aliased Tables—Here you'll find out how to create relationships to tables in other database files as well as multiple relationships to tables within your own database file.

▶ Using File References—If you are accessing other database files, you need to create file references.

▶ Using Self-Joins—Self-joins can provide simple error-checking and data manipulation within a single table.

▶ Working with Contexts—Contexts locate a layout on the relational graph. You'll see what this means in this section.

▶ Using `Lookup` and `LookupNext` Functions—These functions let you retrieve related data and manipulate it.

The examples so far in this book have consisted of simple databases, most of which contain a single table. That's fine for many purposes, but to really unlock the power of FileMaker (or, indeed, of any relational database), you need to move on to multiple tables and relationships. This hour shows you the basics of creating relationships.

In Hour 15, "More About Layouts," you'll see how to create layouts that display the relationships. You might want to work through both hours together—creating a relationship and then viewing it; then creating another one and viewing it.

> The Parties database in Hour 14 on the Web at the publisher's Web site, www. samspublishing.com, or the author's Web site, www.philmontmill.com, is the database described in this hour. A separate and simpler Parties database is located in Hour 13, "Creating a FileMaker Database," on the Web site and accompanies the preceding hour.

Introducing the Relational Model

In the activities at the end of Hour 13, you thought about how to add guests to the Parties database. What strategy did you pursue? A common approach is to add a repeating field (like the Menu field) to each record to use to store the guest names. That's fine, but what do you do if you need to store additional guest information such as phone numbers, dietary preferences, and the like?

One solution is to add that data to additional repeating fields in each event record, but that winds up storing a lot of duplicate data. Someone invited to five parties will have five entries containing phone number, dietary preference, and so forth. Not only does this waste space, but it also takes time to enter the duplicate data.

And there's more: What if the data isn't duplicated exactly? What if there's a typo in the phone number in one of those records? Or what if the phone number changes? Do you need to change it in five records?

Creating a Relationship

What's needed is a *related table* or a *relationship*. To the Parties database that contained only a Parties table at the end of Hour 13, you can add a People table that contains names, addresses, dietary preferences, and so forth. You *relate* records in the People table to a record in the Parties table by using a *key*. (All this is described in detail as you go through this hour; this is the overview.)

A relationship specifies that record(s) in one table are related to record(s) in another table: It's as simple as that. The relationship can be simple or complex, although up until FileMaker 7 it could only be one of equality.

A simple type of relationship can be used to relate multiple records in one table to a single record. (This type of relationship can replace repeating fields in some cases.) Take the common situation in which people have multiple phone numbers for varying types of phones. Rather than try to squeeze all that into a fixed-size record for each individual, you can create a related table for phone numbers. Such a table might have three fields:

▶ Type of phone number—Home, work, mobile, fax, and so forth

▶ Phone number—The actual number

▶ Person ID—The key that relates to the table containing information about people

In the basic table containing names and other identifying information, you create a unique key (or serial number) for each record. That value is used in the phone numbers table as the Person ID.

Thus, if Person ID 42 has three phone numbers, there would be three records in the phone numbers table with Person ID 42. After you defined the relationship, all three records would be related to the basic record for Person ID 42. If Person ID 57 has eight phone numbers, there would be eight records in the phone numbers table with Person ID 57.

Any other method of storing data would entail some form of waste. If a maximum of eight phone numbers can exist for one person, the person with only three phone numbers would waste the space for five phone numbers. Also, if you limit the number of phone numbers to eight, what happens when someone with nine shows up? By using a relationship of this sort, you use as many—and no more—records in the phone numbers table as you need.

Characteristics of Relationships

This simple yet common relationship of person to phone numbers demonstrates several aspects of relationships that you will encounter repeatedly.

First, relationships can be characterized by the possible number of records on each side; this is called *cardinality*. Depending on your point of view, the name/phone number relationship is a *one-to-many* (person to phone number) or *many-to-one* (phone number to person) relationship. There are also *one-to-one* and *many-to-many* relationships. (Note that "many" in each of these cases may actually consist of only one if the data does not have multiple records, but creating a many-to-many relationship allows for multiple records. There may also be cases in which one or many is actually zero—someone might have no phone number.)

Furthermore, in FileMaker 7, there can also be a *one-to-table* or *many-to-table* relationship in which the relationship is between an entire table (using a global value) and record-level values.

Another critical aspect of a relationship is that it must be defined based on specific fields in two tables. Here, the Person ID field in one database is used to match a similarly named field in the other database. The field names need not be the same, and equality (a match) is not required. However, because that's the simplest relationship, it will be dealt with in this hour.

If you are using a field in a relationship, it is important that the field be controlled. In this case, the Person ID field in the basic personal information table would be a *unique key*, probably assigned using FileMaker's auto-enter option to create a unique serial number. That field is not unique in the phone numbers table because multiple records can have the same Person ID value. If the key is not unique, data can be muddled. That is one reason why many database designers never use anything with intrinsic meaning as a unique key. Names need not be unique; they're a bad choice for unique keys. Meaningless numbers (such as serial numbers) generally make the best keys. Fortunately, FileMaker not only has the auto-enter feature to generate them, but it also allows you to create a validation edit to enforce uniqueness of values. In addition, you can prohibit modification of the value in the Options dialog of the Define Database dialog Fields tab.

Adding People to Parties

You might be wondering how to add people to parties using a relationship. The people/phone numbers scenario in the previous section works up to a point. If someone can attend only one party, all is well. But what if someone can attend multiple parties? In this case, you have a many-to-many relationship (many people can attend many parties). How do you create the relationship?

The most common way of creating many-to-many relationship is to use a third table, a *join table*, to store the relationships. For the Parties database, you will add a People table to the Parties table in the database. (If you want, you can add a one-to-many relationship to a related telephone numbers table from the People table as described in the previous section, but for the moment, assume that the People table is self-contained.)

To create the many-to-many relationship, you create a join table that consists of two fields: Person ID and Party ID. To find all of the people attending Party ID 7, you simply find all the join table records with Party ID 7: The corresponding People ID fields show you who's attending. The same works for any other Party ID.

And it also works in the other direction. Want to see what parties Person ID 98 is invited to? Select all the values from the join table with Person ID 98, and the Party ID values show you the parties.

Normalizing a Database

You'll see how to implement these relationships later in this hour. Before leaving the important background issues, it's important to talk about database *normalization*. Normalization is a set of structured processes to help you design database tables optimized for performance and integrity.

> You might hear some people state that normalization not only does not contribute to performance improvements but in fact can degrade performance. There are some cases (described in this hour) in which complete normalization can adversely affect performance, particularly in a networked environment. Nonetheless, these are the exceptions rather than the rule. Longtime database designers generally agree that savings in design and maintenance are significant with normalized data, and that the few cases where performance problems arise can be dealt with on a case-by-case basis. Further, most database management systems today handle relational data and are optimized for the cases in which that data is normalized.

By the Way

There are five forms of normalization. The first three are the most basic, and most people apply them in sequence as they design their databases. Strict definitions build on one another, so a database that adheres to third normal form must adhere to first and second normal forms.

First Normal Form

The cardinal rule of first normal form is to eliminate repeating groups. A *repeating group* is a set of data stored within a record that itself consists of similar data. Phone numbers in a repeating field are a repeating group, and the example given in the previous section shows you how to eliminate a repeating group: Create a related table with one row for each element of the group (the phone number) and relate it to the primary table with a unique key.

Unique keys make this possible, and unique keys are part of the first normal form. (Unique and meaningless is the best.) Most database designers automatically add a unique key (implemented as an auto-enter serial number in FileMaker) to every table that they design. Often, it is given the name ID. When you create a relationship that matches it from another table, you can name the matching field in the second table PartyID, PersonID, or whatever. PersonID relates to ID in the Person table.

By the Way

> Repeating fields in FileMaker may indicate violations of first normal form, but they also can be valid tools and not violate first normal form. A repeating field with three values to represent a color (red, green, and blue) is an excellent example of such a positive case. Another such case is the use of a repeating field to store a primary and secondary telephone number. This is different from storing a varying number of telephone numbers in a repeating field. In the primary/secondary case, there are only two phone numbers, and their order matters. If you're storing home, work, fax, and mobile numbers, you want a related table.

Second Normal Form

Second normal form requires that you remove redundant data. It's amazing how easily such data can creep into a database design. Take the person/phone number example from the previous section. In the Person table, a Person ID identifies each person—as well as a name, address, and so forth. In the Telephones table, a Person ID identifies the person to whom an individual phone number record belongs. Is it worth adding the person's name to that phone number record? In most cases, no—and not just because it violates the second normal form.

The theory goes that it's faster to get the name from the duplicate entry in the Telephones table than to get it from the related Person table. However, because the same information is stored in two places, you use more disk space and allow for the possibility of inconsistent data.

There are two cases in which violating the second normal form is a good idea:

▶ In some extreme cases, network performance can outweigh the logic of the database design. If your phone numbers table is stored on a PDA, it may take a long time—or even be impossible—to find the related record in the Person table stored on a desktop computer. In such a case, the duplication of data is necessary. Even if both tables are available on a network, there may be enough of a time lag that you need to store the duplicate data.

▶ You also sometimes apparently violate the second normal form when you need historical data. For example, instead of storing phone numbers for people, you can use the same design to store prices for inventory items. When you change the prices, they are automatically updated in the related inventory records. (In the same way, if you change a phone number, the related Person record sees the new phone number.) However, what if you want to freeze the value? If you are processing an invoice, you might want to copy the price into an inventory item record on an invoice with the explicit understanding that it might become inconsistent with the data stored in a prices table. The reason is that you are not storing duplicate data of the current price; rather, what you actually are storing is-now-duplicate data, but over time it will be recognized as the price that you actually charged on that invoice. You don't want the value to change when the pricing data is updated because the invoice has already been processed.

Except in these two specific cases, you should always adhere to the second normal form.

Third Normal Form

Third normal form is the limit of normalization for many people. You don't store information that can be derived from stored information. A classic case is a table containing postal codes and place names. If you can derive the place name from the postal code, you don't need to store it in this table. (This situation often does not apply in reverse: Given a place name, you cannot necessarily produce a postal code because one place might have several postal codes.)

FileMaker's Lookup capabilities (described later in this hour in "Using the Lookup and LookupNext Functions") help you adhere to third normal form.

Normalization Guidelines

This section describes the process involved in normalization. Although normalization and relational databases arose from set theory in mathematics, normalization is not an arcane discipline. You can translate most of the principles of normalization into some simple guidelines:

▶ Don't store the same information in two places. It wastes space and can get out of sync.

▶ Don't store information that can be easily derived, looked up, or calculated. (FileMaker gives you significant tools in this area.)

▶ Store information in the simplest way possible. "Simple" usually means compact tables without large sections of blank fields in many records. Except for the case in which data has not yet been entered, large sections of blank fields often mean that the table can be normalized so that unused space isn't required.

▶ Consider unique, meaningless keys for your database tables. FileMaker doesn't require this and manages meaningful keys well, but you will probably be better off with unique, meaningless keys such as are assigned by FileMaker in the auto-enter serial number option.

Add Tables to a Database

In Hour 13, you saw briefly how to use the Define Database dialog to examine the tables in a database. Because there was only one table, you couldn't see any relationships. Now you'll create multiple tables and use FileMaker's relationships graph to view them.

In this section, you'll expand the Parties database along the lines suggested in the first part of this hour. Specifically, you will

▶ Modify the Parties table to add a unique and meaningless ID. After the relationships are created, you'll see that you'll also be able to remove some of the fields.

▶ Create a Guests table to store guest information.

▶ Create a Telephone Numbers table related to the Guests table.

▶ Create a PartiesAndGuests table to join the many-to-many relationship between Parties and Guests.

Next, you'll create relationships among these tables. But first, you need to modify the Parties table and create the others.

Modify the Parties Table

The first step is to modify the Parties table to add EventID—a meaningless and unique ID number. You need it to create a relationship. Specify that it is an auto-enter serial number that must be unique and cannot be changed. You can see that it has been added in Figure 14.1.

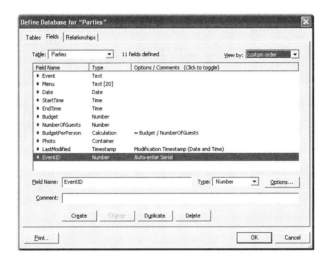

FIGURE 14.1
Add a unique ID to
the Parties table.

Create the Guests Table

Next, create the Guests table. Using the Tables tab of the Define Database dialog,
type the name of the table in the lower left and click Create as shown in
Figure 14.2.

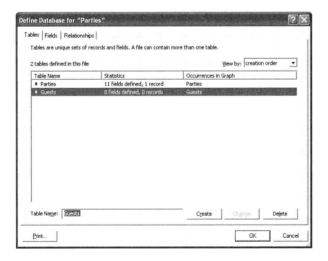

FIGURE 14.2
Create the Guests
table.

If you switch to the Relationships tab as shown in Figure 14.3, you'll see that the
new table has been added to the database graph. You can resize the tables by
dragging any of their borders; you can move them by dragging their titles. In
Figure 14.3, the tables have been reshaped and moved to make the graph clearer.

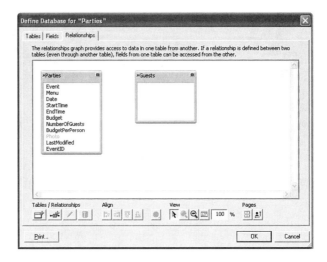

FIGURE 14.3
FileMaker adds the
table to the graph.

Create fields for the Guests table. (If you need help creating fields, refer to Hour 13.) The fields created in this example are

- GuestID
- FirstName
- LastName
- Address
- City

- State
- ZIP
- Email
- DietaryPreference

These are mostly self-explanatory; however, do remember that the GuestID is a unique, auto-entered serial number that cannot be modified.

Create the Telephone Numbers Table

Using the same process, create the Telephone Numbers table. Its fields should be

- PersonID
- TypeOfTelephone
- TelephoneNumber

Figure 14.4 shows the graph as it should exist at this point. You can see the fields added to Guests and Telephone Numbers.

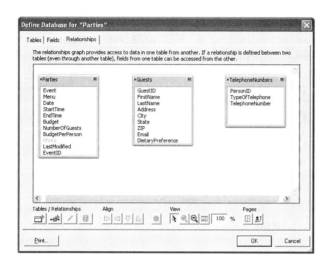

FIGURE 14.4
Review the graph
with all three tables
created.

Create Relationships

The relationship described previously between people and phone numbers can now be created. As shown in Figure 14.5, draw a line from the field in one table that you want to relate to a field in another. In this case, GuestID in Guests is related to PersonID in Telephone Numbers.

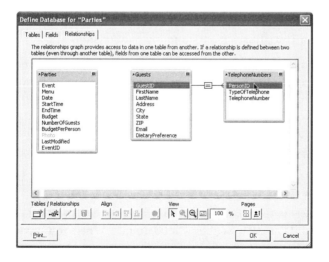

FIGURE 14.5
Draw the relation-
ship.

When you release the mouse button, the relationship will be highlighted. (It is shown in the box in the center of the link, as shown in Figure 14.6.) Furthermore, the keys used in relationships are now shown at the top of each table.

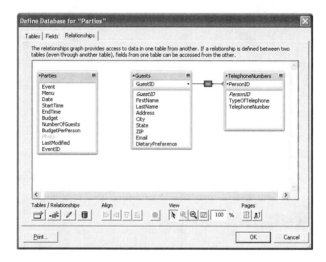

FileMaker uses standard database notation to indicate the cardinality of the relationship. In this case, you see that the relationship pointing to the Telephone Numbers table has three lines at the end; that indicates a many relationship. The end of the relationship pointing to the Guests table has only one line; that is a one relationship. Thus, this is a one-to-many relationship.

How does FileMaker know this? You tell FileMaker as you create a table whether you have a one type of relationship; if not, it is assumed to be a many relationship. The "one" part of this relationship derives either from your choosing that Guest ID values are to be validated as unique or that the field is to be auto-entered as a serial number. Either choice indicates that the field is to be considered a unique key, and thus is one part of a relationship.

Create the PartiesAndGuests Join Table

In a similar way, create the PartiesAndGuests join table. It will consist of only two fields: PartyID and GuestID. Neither will be unique. When you have finished creating the table, create its two relationships (to Parties and to Guests) as shown in Figure 14.7.

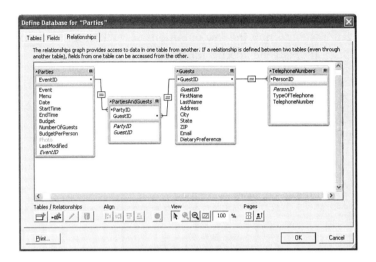

FIGURE 14.7
Create relation-
ships for the
PartiesAndGuests
join table.

In the examples shown here, notice that related fields may or may not have the same names. EventID and PartyID refer to the same logical entity; when you create a relationship, you create the relationship between the entities, and the name doesn't matter. For similar demonstration reasons, you'll find GuestID and PersonID in the example. When you build your own relational databases, it is frequently a good idea to use the same names for the same entities no matter where they are. However, when you work on large systems where you may be integrating tables built by others, you frequently have to integrate your naming conventions with those of others.

By the Way

Relationships to Aliased Tables

So far, you've seen how to create relationships among tables in a single database file. However, there's more to FileMaker now: You can create relationships to tables in other database files as well as multiple relationships to tables in your own file. This section shows you how to do this.

If you used FileMaker before version 7, you are familiar with relationships between various files. With no tables within database files, every relationship involved multiple files (with the exception of self-joins, the topic of the following section).

You never create a relationship to another database file; you always work within your own database's graph in the Define Database dialog using the Relationships tab. However, although you can't place another database into the graph, you can place an *alias* to a table into the graph. You do so by using the Specify Table button; it's the leftmost button in the row of buttons at the bottom of the Define Database dialog. It opens the Specify Table dialog shown in Figure 14.8.

FIGURE 14.8
Specify a table for
your database
graph.

You can use the File pop-up menu at the top of the dialog to navigate to the database from which you want to create an alias. You then select the table from the list of tables in the center of the dialog.

You can also create an alias to a table in your own database. To do so, just select the table in the list. A unique name appears at the bottom (such as PartiesAndGuests 2). In most cases, you'll want to immediately change this to a more meaningful name.

Why would you want to add an alias to one of your own tables? The answer is simple. Sometimes you want to have two or more relationships between a given pair of tables. To have multiple relationships, you'll need aliases because each pair of tables (including aliases) is used for a single relationship.

Using File References

A file reference identifies a file that you will use. In its simplest form, it simply consists of a filename. However, you can add multiple files to a single file reference; FileMaker searches for each of them in order, and it uses the first one that it finds.

Creating a File Reference

In the Specify Table dialog that opens when you click the icon to add a table in the lower left of the Define Database dialog, choose Add File Reference as shown in Figure 14.9.

You are prompted to select the file using a standard file selection dialog. After you select it, the file appears in the File pop-up menu at the top of the Specify Table dialog; all the tables within that file are visible. In Figure 14.10, you can see the single table that is available in the Contact Management template.

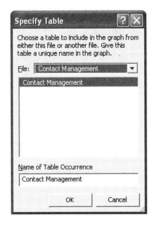

FIGURE 14.10
All the tables in a file are shown.

You can use tables in other database files in your FileMaker solution just as easily as tables in your own database file. Figure 14.11 shows how you can create a relationship to the Contact Management template just as easily as to your own table. (Note that the name of the alias table in another file is italicized.)

FIGURE 14.11
You can incorporate FileMaker template databases into your own solutions.

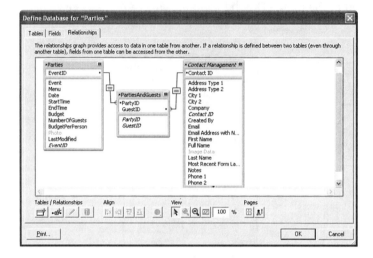

Adding Files to a File Reference

You can edit the file references (either by choosing File, Define File References from the menu or by using the Define File References command in the File pop-up menu at the top of the Specify Table dialog shown previously in Figure 14.9). Figure 14.12 shows the Define File References dialog.

FIGURE 14.12
Define file references.

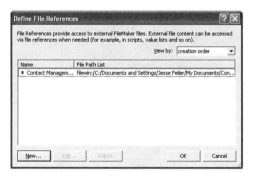

FileMaker lets you associate any number of files with a file reference. When it needs to open the file, it searches for the first available file in the list. By using the appropriate prefixes (shown at the bottom of the Edit File Reference dialog in

Figure 14.13), you can specify local files, files in another directory, and files on a network. This sequential searching provides a convenient way for you to create test environments and multiuser FileMaker solutions.

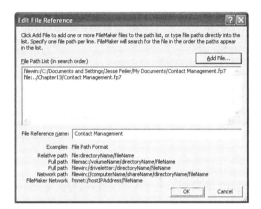

FIGURE 14.13
A file reference can contain many alternative files.

Using Self-Joins

A special type of relationship always requires an alias: a *self-join*. This is a relationship from a table to itself. The PartiesAndGuests table simply lists pairs of data values—parties and guests. Relationships link Party ID to the Parties table and Guest ID to the Guests table. With a self-join, you can link them to an alias of the table. This allows you to display all the parties to which a specific guest is invited as well as all the guests invited to a given party.

Self-joins also are useful in implementing edits. For example, a purchase order might consist of a variety of items that are ordered; some might be mutually exclusive. (If you order A, you cannot order B.) Using a self-join, you can find all the records that contain both A and B: If there are any, the edit fails.

You can see self-joins in use in the Time Billing template.

Working with Contexts

Before FileMaker 7, a layout displayed data from a single database file. You could add related data to the layout, but the layout and the database file were tied together.

With FileMaker 7, a database file can contain many tables. Each layout needs to be linked not to the database file but to a specific table within it. That table is called the *context* for the layout. Just as before, you can add related data to the layout, but its context—its location in the relationship graph—must be specified.

Fortunately, the default behavior in creating a layout (setting the context to the currently viewed table), is usually correct. If it is not, you can choose Layouts, Layout Setup in Layout to change the context (in the Show Records From pop-up menu).

Calculations, too, need a context. You set this from the pop-up menu at the top of the Specify Calculation dialog. But, again, the default—the current table—is usually correct.

Using Lookup and LookupNext Functions

When you have a relationship, you can insert related data into a layout to display it. The Lookup and LookupNext functions let you retrieve that data and massage it.

In the case of Lookup, you specify the related field that you want to retrieve. What is particularly useful about Lookup is that if there is no related record, you can return an error result, as in

```
Lookup (Parties::Event; "no data")
```

If there is a related record, the related Event field is returned; otherwise, the "no data" text string is returned.

You can also use the LookupNext function to get the next or prior value for a related record. Its syntax is

```
LookupNext (Parties::Event; Higher)
```

or

```
LookupNext (Parties::Event; Lower)
```

Summary

This hour introduced you to relational databases in FileMaker. Relational databases provide a quantum leap forward in your ability to manage data with a database. You've seen how normalization can help you to improve your database design, how to add tables to your database file, and how to create relationships.

Aliases let you create multiple relationships to a single table as well as to create relationships to tables in other database files. In the latter case, you need to create file references.

Finally, you saw how self-joins can provide sophisticated searching and data management within a single table.

Now it's time to look at how the data in your multitable relational database will be entered and displayed. That is the topic of Hour 15, "More About Layouts."

Q&A

Q *Why does normalization matter?*

A Normalization is based on the logic of mathematical set theory, and it has a rigorous theoretical background. By using the rules of normalization, you can optimize data storage and retrieval. Perhaps even more important, most people who do any degree of work with databases understand normalization. If you use the process, your colleagues will be able to understand your database design more easily than if you use an idiosyncratic design.

Q *Do relationships always replace repetition fields?*

A Repetition fields used to store specific sets of values (such as the red, green, and blue coordinates of a color) almost always should not be replaced by a relationship. However, repetition fields used to store a variable number of items (such as the Menu field declared in Hour 13) are prime candidates for relationships. If you're never going to access the elements of a repetition field individually (that is, you will enter and display either all 20 menu items or none at all), you might not want to use a relationship.

Q *All the relationships in this hour used the default equality relationship (PersonID equals GuestID, for example). You can have other relationships. Why would you do so?*

A You can define a relationship consisting of all the account balances over a credit limit field. That relationship would identify accounts that need to be attended to. Generally, relationships in FileMaker 7 are comparable to queries in SQL.

Workshop

Quiz

1. How many forms of normalization do most people use?

2. Does FileMaker use standard database normalization?

3. How many relationships can exist between any two tables in the relationship graph?

Quiz Answers

1. Most people use the first two or three normal forms.

2. Yes. A normalized database in FileMaker looks pretty much like a normalized database from another database manager in its structure.

3. One. To create a second relationship, create an alias to one of the tables and create the relationship to the alias.

Activities

One-to-many and many-to-many relationships sometimes aren't as clear-cut as they might seem. For each of these real-life relationships, decide whether they should be categorized as one-to-many, many-to-many, or many-to-one for database design:

▶ A father to his children.

▶ Children in a family to their father. (This is a trick question.)

▶ Coffee cups and saucers in a complete dinner service (that is, no loss or breakage).

▶ Students' grades in a class.

HOUR 15

More About Layouts

What You'll Learn in This Hour:

▶ Using Default FileMaker Layouts—FileMaker's default layouts are powerful and complete. You may be able to use them as is or to make minor modifications that do exactly what you want.

▶ Using FileMaker to Create Customized Layouts—You have almost unlimited choices when you use FileMaker's layout tools. This section shows you how.

▶ Other Layout Settings—These settings let you configure the interface that you'll use to create layouts. Unlike other settings, these are for you, not for the end user.

▶ Using Related Fields in Layouts—The default layouts don't show related fields. You'll always have to customize layouts to show them.

▶ Using Portals for Relationships—Portals let you display (and sometimes enter or edit) data from the many sides of a relationship.

Previously in this book you've seen how to make modifications to layouts in the templates. In this hour, you confront a blank or default layout for a new database. You'll see how to use FileMaker's tools to create a customized layout. Of particular importance is the ability to show data from related tables in layouts. Here's where you'll see how to display the relationships you created in Hour 14, "Working with Relationships."

> **By the Way**
>
> Unless otherwise indicated, all screen shots in this hour show Layout mode, and you should use Layout mode in all cases in working through the hour's examples.

Using Default FileMaker Layouts

If you created the tables in the Parties database as described in Hour 14 (or if you've downloaded the database from the Web using the publisher's Web site, www.samspublishing.com, or the author's Web site, www.philmontmill.com), you already have a default layout for each table. FileMaker creates layouts using the current settings in the status area in Layout mode. (If you want to change those settings, you can customize each field as described in Hour 4, "Introducing Layouts." Alternatively, set font sizes and so forth as you want them before creating fields in the Define Database dialog. FileMaker picks up the current settings.)

In Figure 15.1, you see the default layouts created. Note that the Layout pop-up menu in the status area shows which layout is in use; by default, each layout is given the name of its underlying table.

FIGURE 15.1
FileMaker creates default layouts for you.

As you can see, these layouts are basic—just the field names and standard-sized fields. Many people are happy just to use the defaults. However, it's not difficult to go a step or two further and customize the layouts.

You can customize layouts using the formatting techniques described in Hour 4. There you saw how to add fields as well as how to format fields for various types of data.

General Layout Settings

Now, you'll see how to customize the layout itself. Start by choosing Layouts, Layout Setup from the menu. The Layout Setup dialog opens, as shown in Figure 15.2. Choose the first tab, General, to set basic settings.

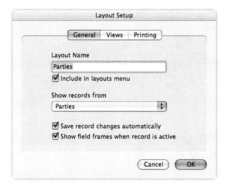

FIGURE 15.2
Set general settings such as the layout name.

By default, the layout name is set to the name of the underlying table, and it is displayed in the Layout pop-up menu. You might want to change either of those settings. The other settings can also be changed, but the name and Layout menu settings are most commonly changed.

Adjust View Settings

In Find and Browse modes, users can choose from different views in the View menu. The basic views (Form, List, and Table) are constructed by FileMaker from the current layout. If you use a default layout such as the ones shown so far in this hour, you often want to allow users to select from alternative views. If you are carefully creating a totally customized layout, you might as well not allow alternative views of it.

You can choose whether to allow each of those views to be shown using the Views tab in the Layout Setup dialog, as shown in Figure 15.3.

FIGURE 15.3
Adjust Views settings.

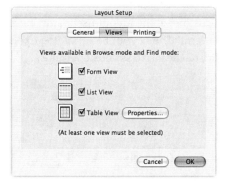

The Table view has additional properties that you can set. When you click the Properties button, the Table View Properties dialog opens, as shown in Figure 15.4.

FIGURE 15.4
Set table view properties.

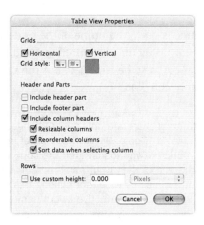

The checked properties in Figure 15.4 are those you often set. They allow the spreadsheetlike Table view to be automatically sorted when you click on each column header and the columns to be rearranged at will.

Modify Print Settings

Finally, on the Printing tab of the Layout Setup dialog, you can set options for multipage printing as shown in Figure 15.5.

FIGURE 15.5
Modify print settings.

Using FileMaker to Create Customized Layouts

So far you've seen how to work from the basic layouts that FileMaker creates for you. You can also create new layouts that can incorporate significant preformatted features. To do so, choose Layouts, New Layout from the menu to open the New Layout/Report dialog, shown in Figure 15.6.

This first screen lets you choose the type of layout to create. The first layout is the default layout created as you define your database fields. You can create another one at any time. The layout being created here is called Data Entry. It contains all the fields in the Parties table.

As you step through the screens, you are asked first to choose the fields to include on the layout. You can choose from any table in your database, whether it is related or not, and whether it is an alias or not. Figure 15.7 shows that interface.

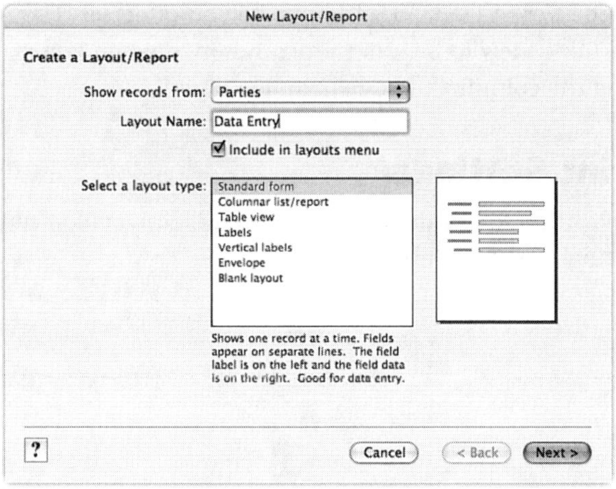

FIGURE 15.6
Create a new layout.

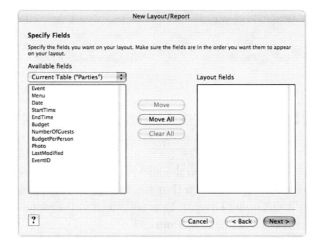

FIGURE 15.7
Select fields for your layout.

Next, you can choose a predefined theme as you can see in Figure 15.8.

You create a Table view in a similar way. You saw how to work with labels, vertical layouts, and envelopes in Hour 5, "Printing Data," and you'll see how to work with columnar list/reports in Hour 17, "Working with Summaries and Layout Parts." (That's how you create automatically summarized layouts and reports.) And, just to complete the choices, you can create a blank layout, which has nothing set in it.

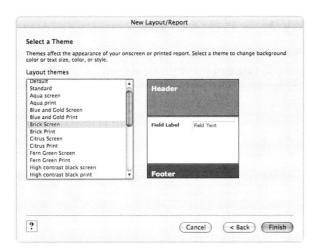

FIGURE 15.8
Select your layout theme.

After the layout is complete, you can modify it as you see fit. If you followed the steps in this section, the layout you created is identical to the default Parties layout shown previously in the upper left of Figure 15.1. By moving a few fields around, you can modify it so that it looks like Figure 15.9. Grouping related fields together can make the layout much easier to use. (You'll find more on interface design throughout this part of the book.)

FIGURE 15.9
Group fields and rearrange them to make the interface easier to use.

Other Layout Settings

Whether you work from a blank layout, the default, or one of the other layouts that you have created, you can set any options you want. Two dialogs may appear as you are working with layouts. The first one, shown in Figure 15.10, asks you whether you want to save a layout. You can turn off this warning message if you want (either from the dialog shown in Figure 15.10 or from the General tab of the Layout Settings dialog). If you used FileMaker in the past, you might notice that this feature is new. If you've been waiting for it, leave the dialog on, but if it changes your work habits, you can suppress the warning.

FIGURE 15.10
FileMaker can prompt you to save layout changes.

As you move items around and resize them, the layout might need to be enlarged. If that is the case, the dialog shown in Figure 15.11 allows you to automatically make that change.

FIGURE 15.11
FileMaker can automatically resize a layout.

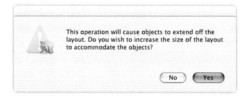

Choose Layouts, Set Rulers from the menu to change the units in which the layout is displayed, as shown in Figure 15.12.

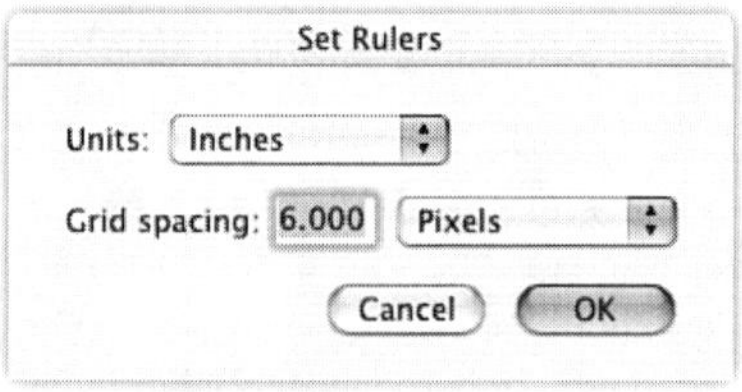

FIGURE 15.12
Choose Layouts, Set Rulers to adjust the units displayed.

FileMaker offers a host of other formatting tools ranging from toolbars to T-squares, grids, and the ability to show sample data in the layout. You can group, ungroup, and lock selected objects; you can move them forward or back; and you can align them in various ways. These tools are similar to those found in many graphics programs. You'll find most of them in the View menu when you're in Layout mode; a few (such as Set Rulers) are in the Layouts menu itself.

One particularly useful tool in the Format menu is the Format Painter. Use it to copy format attributes from one field to another. Select a field, and then choose Format Painter. The pointer changes to a painting icon; when you click on another field, formats such as background colors and fonts are applied to the new field. This can allow you to create a consistent look for your FileMaker solutions.

Because they are comparable to tools in programs that many people have used, these tools are not described in detail here. As you'll see in the activities at the end of this hour, it is useful for you to explore these tools and their uses.

One of the most useful of these tools is the Object Size palette shown in Figure 15.13; you open it by choosing View, Object Size from the menu.

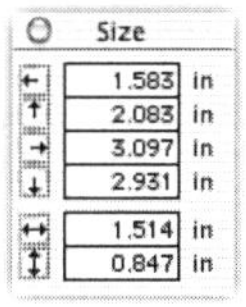

FIGURE 15.13
Use the Object Size palette to carefully position objects.

The Object Size palette displays settings for the currently selected object in the layout (if any); you also can use it to type in new settings. From top to bottom, the settings are

▶ Distance from the left of the layout

▶ Distance from the top of the layout

▶ Distance from the right of the layout

▶ Distance from the bottom of the layout

▶ Width of the selected object

▶ Height of the selected object

Note that if you are dealing with a text field, FileMaker may round your typed-in settings to accommodate the current font and font size. Not all settings are valid, so if you cannot get your typed-in value to stick, remember this. Either use the rounded value or change the font size.

Many FileMaker layouts use tabs to show and hide many settings in a single layout. In fact, this is done with multiple layouts as you can see from the templates. One way to do this is to create the master layout and then copy it. Replace the tab sections on the copies with alternative values. This is, conceptually, a simple way of doing things. But what happens if the master layout changes? (These things do happen!)

Use the Object Size palette to inspect the current settings for objects on the master layout and copy those settings onto the corresponding objects on the copies. When you switch from one layout to another, the identically sized and located objects appear not to move. (You can also achieve the same effect by copying objects, but this can sometimes be faster.)

Using standard settings for field sizes and locations throughout a FileMaker solution can make for a more professional and finished look—and can make the solution easier to use. If people can expect similar fields to be in similar locations, they will find it easier to use your solution.

Choose View, Show to control the appearance of the layout as you are editing it. Of particular interest is the Show Sample Data command. If you select it, data from the current record (if any) is shown in the appropriate fields of your layout. If there is no current record, FileMaker just inserts standard text into the fields. This is useful for verifying that field sizes are adequate (and not too big) for the data that will be displayed. If Show Sample Data is not selected, the field names are displayed in the layout fields.

Using Related Fields in Layouts

You saw in Hour 4 how easy it is to add a field to a layout: You just drag the Field button from the status area to the position that you want and then choose your field from the dialog that appears.

In fact, there's more to the Specify Field dialog than you saw in Hour 4. In the pop-up menu at the top, you can choose fields not only from the current table but also from related tables as well as other tables in the current database file that are not related at all. And, if you need to make a change to the database, you can open the Define Database dialog from here as shown in Figure 15.14.

The default layouts only show fields from a single table; the Specify Field dialog is how you add fields from other tables.

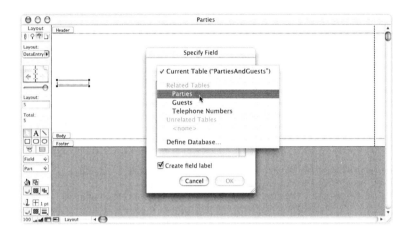

FIGURE 15.14
Select a field to
add to a layout.

But this is usually only part of the answer. In the case of a one-to-one relationship, for a given record in one table, there's at most one related table and thus
one related field to display. Adding a field with the Specify Field dialog works in
that case.

In the case of an unrelated table, adding a field with the Specify Field dialog
works in either of two cases:

▶ If only one record is in the unrelated table, there is only one field value to
display, and this method works to display it. (That might be the case in
which the single record contains status or help information, and there is
never more than one record in the table.)

▶ If the unrelated field is global—that is, a single value for the entire table—it
doesn't matter which record you use to display the value because there is
only one.

But what about the common situation of one-to-many or many-to-many relationships? The Specify Field dialog displays a single field value, and it won't work in
those cases. For those cases, you need to use portals.

Using Portals for Relationships

Portals are layout objects designed to display fields from more than one related
record. They frequently contain scroll bars so that you can scroll through the
data. Figure 15.15 shows a portal displaying the many telephone numbers associated for a single Guest ID using the relationship created in Hour 14. The portal

happens to display two related records, but it could contain any number. A portal can allow the creation of related records. If so, one blank record is always displayed below the data records. You can see a data entry field in the blank third record in Figure 15.15. (Unlike most other figures in this hour, this one displays Browse mode.) You'll see how to create and manage portals in this section.

FIGURE 15.15
Use portals to display multiple related records.

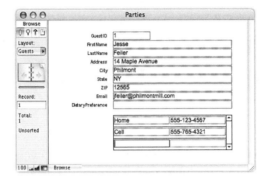

The steps to using a portal in a layout are as follows:

1. Create the portal.
2. Set up the portal with a related table.
3. Add fields to the portal.
4. Allow editing of the portal if you want.

Create a Portal

Start by selecting the Portal tool in the Status area. The Portal tool is highlighted under the pointer in Figure 15.16.

Draw the portal where you want it to be in the layout. (Remember you can always move and resize it just as you would any other layout object.)

Set Up the Portal with a Related Table

As soon as you finish drawing the portal, you are asked to set it up with the Portal Setup dialog shown in Figure 15.17.

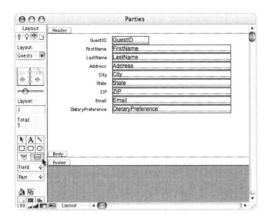

FIGURE 15.16
Select the Portal
tool.

FIGURE 15.17
Set up the portal.

The most important choice here is to determine the related table to use. You can select it from the pop-up menu at the top of the dialog. FileMaker automatically sets the starting row and the number of rows displayed, based on the current field and font sizes as well as the size of the portal that you've drawn. You can modify these numbers.

Note that in setting the starting row number, you can create several portals containing different sets of related data. One portal, for example, might show the first 10 related records, and the second might show the second 10—you would set the initial row for the second portal to 11 and the number of rows shown in both cases to 10. The reason you might want to do this is to arrange the space on your layout effectively. If you want to display 20 rows in a single portal, you need the vertical space for those 20 rows. You can display two sets of 10 side-by-side. (Note that if you have scroll bars in the portals, people can scroll beyond your settings in each one. You might want to eliminate scroll bars from the portals or only use them in the final portal.)

If you want, you can set a sort field for the portal. (This differs from previous versions of FileMaker in which you could only sort the relationship and that sort order applied to all portals in which it was displayed.)

Add Fields to the Portal

After you set up the portal and optionally set the sort order, the Add Fields to Portal dialog asks you to add fields to the portal, as shown in Figure 15.18.

FIGURE 15.18
Add fields to the
portal.

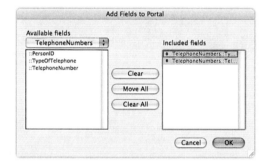

As you select fields to add, note that in the right-hand column they are shown with their related notation: The name of the table in which the field is located is shown before the field name and is separated from it with ::.

Figure 15.15 showed the completed portal in Browse mode. Figure 15.19 shows it again in Layout mode.

Several points are worth noting:

▶ The portal itself can be selected by clicking anywhere in its bounds except within a field. Clicking a field within a portal selects the field.

▶ When selected, the first row of the portal has handles (the small rectangles) that you can use to resize it. You can widen it or drag one of the handles to increase the height of the row. If you increase the row's height, you can move fields around so that they are displayed in two or more lines in the row.

▶ At the bottom of the portal, FileMaker displays the name of the related table displayed in the portal as well as the range of rows to be displayed.

▶ The fields that you place in the first row of the portal are repeated for each row displayed in the portal. If the field boundaries extend beyond the boundaries of that row, they are not shown in the portal. Be careful that the top edges of portal fields remain within the top boundary of the portal.

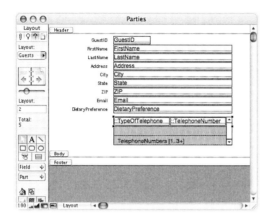

FIGURE 15.19
Adjust the portal.

Allow Editing of the Portal

In addition to displaying data in a portal, you can use the portal to edit data and even enter new rows. To edit data, you simply make the field inside the portal editable just as you always would.

To allow people to add new rows to the portal, you need to make sure that the relationship allows such editing. Open the Relationships tab of the Define Database dialog, and then click on the relationship to open the Edit Relationship dialog as shown in Figure 15.20.

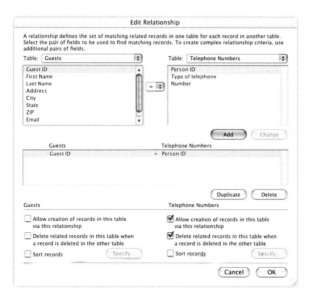

FIGURE 15.20
Allow creation of related records.

Here you see the relationship between Guests and Telephone Numbers. At the bottom of the dialog are two sets of checkboxes; they refer to each side of the relationship. As you can see in the lower right, the relationship allows creation of related records in Telephone Numbers. If you have a portal displaying the Telephone Numbers relationship to Guests, you can add more numbers. That is the case here.

You can't add records on the other side—in Guests when it is displayed in a portal of a layout based on Telephone Numbers. It's common that one side of the relationship determines the other. (Certainly in a one-to-many relationship as you have here, it is unusual to allow creation of records on the one side from the many side. It's not impossible, but it is unusual.)

Note the second checkbox, which lets you control deletions. Here, it is set so that if a Guest record is deleted, all the related telephone numbers are deleted. (They have no meaning without a related Guest ID.)

If you have set up the relationship in this way, you'll find that the portals you create all have a blank row at the bottom. If you click in the blank row, you'll see the outlines of all the fields you've placed in the portal. You can enter data, and it will be stored in a related record automatically.

When you work in a portal in Browse mode, the File, Delete Record command in the menu changes. If you select a field in a portal row and choose Delete Record, you see the dialog shown in Figure 15.21. It allows you to specify whether the master record or just the portal row should be deleted.

FIGURE 15.21
Delete Record can apply to the master record or to a single portal row.

In Hour 16, "Advanced FileMaker Scripting: Design Issues, Script Parameters, and Working with Related Records," you'll see how to write scripts that delete portal records or display their data in another (or the same) window.

Summary

In this hour, you saw the power of FileMaker layouts. You saw how to start with a default layout and how to customize it. You can also create a layout from scratch, adding fields, layout parts, and graphic elements as you see fit.

The power of FileMaker and its layouts really shines when you start to deal with relationships and related records. You saw how to display fields from related records on their own; you also saw how to create portals to create a view onto related records. You can even use portals to create new records in related tables.

Layouts can help you organize FileMaker data so that people can see their data in various ways. You can use interface elements such as buttons to quickly switch from one layout to another depending on what people want to do with their data. You can also organize data and the interface by using FileMaker scripts. Hour 16 provides more information on scripting.

Q&A

Q *What's the easiest way to develop a customized look for a FileMaker solution?*

A Select typefaces, colors, and general layout guidelines for yourself. Don't use all the options; rather, use a subset of them and use them consistently. Look at the templates provided with FileMaker; they all use a standard design. You can reuse that design or modify it for your own purposes.

Q *I showed a client a customized layout and the reaction was "the type's too small." It's the same size as the FileMaker templates. What am I doing wrong?*

A This is one of the most common issues that comes up with layout design. There are two steps to take. The first is preventive: Make sure that your type sizes, fonts, and styles are, indeed, the ones you want. Boldface type, for example, frequently appears muddy on the screen. The second step is to remind people that they should not react to an intellectual idea of whether the layout is too big, too small, or too anything else; they should try to use it and see what works and what doesn't. (And, of course, you should have already done your homework in this regard so that you're sure that your choices are correct.)

Q *What's the first thing you do in creating a layout?*

A If the layout is not for a printed report, the first thing I do is size it to the screen and make it wider than tall (as most screens are, but most printed pages are not).

Workshop

Quiz

1. What is the difference between showing related records in a portal and showing them in fields?

2. What is the limitation of using default layouts?

3. How many layouts can you have for a table?

4. How many tables can you have for a layout?

Quiz Answers

1. A portal can show more than one related record (the many side of a relationship), whereas a field shows only one related record (the one side of a relationship).

2. You can't show related records in the default layout without modifying it.

3. Any number.

4. One base table; all others must be shown through relationships to the base table or as unrelated tables in the same database file.

Activities

Get in the habit of observing and critiquing interface designs. See what works and what doesn't; decide what styles you like and which ones you don't.

Take an interface design that you particularly like that is not implemented in FileMaker and attempt to duplicate the interface in FileMaker.

In the same way in which you added a portal for telephone numbers to the Guests table, add a portal for Guests to the Parties table.

HOUR 16

Advanced FileMaker Scripting: Design Issues, Script Parameters, and Working with Related Records

What You'll Learn in This Hour:

▶ Designing Scripts for FileMaker Solutions and Vice Versa—Here are some design tips that will make your interface easier to use.

▶ Using Scripts to Manage Related Records—One of the most frequent tasks for which you use scripts is managing relationships.

▶ Using Script Parameters to Add Related Records—A new feature of FileMaker 7, script parameters help you consolidate scripts that have only minor variations.

▶ Importing Scripts—You can reuse scripts from one database in another.

Hour 9, "Working with Scripts," and Hour 10, "More on Working with Scripts," provided the basics of scripting. You saw how to use ScriptMaker, attach scripts to interface elements, and create scripts to automate processes such as finding data.

In this hour, you'll move on to the more sophisticated scripting that you may want to do as you develop your own FileMaker solutions. You'll see how to use more sophisticated scripting features such as parameters (new in FileMaker 7) as well as how to use scripts with relationships and multiple tables.

This hour combines the concepts from the previous hours into a realistic multitable solution. You may need to refer back to those hours, because as everything is put together, the degree of complexity increases.

Designing Scripts for FileMaker Solutions and Vice Versa

So far in this book you've seen how to use FileMaker's powerful tools to create and manage databases; to enter, find, and modify data; and, in general, to organize large or complex bodies of data for simple use and reporting. In this part of the book, you'll see how to confront that most daunting of database situations—a blank database to which you add tables, fields, and relationships.

When you start to create a FileMaker solution, you generally plan its structure for data storage just as you would with any other database manager. But with FileMaker, you can use two other sets of tools in your design: layouts and scripts. They interact with one another to let you create a solution in which users don't need to use all those FileMaker commands that you've learned to use. A solution that uses customized scripts and layouts can be used by people who have never used FileMaker before (and who, in fact, may not know that they're using FileMaker). Scripts and layouts can be available to people using your database through the Web, although not all script steps and layout features are available over the Web.

With the introduction of the new database structure of FileMaker 7, it is now possible to structure your FileMaker solutions in a modular manner. In view of the fact that you can have multiple tables in one database file, as well as the fact that you can use aliases and file references to access tables from other files, you can structure a solution in two different types of database files. The first file can contain the data itself along with scripts that manipulate the data without interacting with the user.

The second file might have no data contained within it; it can have layouts and scripts that interact with the user. This separation can make development, testing, and maintenance easier. For example, you can add another interface file that uses another language to access the data in the primary data file. You can also add new functionality simply by adding another interface file. The possibilities are endless.

If you take this approach, make sure that the scripts in the primary database file are never interactive. They should capture errors so that no error dialogs appear.

Designing a FileMaker Solution

For a given set of data, there may be only a few—even only one—way to optimally organize the data. However, for any problem, there usually is a wide range of choices for interfaces to the database. Although normalizing database tables generally is done in accordance with normalization standards, designing an interface is done with a recognition of the needs of users, the capabilities of the database developer, and the resources available.

If you are creating a FileMaker solution for yourself, a client, or your colleagues, your choices with regard to interface—scripts and layouts—distinguish your solutions from another. Many books and other resources can help you understand the principles of interface design. Two basic concepts may help you.

First, in designing an interface, design it for the people who will use it. If that's you, fine. However, if you're designing an interface for others, try to understand how they think and the terminology that they use.

Second, make sure that you stretch your mind and skills by exploring FileMaker features and commands that you don't normally use. This provides you with a repertoire of tools to use to accommodate your users' needs. Remember, there is almost never a single right way to accomplish a task in FileMaker.

By the Way

Using Scripts to Manage Related Records

In Hour 15, "More About Layouts," you saw that the Delete Record command has two possible meanings when the current selection is in a portal. (A dialog lets you determine whether to delete the portal row or the master record.)

By now, you know what all that means. But to many people who might use your FileMaker solutions, words such as "portal," "master record," and even "record" may not be common knowledge. When you develop scripts, you can let users click interface elements that you design and name to carry out what might otherwise be obscure commands for users.

In perhaps no area is this so important as in the area of portals and relationships. Although the concepts behind portals and relationships are simple (there are endless real-world examples, such as the case of one person having multiple telephone numbers), the generalized terminology that needs to be supported in any database manager such as FileMaker may prove daunting. That's where you come into the picture with your scripts and layouts.

This section shows you how to accomplish three common tasks you need to do in portals that display relationships. Those tasks are as follows:

- ▶ Create a button to delete a related row in the portal.
- ▶ Create a button to display the related record in another layout (for example, to display all the related record's data, not just the fields that might be displayed in the portal).
- ▶ Create related records with a script.

Creating a Button to Delete a Related Row in the Portal

Figure 16.1 shows a People table layout with a Telephone Numbers portal like the one that you added in Hour 15 to the Guests table.

FIGURE 16.1
Use a Telephone
Numbers portal to
show a relation-
ship.

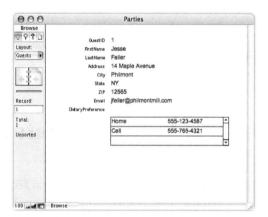

If you have set up the relationship to allow creation of related records in the Telephone Numbers table, you can add a new telephone number. To delete a record, select the portal row by clicking in it, choose Records, Delete Record from the menu, and then choose Row from the dialog that asks you whether you want to delete the master or row record. Alternatively, you can write a script to accomplish the task. Having written the script, you (or a user) can execute it from the Scripts menu, or you can attach it to an interface element.

Writing the Deletion Script

The script is simple. Add the Delete Portal Row from the Records group of script steps to a blank script, and that's all you need to do.

By the Way

> You don't have to worry about the ambiguity that is resolved by the dialog when you use the Delete Record command interactively because a separate Delete Portal Row script step exists next to the Delete Record/Request script step. The FileMaker interface uses one menu command to handle both script steps.
>
> This demonstrates one of the differences between an interactive interface (such as the standard FileMaker interface) and a scripting interface. In the interactive interface, you can assume that the user is there ready to answer questions that you pose in a dialog. When you're writing scripts, there may be no user with whom to interact.

Figure 16.2 shows the script.

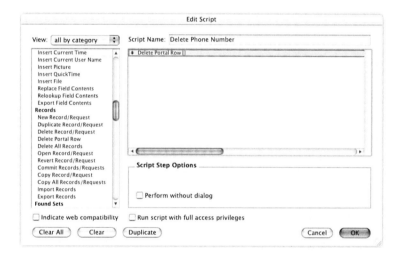

FIGURE 16.2
Create the delete script.

You can experiment with this script. Create new telephone numbers in the portal and then run the script to delete a selected telephone number. You are asked to confirm the delete (as you can see in Figure 16.3) unless you select the Perform Without Dialog option. Thus, you can run the script and click Cancel so that you don't have to keep re-entering data that you're deleting.

Adding the Button to the Portal Row

You saw in Hour 10 how to add a script to an interface element. You do the same thing when you add a script to an interface element, but you must make sure to place the interface element into the first row of the portal along with the fields that will be displayed.

FIGURE 16.3
You are asked to
confirm the dele-
tion.

Figure 16.4 shows an example of this. The fields have been resized in the portal, and a small Delete button has been added. In practice, you might use a graphic or a distinctive color (such as red) for the Delete button. In this case, Delete is simply typed with the text tool, and the font size is reduced to less than the data fields. If you place it inside the portal, it is repeated for each row (including the blank row at the bottom). If your graphic or text does not appear in each row of the portal, it most likely overlaps the boundaries of the portal row in the layout.

FIGURE 16.4
Add a button to the
portal.

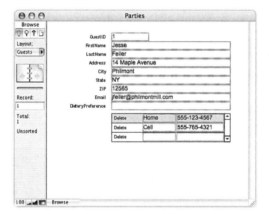

Choose Format, Button from the menu to attach the script you just created to the button, as shown in Figure 16.5.

Creating a Button to Display the Related Record in Another Layout

You can use a similar technique to display a portal row in a different layout. With FileMaker 7, you can choose to open it in its own window or in the window you are using.

In the example shown so far in this hour, all the information from the related file is shown in the portal. But what would you do if additional items were in the related file? This is a common situation, and you can handle it easily with the method shown here.

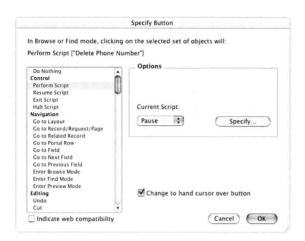

FIGURE 16.5
Attach the script to
the button.

The Parties database provides an opportunity to do this. Figure 16.6 shows that database as modified for this hour. The repeating field Menu has been removed; in its place, a new table, MenuItems has been added using exactly the same relational logic as the TelephoneNumbers table that is related to Guests. Further modifications will be made as this hour progresses.

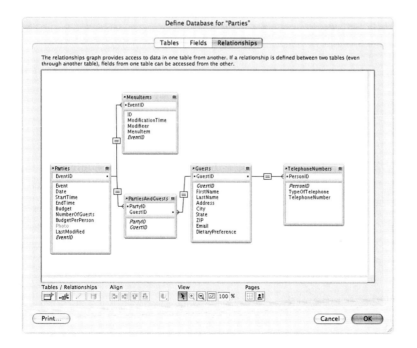

FIGURE 16.6
Replace the repeating Menu field with a relationship to the MenuItems table.

You can create a portal for MenuItems in the DataEntry Layout just as you did in Hour 15 for TelephoneNumbers. In addition, you can create a second portal to display guests. Figure 16.7 shows the revised DataEntry layout. (Other changes made in this layout involve setting date, time, and number formats. The Parties database on the Web at the publisher's Web site, www.samspublishing.com, or the author's Web site, www.philmontmill.com, for Hour 16 reflects these changes.) Figure 16.7 shows some data entered into the portals so that you can see what happens after you implement the code in this section.

FIGURE 16.7
Add two portals to
the layout.

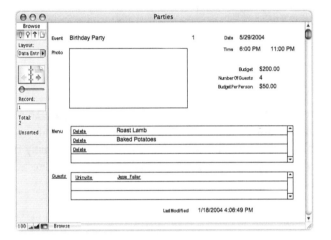

MenuItems has only one field you display in the portal—the name of the menu item. You can use the direct entry mechanism (typing in the default blank row at the bottom of the portal) to enter data.

But the Guests portal is not big enough to display all the guest information. You could make it bigger, of course, but that will not work in all cases. So instead of allowing direct entry into the portal with a blank row always automatically placed at the bottom, the Guests portal allows you to go to the Guests layout by clicking the portal name, which is underlined.

After a new Guest record is added, the name is displayed in the portal row. The name is not going to be editable: All editing of Guests is done in the Guests layout. Because it is not editable, the first and last names are inserted into the portal as merge fields, and they are underlined. As with hypertext links on the Web, you click on the underlined name to go to the data.

To implement this, select the underlined text in the merge fields and choose Format, Button from the menu (in Layout mode) as shown in Figure 16.8. Select the Go to Related Record script step.

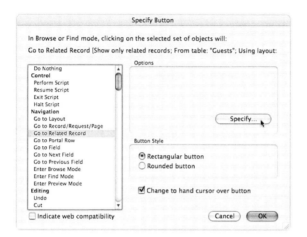

FIGURE 16.8
Choose the Go To Related Record action.

As you can see in Figure 16.9, when you click the Specify button from Figure 16.8, you first specify the relationship to use. Then, you choose the layout to use to display the data. When using a table from an external file, you can use the layouts from that file or from your own file.

> Using layouts from an external file can be a useful way of implementing structured database layouts. If a table is in a certain file, that file can be responsible for its display. All you need to know is the name of the relationship, and the database file is responsible for storing the data and displaying it. This is the same form of encapsulation used in object-oriented programming.
>
> Alternatively, you can use database files for nothing except data storage: You might never implement layouts in those database files. This lets you totally customize the data display each time you use the related external table.
>
> Each of these approaches is useful in various cases. You may want to think about how you will use your data and what internal rules you want to set up for design. It is important to know what parameters you are setting for yourself so that you don't do duplicate work and so that you don't confuse yourself and others.

By the Way

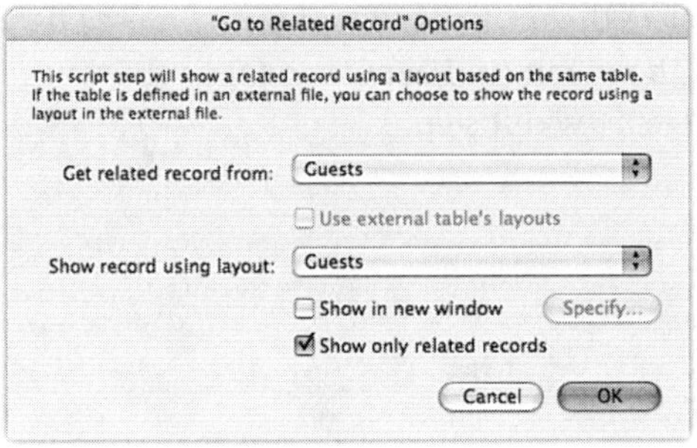

FIGURE 16.9
Specify options for
the Go To Related
Record script step.

The Show in New Window checkbox lets you determine whether the new layout appears in its own window. (In versions of FileMaker before version 7, there was no such choice; all databases opened in their own windows.) By using the same window, users can get a sense of continuity in their work. By using multiple windows, they can compare data in the two windows. The particular circumstances of the solution you're working on determine what choice you make.

If you specify a new window, the dialog shown in Figure 16.10 opens to let you specify the options for that new window. You can type in elements such as the window size or name; you also can use the Specify buttons. Each of those button opens a Specify Calculation dialog that returns the appropriate values—window title, size, location, and so forth. Thus, everything is customizable, and you can size the window appropriately based on the amount of data to be shown.

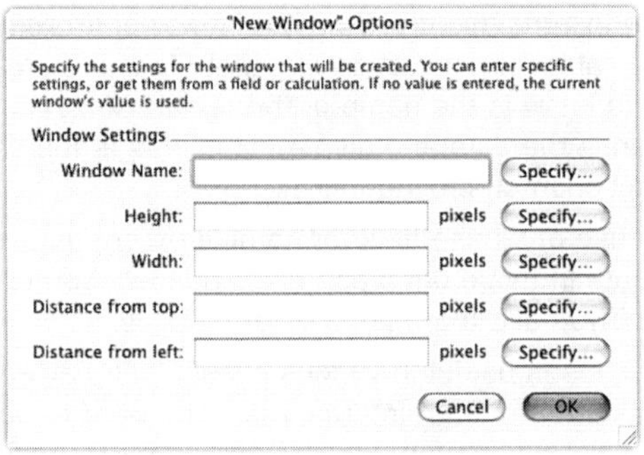

FIGURE 16.10
Set options for a
new window.

This all works well, but how do you get those related records into the portal in the first place? In the case of the party's menu items, you just type. For guests, you need to do something more complex. Script parameters are the key.

Using Script Parameters to Add Related Records

Another new feature in FileMaker 7 is the ability to use script parameters. You specify script parameters when you attach a script to a button or when you use a Perform Script step in a script. Parameters are not specified when you run a script from the Scripts menu.

Before working with scripts and parameters, refer back to the database graph shown previously in Figure 16.6. A join table, PartiesAndGuests, manages the many-to-many relationship between Parties and Guests. In this way, Parties and Guests are defined separately; to invite a guest to a party, you simply add a record to the join table that contains the party and guest IDs. To uninvite someone, you merely need to delete that join table record.

This section shows you how to invite someone to a party and how to uninvite someone.

Implementing Invitations

Sometimes it's easier to work backwards. The final step in the process is to create a new record in PartiesAndGuests and to set the party and event IDs appropriately. You can do this from an Invite button on the Guests layout, because you have the appropriate Guest ID. But how do you get the Event ID?

One way is to script the process of going from the DataEntry layout to Guests. If you underline the Guests portal title in the DataEntry layout to suggest that it's a hyperlink, you can then attach a script to it. The script needs to be created first; it uses a script parameter, which is the EventID, and that parameter is passed to Guests.

Thus, the two major parts of implementing invitations are

1. Creating a script with a parameter.
2. Creating a join table record with a composite script parameter.

Creating a Script with a Parameter

This script collects the data that will be used in the following section to create a join table record. Here are the steps involved:

1. Create a Go to Guests script to go to the Guests table and layout, carrying with it the ID of the current party.

2. When on the Guests layout, you can implement invitations. However, to make the interface easy to use, it is a good idea to display the name of the current party. You'll need to create a new relationship (from Guests to Parties) for this.

3. Create an Invite button and attach the Go to Guests script to it.

4. Specify the parameter for the script.

Create a Go to Guests Script

The script consists of only two lines. The first goes to the Guests layout using the Go To Layout action. You temporarily need to stash the EventID value from the DataEntry layout somewhere: Create a numeric field called CurrentParty in the Guests table and make it global. Then, the second line of the script sets the CurrentParty field to the parameter using the Get(ScriptParameter) function. Figure 16.11 shows the completed script.

FIGURE 16.11
Create a Go to
Guests script.

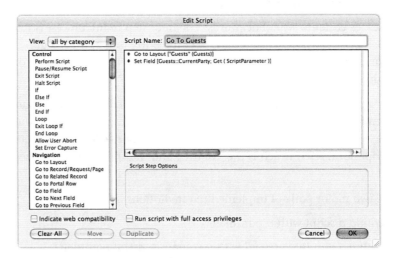

Display the Current Party Name

For the Invite button to work, it should display the name of the current party. To do this, you need another relationship: from Guests back to Parties using the CurrentParty field. If you try to draw this relationship, you are warned that you need an alias table. Agree, and name it CurrentParty. Thus, your graph looks like the one shown in Figure 16.12 (although the spacing almost certainly will differ).

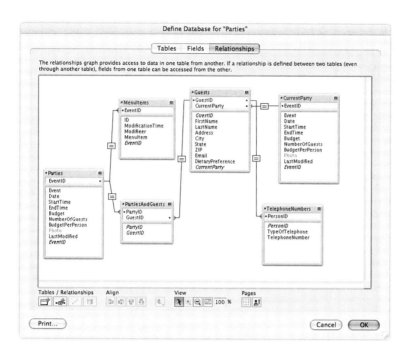

FIGURE 16.12
Add a CurrentParty
relationship.

Attach the Go to Guests Script to the Interface

Now, you can finish up the first part of the process. Attach a script to the under-lined Guests portal title in DataEntry. In the Specify Button dialog, choose Perform Script and select the script you just created as shown in Figure 16.13.

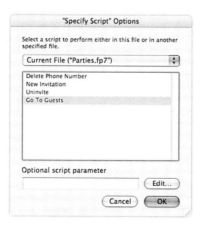

FIGURE 16.13
Attach the script to
a button.

Specify the Script Parameter

Click the Edit button at the lower right to specify the parameter. The Specify Calculation dialog shown in Figure 16.14 opens.

FIGURE 16.14
Specify the parameter for the script.

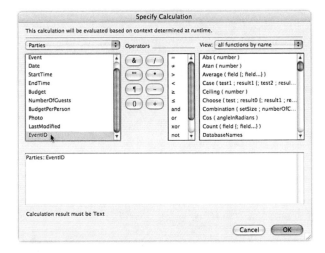

You want to place the EventID field from the Parties table into the parameter, so select it in the scrolling list at the left. (You'll see in the next section that you can create complex parameters with calculations.)

> The reason you had to work backwards here was because you need to create the script before you can attach it to the button.

You can test the whole process. Clicking the Guests portal title takes you to the Guests layout, and the EventID value passed in the parameter should be in the global CurrentParty field in Guests that you just created and used in the relationship to CurrentParty. The Guests layout looks like Figure 16.15 (with variations depending on where you have drawn the button).

Because CurrentParty is a global, its value is the same for each record, and the button appears the same on every record in Guests.

Creating a Join Table Record with a Composite Script Parameter

You're almost finished. You have the EventID for the party stored in the global CurrentParty field. The user navigates to the appropriate guest record and clicks the button. To finish the job, you need to create a script to attach to that button.

That script creates a new record in PartiesAndGuests and fills in the guest and party IDs. For this to work, you need to pass two parameters—but there's only room for one. The easiest way to do this is to use the Specify Calculation dialog to create an easily parsed set of values. Again, you need to work backwards, defining the script before you set up the button and create the parameter.

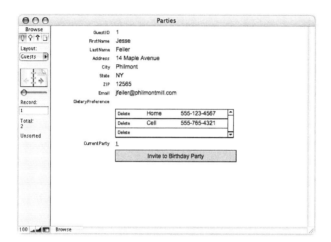

FIGURE 16.15
You can now invite people to parties.

The key to the script is a parameter that consists of two lines: the event ID on the first and the guest ID on the second. You can then use the LeftValues and RightValues functions to split them apart.

Implementing the Invite Button
You have the script to do the invitation. Now, all you have to do is attach it to your Invite button. In Layout mode, select the button and choose Format, Button from the menu to select the script to perform. As in the previous section, specify the script parameter. But now you need a more complex calculation because you need to pass two values.

Create the Script
Figure 16.16 shows the script. It uses script steps that you've seen before in this book to freeze the window, go to PartiesAndGuests, and create a new record. Then, it sets the two values.

The fourth and fifth lines of the script do this. They are complex, so they are parsed here from the inside out.

FIGURE 16.16
Create the join
table record.

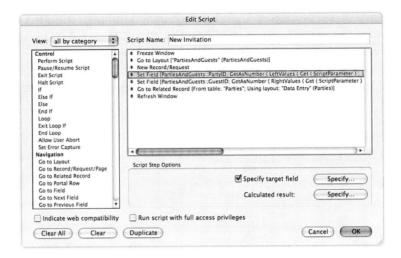

First, you get the script parameter:

```
Get (ScriptParameter)
```

This will be of the form

```
15
2
```

where 15 is the EventID, and 3 is the GuestID.

You split this apart with the LeftValues function:

```
LeftValues (GetScriptParameter), 1)
```

which returns the first left value—the EventID (15).

This is a text value; you need a number. So you need to coerce it to be a number with the GetAsNumber function:

```
GetAsNumber (LeftValues (GetScriptParameter), 1))
```

At that point, you have the event ID as a number, and you can pass it into the Set Field script step.

The fifth line of code is the same, except that it uses RightValues to get the right-most value. (If you have more than two, you can use some combination of LeftValue and RightValue because you control how the parameter is constructed and know the numbers of each value.)

Finish the script by going to the related Parties record using the existing relation-ship you created in Hour 15 from PartiesAndGuests to Parties. Then, unfreeze the window.

Attach the Script and Create the Parameter

Repeat the process you used previously to attach a script to a button. When it comes time to specify the parameter, use the & operator to insert both event and guest IDs separated by the ¶ character as shown in Figure 16.17.

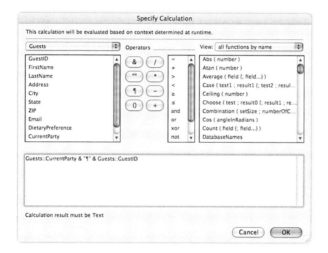

FIGURE 16.17
Create the compos-ite script parame-ter.

Remember that the order of the values is critical to the script operating successful-ly. You should now be able to go to the Guests layout from the DataEntry layout, browse for a guest to invite, click the Invite button, and then be returned to the DataEntry layout. The name of the guest should be in the portal, and if you click on it, you should go to the appropriate guest record in Guests. Try it!

Implementing Disinvitations

Finally, implement the ability to uninvite someone. The techniques are the same as those shown previously:

1. Create an Uninvite button in the Guests portal in the DataEntry layout.

2. Create an Uninvite script.

3. Attach the script to the Uninvite button and pass a composite parameter of both event and guest IDs in exactly the same way you did previously. The only difference here is that because you are building the composite parameter from the portal, you have the event and guest IDs right there, and you don't need to cache the event ID in a global before you get to it.

Figure 16.18 shows the script.

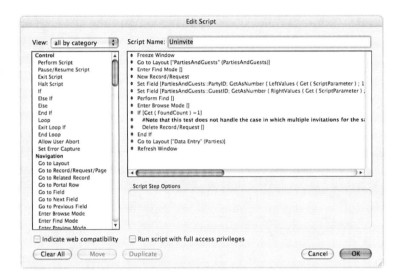

FIGURE 16.18
Create a script to uninvite people.

Importing Scripts

You can import scripts from one database file to another using the Import button on the first ScriptMaker dialog. By importing scripts, you can avoid duplicate work. However, when you import a script, it may have references to layouts, fields, tables, and files that do not exist in its new home.

To avoid problems, carefully examine any script that you import to make sure that it does not have unresolved or incorrect references. When you create scripts that you will share, document them with comments so that people know what you expect.

You can also create dummy scripts with no references in them—just comments where the layout name (or whatever) would be. Those scripts can be easily imported and customized.

Summary

In this hour, you saw how to use scripts with interface elements such as buttons to control records in portals. Because the FileMaker menu interface is ambiguous in these matters, scripts and customized buttons can make your users' lives much easier. You also saw how to use script parameters.

Now it's time to return to layouts and examine how they can help you produce summaries of data. Because summaries are only displayed properly when the table is sorted and because they need to be viewed in Preview mode, a script is often a companion to the layout. (In fact, FileMaker automatically creates a script to produce each layout report if you want.)

You'll be able to apply some of the techniques from this hour to the features described in Hour 17, "Working with Summaries and Layout Parts." For example, instead of using a button in a portal row to display data in a new layout, perhaps you want to attach a script to that button to actually generate a report—and maybe even print it automatically.

Q&A

Q *What are good uses for script parameters?*

A Script parameters work particularly well when you have a number of similar scripts. The example in this hour showed a script that sometimes wants an interactive warning and sometimes doesn't. Another example is a script that creates a new record in all cases and sometimes enters data into it. You could use a script parameter with values "New Only" and "Enter Data" to handle that case. In the "New Only" section, only part of the script would execute; in the "Enter Data," the "New Only" section would execute and an additional part of the script (or a separate script) would then execute.

Q *Parameters are new in FileMaker 7. How did people write FileMaker scripts without them?*

A To pass parameters into scripts before FileMaker 7, many people declared global variables into which they would store the "parameter"; the global variable could then be accessed from within a script. There is now no need to do this. However, if you're looking at a script written for FileMaker 6 or earlier, you may very well see this type of architecture. If you're sure that the global variable is only used as a parameter, you can replace it with a true parameter and remove it from the database definition (but be sure to save a copy of the database first in case it has other uses that you haven't encountered).

This situation is similar to that of relationships before FileMaker 7. Related fields were visible only across the relationship that spanned two databases. To access a field two databases away, you had to create a calculation in the intermediate table, which consisted simply of the field in the third database. By accessing the calculation, you could get to the distant related field. Such calculations are abundant in pre-FileMaker 7 solutions and can be removed as part of the conversion process. Ultimately, it makes for simpler databases, but the process of removing these calculations may unleash changes to scripts, layouts, and other calculations that cause more work in the short term.

Workshop

Quiz

1. What is the consequence of using the Show Only Related Records checkbox?

2. How many parameters can you pass to a script?

Quiz Answers

1. FileMaker performs a find on the relationship so that users can navigate back and forth only within related records.

2. One. But because it's text, you can parse it using the string functions if you need more than one data element.

Activities

If you followed the example in this hour, there's something left to do. When you use the button to go to the related row, you're in the Telephone Numbers layout. You can return to the original layout using the Layout pop-up menu in the status area, but you might want to place a button in the Telephone Numbers layout to return people to the other layout.

Can you do that? You might want to try now. If you have trouble, read on.

You need a reverse relationship on People ID to get you to the People table.

Working with Summaries and Layout Parts

What You'll Learn in This Hour:

▶ Preparing the Parties Database for Reporting—This section explains the steps to take to modify the schema.

▶ Creating a Report with the FileMaker Assistant—The FileMaker assistant can produce sophisticated reports; you can choose from a number of different options as you create the report.

▶ Looking at the Report Parts—After the report is produced, you can see how it was done so that you can modify it or create reports from scratch in the future.

▶ Examining the Script—The optional script that is automatically created can serve as a starting point for your own scripts.

▶ Modifying the Layout—You'll see how to manipulate the layout to further customize it after you're finished with the assistant.

One of the most frequent tasks for database designers is to produce reports summarizing the database and subtotaling fields in it. FileMaker makes this easy to do. In this hour, you'll find a walk-through of creating a summarized report using FileMaker's New Layout/Report assistant. As you examine the report that is built automatically for you, you'll see how the different components work together. And then you'll see how you can modify them and expand the report.

This hour provides many step-by-step figures to guide you through the report creation process. FileMaker has a wide variety of reporting features and options, and that is why they are shown in such detail. Don't let the detail put you off: You can produce simple reports quickly with the assistant, but you won't have to compromise your report design in most cases because you can use these various detailed options to get exactly what you want.

Once again, the Parties database serves as the basis for this hour's examples. If you're following along, make sure to use the version of the database located in the Hour 17 folder because it differs from versions in other hours. Parties Start is the database for the beginning of the chapter. After all the changes are made, Parties represents the database at the end of the chapter.

Preparing the Parties Database for Reporting

In this hour, you'll see how to produce reports that summarize data in one or more tables. The simplest summarization just adds up values from each record in the table. However, in this hour a somewhat more complex summary is demonstrated. (You can use the same techniques with fewer details to produce a simpler summary.)

To allow you to produce subsummaries (summaries of grouped records within the table), you add a new field to the Parties table. Each party will now have a client for whom the party is to be arranged. One client may have several parties scheduled, and the report to be produced in this hour will summarize the budgets for all parties scheduled by each client as well as for all parties for all clients. Figure 17.1 shows one version of the completed report.

FIGURE 17.1
Produce a summarized report.

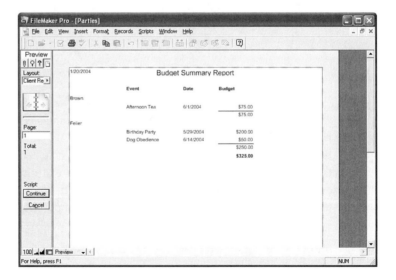

To produce this report, you need to add some fields and relationships to the database. The steps are briefly outlined in this section; they serve as a review of some of the material covered previously in this part of the book.

Add Client Information

First, to be able to summarize by client, you need to add a client field to the Parties table. The simplest way of doing that is by taking advantage of a table you already have: Guests. That table contains names, addresses, and a relationship to multiple telephone numbers. That will serve equally well as a clients table. To use it, create an alias to the Guests table; the default name is Guests 2, but you can rename it Clients.

Add a ClientID field to the Parties table, and create a relationship to Guest ID in the Clients alias to the Guests table. (If you want, you can clean up the database by renaming Guests to something more generic such as people, but that's not necessary.) While you're at it, create a telephone number relationship from the Clients alias to an alias to Telephone Numbers. Figure 17.2 shows the revised database graph. (The relationship from Clients to Telephone Numbers is not shown to simplify the figure. You can rearrange tables, change the scale, and scroll the graph to handle large graphs; however, changing the scale and using the scroll bar result in unsatisfactory images for a printed book.)

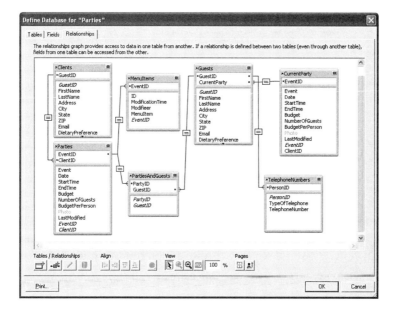

FIGURE 17.2
Create an alias to Guests and call it Clients.

By the Way

> You don't have to start by creating aliases. If you want, just create the new ClientID field in Parties and draw a relationship to Guests. You'll be warned that you need to create an alias, and FileMaker will do so for you at that time if you want.

You may be struck by the fact that when you were actually assigning guests to parties, you needed an intermediate join table (PartiesAndGuests). Why can the ClientID go directly into the Parties table? The reason is that the Parties to Clients relationship is one-to-one, not one-to-many. One party has only one client, although one client may have many parties. In the case of guests and parties, it's a many-to-many relationship.

Add a Budget Summary Field

You need to add a summary field that calculates the budget for the report. Do so by adding a summary field called BudgetSummary, as shown in Figure 17.3.

FIGURE 17.3
Add a summary field.

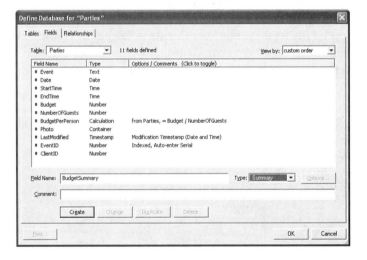

As you can see in Figure 17.4, FileMaker immediately asks you what summary function you want to use and what field to summarize.

FileMaker takes care of calculating the summary as needed. Depending on where you place the summary field in a layout, it summarizes all records or only records in a certain category. You'll see how this works later in this hour.

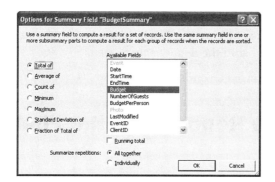

FIGURE 17.4
Choose the summary calculation.

Update the Data Entry Layout

Now that you've added the ClientID and BudgetSummary fields to the database, you need to update the layout so that you can enter the ClientID. In Figure 17.5, you see the DataEntry layout used previously.

A ClientID field is added so that you can choose which client is sponsoring a party. You can create a value list that contains the ID numbers of the clients along with their names as a secondary field to be displayed. (If this isn't familiar, you may want to review the material on value lists in Hour 13, "Creating a FileMaker Database.")

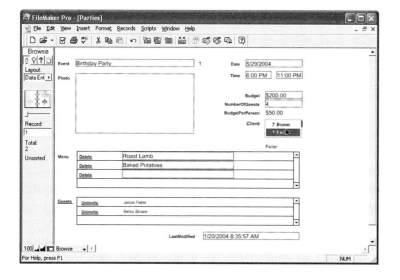

FIGURE 17.5
Add a ClientID field on the layout with a value list–driven pop-up menu.

Below the pop-up menu, the client name appears in the layout. This is not a data entry field: It's created by choosing Insert, Merge Field from the menu. It displays the first phone number in the relationship as well.

Now you're ready to create your summary report.

Creating a Report with the FileMaker Assistant

The simplest way to create a report is with the New Report/Layout assistant in the Layouts menu when you're in Layout mode. Because the report can be customized while you are running the assistant as well as after, you may never find it necessary to start from scratch. This section shows you each step of the process. In the following sections, you'll see how to modify the new report.

When you choose Layouts, New Report/Layout from the menu, the dialog shown in Figure 17.6 appears. You've seen it before; this time, you'll use it to create a report with subtotals and totals.

FIGURE 17.6
Create a new
report.

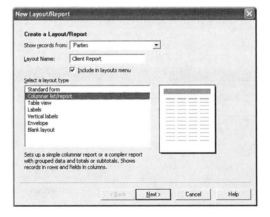

Next, you are asked whether you want to group data and to include subtotals and grand totals. As you click the radio buttons and checkboxes shown in Figure 17.7, the report images change so that you can see what the default layout will be. Note that although subtotals and totals are shown in the schematics at the ends of the sections, you can change the option as you create the report. Experiment with the dialog to see how the default layout changes.

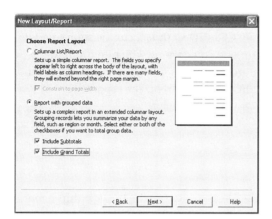

FIGURE 17.7
Choose to subtotal and group your report.

As you see in Figure 17.8, you next are prompted to select the fields to appear in the report. They will be shown in the order you place them here, but you can move them later. (You can use the double-arrow icon to move fields up or down in the Layout Fields list at the right of the dialog.) Using the pop-up menu at the top of the left-hand side of the dialog, you can choose fields from any relationship you have defined in the database.

It's important to remember that fields containing title information need to be made part of the report. Rather than include ClientID from Parties, you'll need to include LastName from the Clients relationship you created at the beginning of the hour.

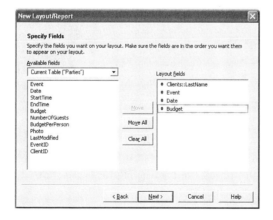

FIGURE 17.8
Select fields for the report.

Next, choose the categories for your report (see Figure 17.9). In this case, you want to group data by ClientID so that it can be subtotaled for each client. You can specify more than one category by which to group the report, but the categories should be hierarchical. Thus, if clients can be corporations rather than individuals, you might choose to group the report by

▶ Client (corporation)

▶ Department

▶ Project

As long as parties are within projects, which are within departments, which are within individual clients, all will be well. If you need to group data by nonhierarchical means (clients and locations, for example), you'll need two reports.

The fields by which the report is grouped are sometimes called *break fields*, and the report is said to *break* on such fields, as in "the report breaks on clients." You may also hear people talk about a report "breaking on departments within clients."

FIGURE 17.9
Select fields by
which to group the
report.

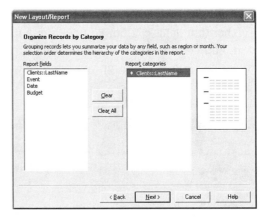

Your next choice is the order by which to sort the report. It is sorted first by the fields you've chosen, but you may choose additional fields by which to sort. One possibility is to sort parties by their dates. Figure 17.10 shows how you specify the sort order.

You've specified the data in the report and how it should be grouped. All that's left is to specify what fields are to be subtotals. The next screen, shown in Figure 17.11, lets you add subtotals to the report. Select a field using the Specify button at the left.

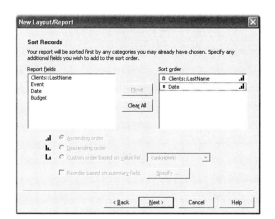

FIGURE 17.10
Specify the sort order for the data.

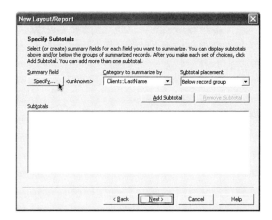

FIGURE 17.11
Specify a subtotal.

When you click the Specify button, the dialog shown in Figure 17.12 appears. The only available fields are those that you created as summaries.

Then, use the pop-up menu in the Specify Subtotals dialog (refer to Figure 17.11) to choose where it appears in relation to the data (above or below) when the report is summarized by the field chosen in the pop-up at the center of the dialog. (Note that the Specify button lets you select only fields that you identified as being summary fields. You can add other fields, such as names, manually later on as you'll see.)

You can add as many subtotals as you want to a group. Simply click the Add Subtotal button when your settings are as you want them, and the subtotal will be added, as shown in Figure 17.13.

FIGURE 17.12
FIGURE 17.12
Specify the summary field for the subtotal.

FIGURE 17.13
Add the summary field to the report.

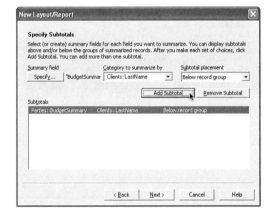

After you add summary fields to grouped data, you add a grand summary field in a similar manner, as shown in Figure 17.14. (In the example used here, only one summary field is declared: BudgetSummary, so your life is simple.)

Choosing a layout template as shown in Figure 17.15 is the same as in other layouts.

You finish up by specifying header and footer information on the next screen, as shown in Figure 17.16. You can choose from standard items such as report date, time, and page numbers. You can also choose to enter customized text.

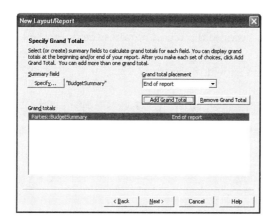

FIGURE 17.14
Add a grand summary field.

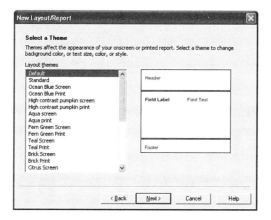

FIGURE 17.15
Choose your layout template.

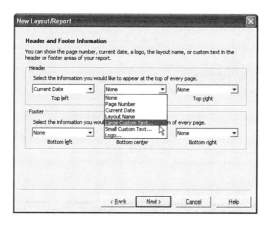

FIGURE 17.16
Specify report headers and footers.

On the penultimate screen, you can choose to have FileMaker create a script that produces the report. Because the report requires the database to be sorted in a specific way (so that your grouped data is together), it's convenient to choose the Create a Script option shown in Figure 17.17.

FIGURE 17.17
FileMaker can create a script for your report.

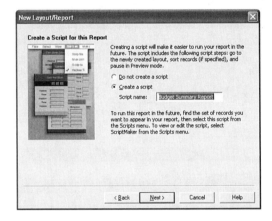

And, finally, as you see in Figure 17.18, you can select whether the script leaves you in Layout or Preview mode. Many report features, including summaries, function properly only in Preview mode.

FIGURE 17.18
Choose whether to end in Layout or Preview mode.

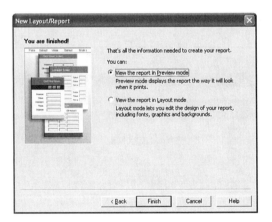

If you run the script, you see the report as shown in Figure 17.19. Yours may differ depending on the default field settings in your layout.

You can do some fixing up; the next sections show you how. (Some of the fix-ups could have been avoided if the report had been created differently. They deliberately are included for tutorial purposes. If everything had worked perfectly the first time, that would have been great—but in real life, that rarely happens, and you need to know how to improve on the first pass of the report.)

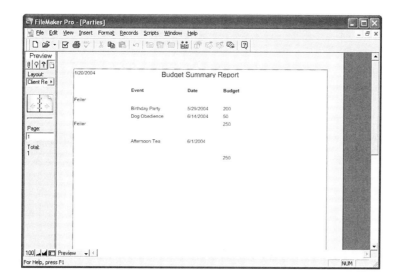

FIGURE 17.19
The report is created for you.

Looking at the Report Parts

If you go into Layout mode, you'll see the report and its parts. Parts are the key to these reports, and they are identified at the left side. In Figure 17.20, the parts are, from top to bottom, Header, Subsummary, Body, Subsummary, Trailing Grand Summary, and Footer. (The parts in the layout in Figure 17.20 have been lengthened to allow more of the part names to appear.)

Double-click on a part name at the left of the layout to open the Part Definition dialog for that part. Figure 17.21 shows the Part Definition for the second subsummary. This has been set up for you by the assistant; you can modify it if you want.

As you can see, in the Part Definition dialog you can specify page breaks and other report formatting features.

FIGURE 17.20
Parts control how
reports are totaled
and subtotaled.

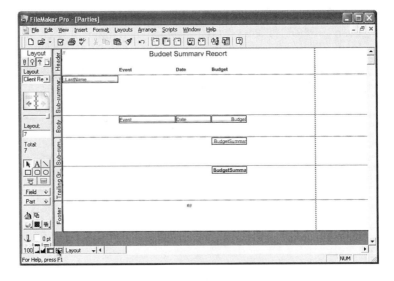

FIGURE 17.21
View and modify
report parts.

By the Way

If you change the break fields for summaries or subsummaries, you also need to change the sort order in the script. The sort order must match the break fields.

Examining the Script

If you chose to have FileMaker create a script for your report, you may want to examine it now. Using ScriptMaker, edit the script as shown in Figure 17.22.

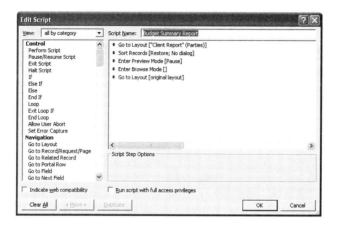

FIGURE 17.22
Edit the script.

The script is a basic script that sorts the database, applies the report layout, goes to Preview mode (if you've chosen that), pauses, and then returns to Browse mode and the original layout. A significant improvement in FileMaker 7 is the fact that you can view the sort specifications in a script. To do so, edit the script (choose Scripts, ScriptMaker from the menu). If you select a Sort Script step, there's a Specify button in the lower right. It lets you view and edit the sort specification as shown in Figure 17.23. (Previously, ScriptMaker attached the last-used sort to the script.)

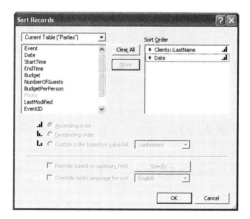

FIGURE 17.23
View the sorting specifications.

Modifying the Layout

You can modify the layout just as you have modified other layouts. For example, the budget numbers and budget summaries will look better formatted as currency and aligned to the right. If you place a border on the top of the summary field, you'll have the underline you want before the total.

The default behavior places the name in subsummary parts both before and after the body of the report. You may want to remove the name from the following subsummary, leaving only the summary field. Figure 17.24 shows the selected field about to be deleted at the lower left.

FIGURE 17.24
Delete unnecessary
fields.

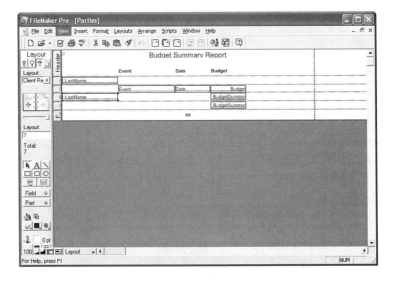

You frequently build layouts on other layouts. Figure 17.25 shows an example of a summarized version of the same report. It provides totals by client, but no specific party information.

First, choose Layouts, Duplicate Layout from the menu; use the Layout Setup command to provide a meaningful name for this layout. Likewise, duplicate the script and rename it. Next, select the Body part by clicking its name at the left. Delete it with the Delete key or by choosing Edit, Cut from the menu. Alternatively, you can choose Layouts, Part Setup from the menu to select the Body part and delete it as shown in Figure 17.26.

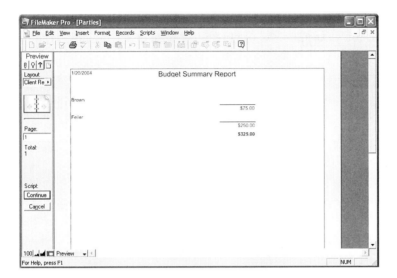

FIGURE 17.25
You can eliminate detail information on a report.

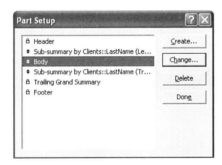

FIGURE 17.26
Delete the Body part.

You are asked to confirm the deletion as shown in Figure 17.27.

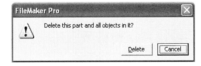

FIGURE 17.27
Confirm that you want to delete the Body part.

Summary

Summaries and the various layout parts are significant features of FileMaker that go beyond mere data manipulation. They are at the heart of many FileMaker solutions.

You've seen how to add fields and relationships to a table to make its reports easier to read. You've seen how to use the assistant to create reports—even complex reports—with just a few mouse clicks.

To modify reports, you need an understanding of the parts of each report such as headers, footers, and summaries. You've seen how to create and modify them, as well as how to modify the scripts automatically generated to create reports.

Finally, you've seen how to modify reports to provide summary data only, detail data only, and various other combinations you can think of.

Now that you've learned how to create databases and relationships, work with complex layouts, and provide sophisticated reports, it's not a moment too soon to start thinking about protecting your data and your work. Hour 18, "Securing Your Solutions and Databases," is all about security.

Q&A

Q *What most often causes perfectly good summary reports to break?*

A If you change the sort in the database (or don't sort it), the report may not break properly. Likewise, if you don't go into Preview mode, the summary fields won't be calculated properly. That's why using scripts to produce summary reports (such as the automatically created ones in the assistant) is so helpful.

Q *What happens if you have two clients with the same last name?*

A In this example, their data will sort together. If that is possible, use the ClientID field to sort the report and display the last name.

Workshop

Quiz

1. Can summary reports contain buttons?

2. How do you decide which summary or total part to place a summary field in?

3. Can you apply number formatting to summary fields?

Quiz Answers

1. Yes, but they won't work in Preview mode, which you need to use to display the report.

2. It goes in every summary or total part that you want summarized. It can appear several times in the layout to produce several different summary values.

3. Yes. They often have different formats than the detail rows. For example, a currency symbol is often omitted from detail rows but included in a summary value.

Activities

Using the example in this chapter, add the additional groups suggested (company, department, project). Experiment with summary reports. Try using ClientID for the sort and displaying the last name.

HOUR 18

Securing Your Solutions and Databases

What You'll Learn in This Hour:

▶ About Security—More than ever, security is essential these days. It's not just about preventing unauthorized access; it's also about keeping your solutions running and protecting them from accidental or deliberate damage.

▶ Overview of FileMaker Security—Totally rewritten in FileMaker 7, the new unified security model is used for individual FileMaker databases, FileMaker Server, and Web publishing.

▶ Defining Accounts—The first aspect of security is setting up who can use your databases.

▶ Defining Privileges—The second aspect of security is specifying what your database users can do.

▶ Defining Extended Privileges—Extended privileges provide a convenient way of combining privileges into sets that can be applied to specific types of access (such as the Web, ODBC, and local area networks).

▶ Turning Security On—You need to verify usernames and activate accounts to use your security model.

Databases store large amounts of data in a manner that makes it easy to retrieve and manipulate. Thus, by their very nature, they are security risks for that data. (You can argue as some do that disorganized data jammed into paper files in a closet is inherently more secure than an efficient computerized database.) In this hour, you'll see how to use FileMaker's new security model to keep your data secure yet accessible to the right people.

This hour uses the Contact Management template to demonstrate the security model.

About Security

Unless you are using a database solely for your own purposes and only on a computer to which you alone have access, you need to consider security concerns for your databases and solutions. Security is more than just a matter of preventing unauthorized access to your data. It includes making sure that your databases are not corrupted either maliciously or inadvertently. It also includes ensuring that your databases and database solutions work and are available at appropriate times (and this vision of security therefore includes availability of network connections as well as of power).

Security can entail making sure that your database solutions, including layouts and scripts, are not appropriated by others without permission. (This is particularly important if you are a developer or consultant.) And, on the other side of the coin, security for a client may mean making sure that the consultant or developer provides sufficient documentation and resources so that a mission-critical FileMaker solution can be maintained in the future.

In short, security is about a lot more than passwords.

As you can see from the points touched on so far, security involves everything from the power supply for your computer to your relationships and contracts with consultants and developers. None of these is specific to FileMaker; however, their absence from this hour's discussion should in no way be taken as suggesting that they aren't important. And, as noted at the beginning of this hour, databases are intrinsically tied up with security issues.

In embarking on any database project or FileMaker solution, you should plan for security from the beginning. In general, three aspects of system design cannot be retrofitted: security, version control, and networking. Thus, you should not leave your security plans to the end of a project. You can implement security at the end of the project, but you should know from the start what you will be doing.

As you'll see in this hour, FileMaker provides a wide range of security features including access controls for individual fields, scripts, value lists, and layouts. Because each of these can contribute to the security picture, you can choose to design your system around security concerns. For example, by securing a specific layout, you may be able to address many individual security issues instead of working at the field level. This might encourage you to create a layout strictly for security purposes. It might almost completely duplicate another layout's design, but many of the fields might not allow data entry. In this way, you can use the layouts to manage access.

Overview of FileMaker Security

Security is one feature that has changed in FileMaker 7 from previous versions. Initially, FileMaker security only had to address issues of security on the desktop and on a local area network. With the addition of Web publishing in FileMaker 4, security was needed for the Web, too. Until now, the implementations of security in the different environments were done separately. Now, however, a *unified security model* controls security in all environments.

There are two primary aspects of FileMaker security:

▶ Accounts

▶ Privileges

These two aspects are managed separately, but both are managed within the Define Accounts & Privileges dialog, which is the topic of this hour.

Accounts

Accounts are about authentication: Who is this user? Each account has a password, although the password can be blank if you want. Initially, two accounts are set up for each database file: an Admin user with total access to the file and a blank password and a second account for a read-only access user. The Admin user is activated by default; the other account is not yet activated.

The consequence of these default settings is that if you do nothing, anyone can open the database file without entering an account or password. That may be what you want. But if you want to implement security, you can set up additional accounts (and even delete the default Admin account if you want—but you will need to have at least one account with full access to the file).

You can set up accounts for individuals, classes of users, or a combination. Thus, you might have individual accounts for Admin or other database administrators, whereas most users might share a Users account (or even the default read-only account).

Privileges

Privileges are about what can be done with the database. (This is sometimes referred to as *role-based security*.) You can define privileges that allow updating, viewing, or no access to individual fields, layouts, tables, and other entities. You can create as many privilege sets as you want.

Implementing Security

Implementing security is simple. After you create your accounts and your privilege sets (or have decided to use the defaults), you link a specific privilege set to a specific account. This architecture makes it easy to define a privilege set that is attached to many different accounts (perhaps a Students privilege set that is attached to each of 50 student accounts). It also makes it easy to copy a privilege set and to make one or two minor changes to create a separate privilege set.

All security controls are implemented in the Define Accounts & Privileges dialog, which can be accessed by choosing File, Define, Accounts & Privileges from the menu, as shown in Figure 18.1.

By the Way

You can start by defining accounts or by defining privileges—or by working on both at the same time. For any security implementation beyond the most basic, you'll probably want to design the accounts and privileges on a piece of paper before starting to work with the dialog.

FIGURE 18.1
Define accounts and privileges.

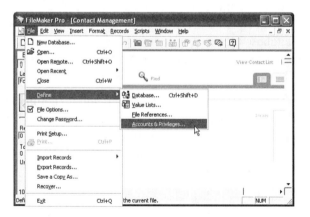

Defining Accounts

To define accounts, choose the first tab, Accounts, in the Define Accounts & Privileges dialog. Figure 18.2 shows the two default accounts, Guest and Admin.

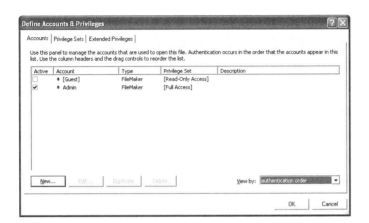

FIGURE 18.2
Manage accounts in the Accounts tab.

The accounts are activated when people log in with a password (if this is necessary). The password can be blank, as it is in the case of the default Guest account. You can reorder the accounts to control the sequence in which they are used (in the case of blank passwords, for example). Note, too, that each account can be marked active or not with the checkbox at the left. This lets you create more accounts than you need right now. You might create a Test account, for example, along with a variety of inactive accounts that will be activated when a FileMaker solution moves into production.

You edit an account by selecting it and clicking the Edit button at the bottom. The Edit Account dialog opens, as shown in Figure 18.3. Here you can set the default password, require the user to change the password on next login, and so forth. Requiring a user to change the password on the next login is an effective way of increasing security: Your default password is used only once, and the user has total control over the actual password used from then on.

You can assign a privilege set to an account using the pop-up menu in the center of the Edit Account dialog; a command in that menu also lets you create a new privilege set. You also can create privilege sets using the Privilege Sets tab of the Define Accounts & Privileges dialog.

At the top of the Edit Account dialog, a pop-up menu lets you choose whether FileMaker manages accounts or an external server is used. If an external server (such as an LDAP server) is used, it is configured in FileMaker Server so that you can use those accounts rather than duplicate your own. More information on this feature is available in the documentation that comes with FileMaker Server; you also may need additional documentation from the network administrator who manages your external server.

FIGURE 18.3
Edit an account.

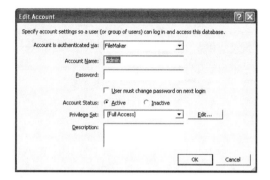

Defining Privileges

You can define privileges either from the Privilege Set pop-up menu in the center of the Edit Account dialog, as shown in Figure 18.3, or by using the Privilege Sets tab in the Define Accounts & Privileges dialog, as shown in Figure 18.4. Three default privilege sets are created for you by FileMaker; they are shown in Figure 18.4. They may be sufficient for all your purposes.

FIGURE 18.4
Manage privilege sets.

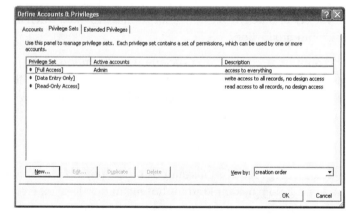

To edit a privilege set, select it in the Privilege Sets tab of the Define Accounts & Privileges dialog, and click the Edit button to open the Edit Privilege Set dialog shown in Figure 18.5.

As you can see, you have a great deal of control over what accounts assigned to a privilege set can do. One of the most powerful choices is in the lower right: the Available Menu Commands. A pop-up menu lets you choose among All, Editing

Only, and Minimum. Many people find that the Editing Only menu commands provide the best security for users who are viewing and updating a database (but not changing its layouts and schema). Whenever you can implement security with a simple choice (such as Editing Only commands) rather than a host of specific controls, your security will be easier to manage.

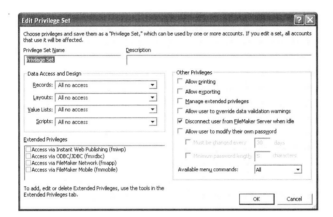

FIGURE 18.5
Edit a privilege set.

The Data Access and Design group of controls at the left lets you manage access to records, layouts, value lists, and scripts. Each of the pop-up menus is slightly different, reflecting the different choices for each of these elements. The choices for each of these menus are described in the following sections.

You can see the choices for records in Figure 18.6.

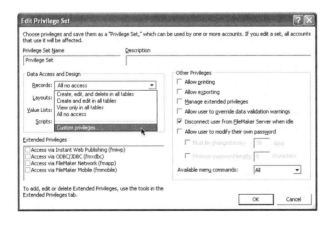

FIGURE 18.6
Configure access to records.

Access to Records

If you choose the final option under Records in the Edit Privilege Set dialog (refer to Figure 18.6), the Custom Record Privileges dialog opens, as shown in Figure 18.7.

FIGURE 18.7
Customize privileges for individual tables.

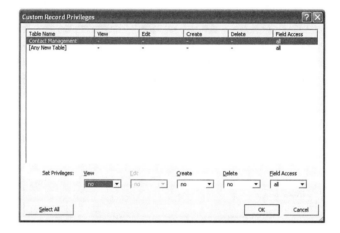

For each type of access (View, Edit, Create, or Delete), you can specify Yes or No for the selected table. In addition, most types of access also allow you to select a Limited choice. When Limited is selected, a Specify Calculation dialog like that shown in Figure 18.8 opens. You specify a calculation, the result of which must be Boolean, that is invoked to determine at runtime whether the specific access is allowed.

FIGURE 18.8
Create a calculation to control limited access.

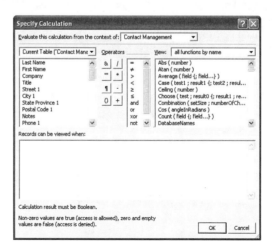

You can base the calculation on data in any table to which you have access. One example of the implementation of limited access might be a calculation that checks the value of a specific field and acts accordingly. This is how you would allow editing of fields with values under $1,000, for example, but would disallow editing of higher values. Another similar type of limited access might allow editing of transactions that have not been billed or shipped.

At the lower right of the Custom Record Privileges dialog is the Field Access pop-up menu. You can use its "Limited" command to open the Custom Field Privileges dialog shown in Figure 18.9, which lets you set access for each field in the table.

FIGURE 18.9
Set access at the field level.

Access to Layouts

The basic choices for access to layouts are found in the Layouts pop-up menu in the Edit Privilege Set dialog (refer to Figure 18.5). They are All Modifiable, All View Only, and All No Access. In addition, a Custom Privileges command is available, which opens the Custom Layout Privileges dialog, shown in Figure 18.10.

Note that you can control access not only to the layout itself but also to the records viewed through each layout. Also, in addition to setting privileges for each layout, a standard entry at the end of the list lets you set privileges for any new layouts that may be created in the future. (This feature is available for all types of privileges—layouts, value lists, and scripts. It is always located at the bottom of the list; you'll see it next in Figure 18.11 in the context of value lists.)

FIGURE 18.10
Customize layout
privileges.

FIGURE 18.10
Customize layout
privileges.

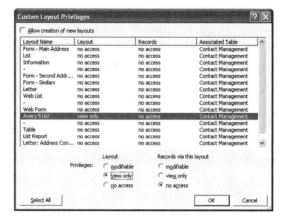

Access to Value Lists

In addition to the basic access choices (All Modifiable, All View Only, and All No
Access), you can set custom privileges for value lists. In the Edit Privilege Set dia-
log (refer to Figure 18.5), open the Value Lists pop-up menu, and choose Custom
Privileges to open the Custom Value Lists Privileges dialog, which is shown in
Figure 18.11.

FIGURE 18.11
Customize value
list privileges.

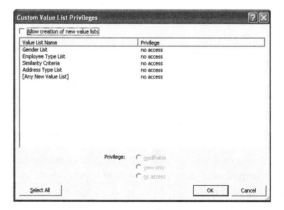

As with layouts, you can set privileges for existing items as well as for new value
lists created in the future (until you change their privileges again in this dialog).

Access to Scripts

For scripts, the access choices in the Edit Privilege Set dialog (refer to Figure 18.5) are similar to those for value lists: All No Access, All Modifiable, and All Execute Only (rather than View only), as you can see in Figure 18.12. As with value lists and layouts, a final entry lets you select privileges for any new script that you create.

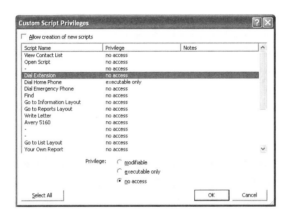

FIGURE 18.12
Customize script privileges.

Defining Extended Privileges

Extended privileges are displayed in the lower left of the Privilege Sets tab in the Define Accounts & Privileges dialog. You can manage and edit extended privileges from the third tab, Extended Privileges, which is shown in Figure 18.13.

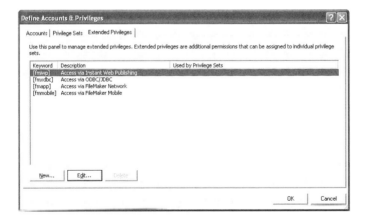

FIGURE 18.13
Manage extended privileges.

Four extended privilege sets are built into FileMaker, as you can see. You cannot delete or modify these sets, but you can create others either from scratch or by duplicating these. When you choose to edit an extended privileges set, the Edit Extended Privilege dialog opens, as shown in Figure 18.14.

FIGURE 18.14
Edit extended privileges.

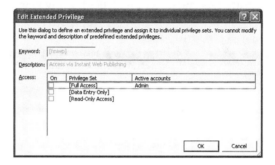

You can turn on existing privilege sets for the extended privilege. In that way, you can group a set of privileges for a specific type of access (for example, over the Web).

Turning Security On

To actually use the security that you've set up, you need to make two sets of adjustments: Verify the username that you (or others) will use to log in, and turn on the security at the database (not the user) side.

Verifying User ID

By default, FileMaker uses the current username in a login dialog. You should verify that each user's name is correct (whether it is a person's name or a title such as Receptionist). You do this in the general Preferences dialog; in Windows it is located on the Edit menu, and on Mac OS X it is on the FileMaker applications menu. The respective dialogs are shown in Figure 18.15 and Figure 18.16.

You do not have to set the name for each user individually; rather, you need to check that the database correctly is picking up a username or the system username. (And you do have to verify that the correct username is set for each computer being used.)

FIGURE 18.15
Set the username
in Windows.

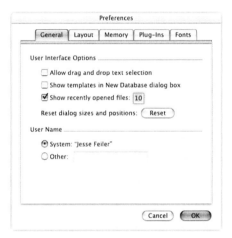

FIGURE 18.16
Set the username
in Mac OS X.

Activating Database Security

You activate database security by using the checkbox to mark an individual account as active (in the Accounts tab of the Define Accounts & Preferences dialog). You also make a default account such as Admin active by adding a non-blank password to it. If you do so, you are prompted to confirm that you know an account and password that lets you access the entire database, as you can see in Figure 18.17.

Thereafter, when you open the database, you are prompted to log in, as you can see in Figure 18.18. If Guest access is allowed, the Guest Account radio button will be available; if not, it will be grayed out. The default username is the name picked up from Preferences (refer to Figures 18.15 and 18.16).

FIGURE 18.17
Verify that you can access the entire database.

FIGURE 18.18
Log in to a database.

Summary

In this hour, you saw how to implement security using the new FileMaker unified security model. It's based on accounts (who you are) and privileges (what you want to do). You can define them separately and then connect them as you want.

In this part of the book, you've seen how to start from scratch to create a database, its tables and relationships, its layouts and scripts, and how to implement security. You need to understand one more set of topics to create powerful and useful FileMaker solutions. Hour 19, "Finishing Up: Help, Testing, and Keeping Things Running," shows you how to add help, as well as how to test and verify your solutions.

Q&A

Q *Isn't this security model very complicated?*

A The FileMaker unified security model is now designed to be able to handle the most complex and demanding security needs. They may be far beyond what you need. You can use default security privileges and accounts for most purposes. All you have to do is add a password to the Admin account and activate the Read-only guest access. But the rest is there in case you need it.

Q *What is the biggest challenge in implementing security?*

A Generally, one of the biggest challenges (other than convincing people that security is essential) is to avoid over-implementing security. It is possible to lock users out of legitimate access. In general, try to use the most broadly based tools for security access (such as securing layouts and the records viewed through them rather than individual fields).

Workshop

Quiz

1. How do you turn on security for the Admin account?

2. If you use group accounts (such as Students), how can you control individual access?

3. Do you have to be able to view a script to execute it?

4. Do you have to be able to view a field to edit it?

Quiz Answers

1. Define a nonblank password.

2. Use the limited access feature and construct a calculation that gets the current username, Get(UserName).

3. No.

4. Yes.

Activities

Pick any three FileMaker templates from different types of applications (perhaps Contact Management, To Do List, and Expense Report). Design security for each template from the standpoint of an administrator (not necessarily the Admin account) and of a user. How do your choices vary from one type of FileMaker solution to another?

HOUR 19

Finishing Up: Help, Testing, and Keeping Things Running

What You'll Learn in This Hour:

▶ Providing Help and Assistance—Here are some tips about how to write help and assistance along with a few different ways of letting people get to the help they need when they need it.

▶ Testing FileMaker Solutions—Your FileMaker solution is only partly done the first time it appears to work. Can you guarantee that it will work as it should under all circumstances? What are its limits? These are the procedures you can follow to verify and validate your solution.

▶ Keeping Things Running—Finally, this section shows you the variety of FileMaker tools and commands that you can use to maintain your database. Everything from the built-in Recover command that can deal with corrupted databases to a variety of commands that let you perform wholesale replaces and updates of data is described here.

In this hour, you'll see how to add the finishing touches to your FileMaker solutions and how to keep the solutions up and running. After you've invested time and energy in developing the solutions, spending a little time to protect that investment is certainly worth it.

Perhaps the most important point to remember is that you should carefully document what you've done—as you go along and when you're finished. What is fresh in
your mind today is likely to be long gone a year from now when you need to make a
small adjustment to the database. As part of this process, make copies of the databases as well as work files you may have created (raw graphics, for example, that
you create in a graphics program and then paste onto a layout—you may need to
modify that logo after a corporate name change).

Providing Help and Assistance

FileMaker provides its own help and assistance through the Help menu. When
you create your own FileMaker solutions, you generally need to provide additional help for your users to help them use the tools you are providing for them.

This section provides a few tips on authoring help; you'll then see two methods of
providing help in your FileMaker solutions. Finally, you'll find some design pointers that help reduce the need for help.

General Help Authoring Issues

Over the years, a lot has been learned about how to provide online help. Here are
some pointers that can make your life easier (as well as make your users' lives
easier).

Types of Help

People need three basic types of help when they're using software products. First,
they frequently need to know how to do something. This may be a theoretical
issue, but more often the user needs to perform a task *now* and needs assistance
in doing so. Perhaps the user has gotten part way into the task and is stumped.
How-to-do-it help needs to be direct and to the point, recognizing the immediacy
of the need. This is the most frequent type of help that you provide online for
your FileMaker solutions.

Second is the more casual "what-is-this?" type of help. Here, the user looks at the
interface (buttons and menus) and wonders what a particular command or button does. In some applications, this type of assistance is provided with help tags
or tool tips; in other cases, illustrations of the interface are annotated.

Finally, users may want to understand what they can do with their software. Did
you know that you can use FileMaker to produce mail merge letters? Did you
know that you can automatically publish your databases using Instant Web
Publishing? These are examples of the third kind of help. This type of help is

usually the most extensive and wide-ranging. It frequently includes examples and tips. (This book is an example of the third kind of help.)

Use the Right Vocabulary

Frequently when you're developing a FileMaker solution, you are the mediator between the world of technology and databases and a particular world of business or other endeavor. Your normal vocabulary may consist of database terminology, but it's a good idea to go out of your way to use the terminology that your users are comfortable with.

Why bother explaining the concepts of match fields and related tables if everyone in the office already knows that all data is filed according to patient ID, property street address, or other such information.

Incorporate Graphics...Carefully

You can create a graphic that illustrates what a user should do. It can contain a section of the actual layout that the user will see, and you can use a graphics program to add text to it.

If you are using graphics that show parts of the interface, make sure that you make it clear that this is illustrative, and not a live part of the interface. In Figure 19.1, you see three different approaches. First, you see part of the interface. If you insert this graphic into a help screen, you may find people clicking on it. Below it, you see a similar graphic; however, note that the cursor is positioned over the Print Purchase Order button, and the screen shot was taken with the mouse button held down so that the button is highlighted. Few people will click on this graphic. Finally, an arrow points to the Print Purchase Order graphic. In this case, the graphic is framed with a rectangle; furthermore, it is slightly reduced in size from the actual interface. Because the arrow breaks the frame of the graphic (that is, it extends beyond the graphic itself), the frame itself, and the reduction in size, most people recognize that it is an illustration, and not a live part of the interface.

Providing Help in a Global Field

A simple way of providing help is to create a global field in a table. It can be text, or it can be a container for a graphic, PDF, or even a movie. The field is available from all records, but only takes up space in the table for one item. If it's text, you can place the global help field at the bottom or side of your layout; when people need it, they can scroll through it. This is suitable for small help texts—such as are needed when people are stuck (see the section "Types of Help" earlier in this hour).

FIGURE 19.1
Make illustrations in documentation distinct from the interface itself.

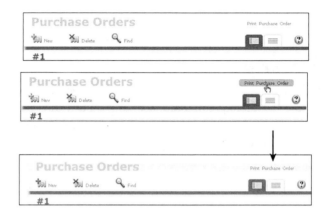

An advantage of using a global text field is that if you have several layouts, you can make consistent help text available in all of them. Alternatively, you can type help text directly onto a layout, but you'll have to add it for each layout.

Providing Help with a Script and a Layout

Rather than leaving help visible in a global field on a layout, you can prepare a separate layout that contains help. It can display a global field, or you can type the text right on the layout. The layout might contain different sections of help—in fact, it might be a control center with buttons users can click to go to other layouts for additional help.

To implement this, you need to create the layout and then add a button to the primary layout(s); when users click the button, they'll go to the help layout. And from there…? You must enable them to get back to whatever layout they started from. There are two ways to do this.

Use a Script Step to Return to the Original Layout

You can use the Go to Layout script step from the help layout to return to the layout from which users started. In the ScriptMaker window, specify Original Layout as the layout to which to return. This returns the user to the layout in use when the script started.

For simple help layouts, this is fine. However, if you allow users to navigate through a variety of help layouts, you may wind up launching other scripts as well as allowing users to navigate by themselves to other places. In such a case, you might want to consider the following procedure.

Use a Global to Return to the Original Layout

To do this with a global, you'll need to attach a two-step script to the button that goes to help. First, store the current layout number in a global; then go to the help layout. When the user clicks to return to the initial layout, execute a script step to return to the layout number in the global field.

Here are the details. First, create a global field—call it CurrentLayout. Its type is numeric because it will store the number of the current layout. You don't have to worry about setting its value except when the user is going to go to the help layout. Here's the script to attach to the Help button or whatever other interface element you want to use to go to the help layout. Assume that the help layout is named HelpLayout.

```
Set Field ["CurrentLayout", Get(LayoutNumber)]
Go to Layout ("HelpLayout")
```

The return script simply consists of

```
Go to Layout [CurrentLayout]
```

The advantage of this procedure is that you can place return buttons throughout your help layouts and be assured that clicking any of them returns the users to the appropriate layout.

Providing Help with a Custom Dialog

The simplest way of providing brief help is with a custom dialog. It can display text or the contents of a global field. The disadvantages are that it cannot include graphics, the text must be short, and it cannot easily contain links to further assistance.

Use a Script Parameter to Provide Help

You can write a help script that is accessed from various interface elements and that takes a script parameter to indicate what should be displayed. You would invoke the script with a script step such as

```
Perform Script ["Provide Help", Parameter: "Input Formats"]
```

The script can then decide whether to use a global field, a layout, or another technique to provide help. This is the most robust method, in view of the fact that it allows you to attach the script to interface elements and change the help delivery system by modifying only the script—not the interface elements.

Preventing the Need for Help

Finally, remember that it's easier to prevent problems than to solve them with help. Although you can get away with FileMaker's automatic type coercion, make your field types as specific as possible—dates for dates, rather than dates in text fields, for example. Use the built-in validation routines so that you know that the data in a field is what you expect it to be. Don't let the user enter "Rosemary" as a date. (A further advantage is that you let FileMaker perform the error checking and provide the error messages instead of duplicating their effort.)

If you make any assumptions about data that can't be caught with validations, at least provide clear instructions on the layout. If you expect names to be entered as Last Name, First Name, say so right next to the field in small type.

Finally, as you are designing your database and your solution, keep track of the inherent limits you are placing on data. FileMaker doesn't require you to specify the number of digits in fields as some other database managers do (although you can specify a valid range of values). But if your solutions assume that all dates are in the current year, that all addresses are in the United States, or that all inventory items have a price greater than zero, keep track of these limits on a piece of paper (or at least in the comments in the Define Database dialog's Fields tab). When you repurpose your database or expand it in one way or another, these items can become important.

Testing FileMaker Solutions

Testing your solutions is more than just checking that some sample data works as you expect it to. This section shows you how to go about testing your solutions.

By the
Way

Testing Lessons from Y2K

The Y2K problem really did exist. Extensive testing and remediation (at the cost of billions of dollars worldwide) helped to mitigate the problem.

For many systems—particularly older ones—there was no substitute for simply reviewing the code manually. In other cases, systematic testing was done. Because the risk of Y2K failure was significant, particularly in older systems and in industries such as financial services, testing was done on a larger scale than had been done before in many organizations.

Many bugs were found. On review, it turned out that a significant number of those bugs had nothing to do with Y2K. They were bugs that had never been noticed before for one reason or another. Only the intense testing regime uncovered them.

Even FileMaker had Y2K vulnerabilities. The issue arose in FileMaker and in many other products when people used two-digit years. In computing the number of years between two given dates, it was always easy to subtract. However, when the later two-digit year had a lower value than the earlier two-digit year (as in 04 for 2004 versus 89 for 1989), the results of these computations were erroneous. Try it yourself: 2004-1989 gives you 15. 04-89 gives you -85. This is not a problem within FileMaker itself so much as a problem that could arise with implementations that people developed without worrying about this issue.

Types of Testing

Testing is far more than just checking to see that things work the way you expect them to. There are many ways of describing testing; here is one way of breaking down the tasks. You'll find many books and articles about software testing in your library or bookstore; the field is sophisticated.

This section is designed to give you an overview of the basic issues. You can create a complete test plan based on the points in this section; for a rigorous test plan, you'll need to get additional guidance both from general references and from specific sources related to the type of solution you are developing.

Decide what you'll be testing and create a test plan. The plan should make clear the objectives of the testing (that is, which of the following types of testing you'll be doing), and what their results should be. In a formal system design process, the development of the test plan proceeds hand-in-hand with the development of specifications. In some cases, the same people who develop the specifications start to work on a test plan as the developers start to implement the specifications.

Performance Testing

Performance testing tests to see that the solution does what it is expected to do. If there is a formal specification, are all the issues in the specification addressed? In many solutions that evolve over time, there is no formal specification, so basic testing is a matter of users reviewing the system for accuracy and reasonability.

Parallel Testing

If you are automating an existing system (either manual or implemented with other software), it is frequently a good idea to conduct a parallel test to make sure that the old and new systems produce appropriate results. (Sometimes the results should be different—as, for example, in the case in which you are adding functionality or replacing a system that sometimes misbehaves.)

If yours is an accounting system, it is usually a good idea to run in parallel for at least one complete accounting cycle. This involves entering the data twice and comparing the outputs.

Parallel testing of this nature is possible for structured systems such as accounting systems. It's frequently not possible for systems that support ad hoc queries and analysis.

Stress Testing

It's important to test the limits of a system in many cases. After you've determined that the system is doing what it should do, stress testing helps you see what happens when a lot of people enter a lot of data in a short period of time. Many performance problems materialize only under conditions of stress. (Entering one data record is unlikely to uncover a severe performance problem.)

Failure Testing

One area frequently missed in testing is the proper handling of failures. When you test your solution, you are tempted to test it by doing what you're supposed to do. But what happens if the user enters incorrect data? Does the appropriate error message appear (does *any* error message appear)?

Regression Testing

Regression testing is the process of testing all the old functionality of a solution after changes have been made. There are many horror stories of minor changes that inadvertently create problems seemingly unrelated to the changes that were made.

Prepare a Test Suite

Now that you've developed a test plan, the next step is to develop one or more test suites. These are sets of data and procedures used to repeat tests from one version of the software to another. (This is how you can easily implement regression testing: Just run the test suites again.)

A test suite consists of data as well as a sequence of steps in which the data is entered and modified. The results should be specified so that it's easy to see whether the test has passed. (If you are converting an existing system, the output from the existing system may serve as the expected results in many cases.)

Test data isn't a matter of typing in "John Doe" for a customer's name. It should be thought out carefully so that it lets you perform the needed tests. There are two basic categories of test data: real data and exceptional data.

Real Data

This is just what the name says: actual data either from an existing system or from your records. Why use real data? Real data often reveals flaws in logic and other problems that simplified, made-up data doesn't expose.

Exceptional Data

This is data—real or made-up—specifically designed to test potential problem areas. You may want to create two people with the same name and make sure that the solution doesn't confuse them. (You also need to make sure that the interface provides some way for users of the solution to understand the difference between the two identically named people.) Another common type of exceptional data is data that tests limits (very long and very short names, for example). If you are working on a solution that automates or re-automates an existing system, talking to the people using the system can be helpful. The strange cases that caused problems with an existing system have probably stuck in their memories (and even become part of office lore).

Usability Testing

Another type of testing is usability testing, also known as interface testing. This type of testing is frequently done with an early version of the solution to test whether the design of the application is appropriate. In its most complex incarnations, usability testing involves video cameras trained on testing subjects, two-way mirrors, and many other behavior recording devices.

One of the great features of FileMaker is the ease with which you can put together a prototype. Do so, and then let people play with it. It's important to try to provide the level of support and documentation that you expect people will have when they start using the solution. You probably won't have a manual or online help at this stage, but decide what will be in the manual and verbally tell the testing subjects what they'll find there. Then step back. Unless you plan to coach all the people who'll use the solution, they should be able to use the solution based solely on what you've told them. If they can't, it's back to the drawing board—either for documentation or for a revision to the interface.

Above all, watch for consistent errors. At this stage of the process, if most of your testers enter names in an address field, it's probably your fault as the interface designer.

Tracking Problems

Testing may be complete when you release your FileMaker solution, but it's wise to track problems that people have as they use it. Record complaints and bugs (in a FileMaker database, of course), and periodically browse through it. Set up a categorization scheme or use Find to search for keywords in the descriptions of problems. Here's where you'll uncover consistent errors that you may be able to fix either in documentation or with small interface tweaks.

Keeping Things Running

This section provides a look at the various tools that FileMaker provides to help keep your solutions running and your databases in prime condition. The first one, the Recover command attempts to repair inconsistencies and errors within a database automatically. The others are various commands that you can use to manipulate data; many of these commands operate on several records at a time.

Recovering Databases

The Recover command in the File menu lets you open a database that has been corrupted. You may receive a message that a database has problems and that you should try to recover it; in other cases, problems with finding and sorting data indicate the need for recovery.

Recovery is a drastic step: It's not for routine maintenance. Suspect parts of the database will be removed if they cannot be fixed. When you choose the Recover command, you'll be asked to locate the database you want to recover. You then have an opportunity to name the recovered database. Remember the name you've chosen and where you've placed it.

When recovery is complete, rename the original database (perhaps MyDatabaseBad), and then rename the recovered database to the name of the original database. (If you don't do this, relationships based on filenames can break.) Finally, place the recovered database in the same location as the original database. When you open the database, check that all data is present and that everything works as it should.

It's important to keep copies of your databases and to perform regular backups. After recovery, how will you know whether all the data is there? If you have a copy from yesterday that contains 1,425 records, and the recovered database has 1,425 records, you may be okay (if no records have been added or deleted). Certainly, if you wind up with 823 records, you'll know there's a problem.

Also be aware that the recovered database is likely to be approximately the same size as the corrupted database. If there isn't enough room on your primary disk for this database, locate the recovered database on another disk. You can use low-speed removable disks for this process because, although recovery is usually lengthy, you can let it run overnight while it attempts to undo whatever damage has occurred.

By the Way

Replace Field Contents

Sometimes you want to change values in a given field for a number of records. The Replace Field Contents command in the Records menu lets you do so easily. First, select the records in which you want to replace the field value. This could be all of the records in the table, or you can use Find and Omit to create a found set of records. If you do not have the right records in the found set to start with, you may not be able to undo the Replace, and you could wind up destroying valid data.

Next, select the field you want to work with. If you want to place a certain value into that field in all of the found records, type that value into the field. Then choose Records, Replace Field Contents from the menu to open the Replace Field Contents dialog shown in Figure 19.2.

FIGURE 19.2
Replace field contents in multiple records.

You can choose to use the current value in the field for the replaced value. The second radio button lets you enter serial numbers in any range that you want;

you can optionally update the auto-enter serial number. (This is a convenient way of renumbering a table that has merged data from a variety of sources and may have duplicate numbers. However, be aware that if you're using serial numbers as a match field for a relationship, renumbering the records may break the relationships.)

Finally, the third choice is to place a calculated value into the field. The calculation can involve other fields in the records; thus, its result may be different for each record.

Relookup Field Contents

FileMaker provides the lookup feature to let you copy data from a related table as an auto-enter value when a new record is created. Lookup is one of the Auto-Enter choices that you can set with the Options button for a selected field in the Fields tab of the Define Database dialog. Figure 19.3 shows the Lookup dialog.

FIGURE 19.3
Use the Lookup dialog to auto-enter values from a related table into the field of a newly created record.

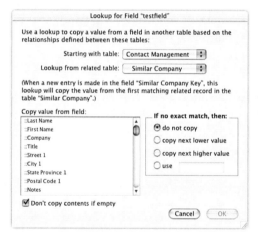

The value from the related record is placed in the field of the newly created record, and that's the end of the use of the relationship. You can modify the looked-up value. Indeed, if you look at the options in the Lookup dialog shown in Figure 19.3, you'll see that you can control behavior in cases for which no precise lookup value is found. Often in such cases, users need to be able to modify this initial value.

Sometimes, the lookup values need to be replaced. There are two general cases where this occurs. In the first, the match field (that is, the field that specifies the relationship on which the lookup was performed) changes its value. Instead of looking up the postal code for one street address, you need to look up the postal code for a changed street address.

The second case is one in which the lookup values themselves have changed. To continue the postal code example, if the post office has remapped codes (perhaps adding new postal codes to accommodate new buildings), even though the street address is unchanged, you'll need to look up revised postal codes.

A third common case also arises: Data has been entered incorrectly in one way or another.

For any of these reasons, you may need to redo the lookups. This replaces the values in the lookup field—even if it has been changed by the user. For this reason, you need to be clear about how the data has been entered and modified.

To relookup data, select all the records on which you want to perform the new lookup. This might be all the records in the table; it also might be a found set that you create with Find and Omit.

After you select the records you want to deal with, click in the field that is the match field (that is, part of the relationship); don't select the field with the lookup value. Then, choose Records, Relookup Contents from the menu. You are asked whether you want to continue; if you agree, the new values are placed in the lookup field(s).

Replace replaces values in a field; Relookup up may or may not replace values in one or more fields. Relookup works by reinspecting the field that controls the relationship.

By the Way

Insert from Index

If a text field is indexed, you can see the contents of the index. Figure 19.4 shows the View Index dialog.

You may want to view the index because the index shows all the values currently entered into the selected field in every record in the table. If you have chosen to use indexes, FileMaker automatically updates them as necessary so that you can rely on the index being accurate. Internally, FileMaker uses indexes to manage relationships and implement finds, but by allowing you to see the contents of the index, one additional feature is provided to you.

FIGURE 19.4
Use index values.
The word index is
shown at the left;
the value index is
shown at the right.

If you want to make sure that like-named data is entered identically, use the View Index dialog to see how existing values have been entered. For example, if you're about to enter the address, "500 Fifth Avenue," seeing that there's already an address of "500 Fifth Ave." can be useful. You might want to modify the existing record(s); more likely, you'll just go with the spelling and punctuation that already exists in the database.

Choose Insert, From Index to display the View Index dialog. Then, select an existing value by clicking on it; when you click Paste, that value is pasted into the currently selected field in the record you are browsing.

Note that the View Index dialog has a checkbox at the bottom left that lets you switch between the value index and the word index.

Insert from Last Visited Record

This is another useful feature for keeping data consistent in a database. Choose Insert, From Last Visited to copy the value from the last-visited record into the selected field. (This works only on a single field; to copy all fields, duplicate the last-visited record.)

You can set an auto-enter option to carry forward data in this way, but it can also be useful to manually carry forward one or more records. Certainly if you are entering a new record that is similar to an existing one, this command is easier than copying and pasting the data.

Summary

In this hour, you saw how to finish up your FileMaker solutions and how to keep them running. First, you saw several approaches to providing help and assistance. If no one can use your solution, you've wasted your time.

You saw how to test your solution. Not only do people need to be able to use your solution, but also they need to be able to rely on it. By testing conditions—both positive and negative—you can assure users (and yourself) that your solution can handle everything from correct input to user errors.

Finally, you saw some of the keep-running commands in FileMaker that help your solutions stay up and running. The Recover command automatically recovers databases. Other commands, such as Insert from Index, Relookup Field Contents, and Replace Field Contents let you put on your database administrator's hat to periodically clean up the database and make the values consistent. A lot of this can be done with validations and with scripts, but—particularly if many people are entering data and if it involves judgment with regard to spelling or abbreviations—someone periodically has to clean up the data by hand.

Q&A

Q *What is the best way to document a FileMaker solution?*

A There are several ways to document a solution. The first and most basic way is to keep the specification document along with any revisions to it that have been made along the way. In large installations, there is a formal process for maintaining this documentation. In smaller environments, it's often a problem to find the time to do this sort of clean up. One way to handle it is to simply save all the documents and email messages that surround development. At some time, you can organize them into a coherent report. If you don't have the time, when you need to refer to them, you'll at least have the raw material.

Another excellent way of documenting a solution is to use the reports in FileMaker Developer, which is described in Hour 20, "Creating Solutions with FileMaker Developer."

Q *How important is it to have a test suite of data?*

A For most FileMaker solutions, it's critical to create this body of data that you can use to validate the solution. If you have several people working on the project, the end-user is often a good candidate for someone to create the test data. Remember that you want a lot of data (for stress testing), common data conditions, and exceptional data. Often, preparing the test data results in modifications to the system specifications as people start to understand special cases that the software needs to address.

Workshop

Quiz

1. How do you replace values for a field in several records at a time?

2. Why do you use Insert from Index?

3. When do you use regression testing?

Quiz Answers

1. Choose Records, Replace Field Contents or Records, Relookup Field Contents from the menu after you have selected the field in question and have selected the appropriate records to replace or relookup.

2. Because the View Index dialog shows you all the values or words entered into the selected field in every record in the database, you can select existing values or words and paste them into the field in the current record. This manual process keeps data consistent in spelling, spacing, abbreviations, and capitalization.

3. Regression testing should be used whenever a change is made. It tests that all previous tests—whether affected by the change or not—still pass.

Activities

Take one of the solutions that you've built while working through this book and prepare a test suite of data for it. Document the solution and the test suite and prepare a user guide.

HOUR 20

Creating Solutions with FileMaker Developer

What You'll Learn in This Hour:

▶ Database Design Report—Produce complete documentation of your FileMaker solution.

▶ Using Developer Utilities to Create Standalone Solutions—Create a stand-alone version of your FileMaker solution.

▶ File Maintenance—Optimize your database file's performance.

▶ Custom Functions—Add your own functions to those built in to FileMaker.

FileMaker Developer consists of FileMaker Pro along with some additional functionality that lets you build and manage FileMaker solutions. With FileMaker Developer, you can create a standalone FileMaker solution; with a standalone solution, users can double-click the solution icons and access the database without needing to have a copy of FileMaker. You also can manage your solutions with reports and file maintenance. If you are building FileMaker solutions of any complexity (or any significant number of them) you'll probably find that you need FileMaker Developer for these tools.

In addition to the features described in this hour, FileMaker Developer provides the script debugger described in Hour 10, "More on Working with Scripts."

 By the Way

Database Design Report

As you develop FileMaker solutions, it's important to document what you're doing, what various fields are used for, and the assumptions made in scripts. You can use comments in scripts, and, starting in FileMaker 7, you can add comments to field names in the Define Database dialog.

But for an overall picture of your FileMaker solution, nothing beats the Database Design Report in FileMaker Developer. It can run against any FileMaker solution—you don't need to have created it in FileMaker Developer.

Launch the Database Design Report by choosing File, Database Design Report from the menu. The dialog shown in Figure 20.1 opens.

FIGURE 20.1
Specify the Database Design Report.

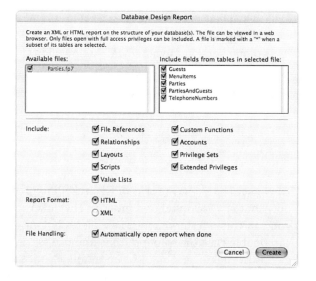

As you can see, you can choose to run a partial report (perhaps just displaying scripts or maybe only selecting certain files and tables). It is a good practice to run a complete database report when you reach a milestone in a project (such as moving the solution into production).

By the Way

At such a milestone, it is often a good idea not only to run the Database Design Report, but also to copy it and the entire FileMaker solution to a safe place (such as a CD). In that way, you know that the report and the saved solution are identical.

The report can be produced either as XML or HTML files. When you are asked to name the files, it is usually a good idea to create a new folder into which the files will be placed. (This is the folder that you can copy to your archive CD.)

The HTML version of the report is the easiest one to use for most people. It produces an interactive series of HTML pages that let you quickly locate the information you need.

Figure 20.2 shows the starting page.

FIGURE 20.2
The Report Overview lets you select what you want to see.

This summary simply provides a count of the number of tables, relationships, and the like in the database (depending on what you have selected in the Define Database Report dialog). Note that each number is a hypertext link that takes you to more details when you click on it.

In Figure 20.3, you see the overview for the file. Again, links are available so that you can drill down further into the report.

Clicking on a table's fields link (under the pointer in Figure 20.3) moves to more detail for an individual table's fields as shown in Figure 20.4. Note that the validation and storage options are displayed along with the comments (if any). This section of the report can be important for users to review; the validation rules implement their business logic, and they should be confirmed by the user.

FIGURE 20.3
The Overview/File
section provides
information about a
single database
file.

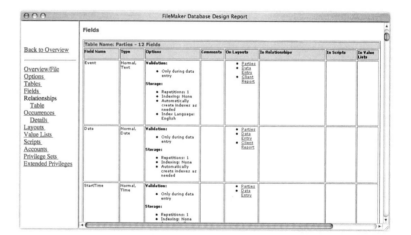

FIGURE 20.4
Confirm field
options and valida-
tion rules.

Using Developer Utilities to Create Standalone Solutions

Choosing File, Developer Utilities from the menu lets you create standalone FileMaker solutions. You can distribute them as you want: People do not need a copy of FileMaker to run them. In this section, you'll see the process involved in creating standalone solutions. There are two steps:

1. Specify the solution name and the files needed.

2. Set solution options.

The solution and the database files are placed in a folder that you specify. If you are running on Windows, the solution created will be for Windows; if you are running on Mac OS X, the solution created will be for Mac OS X. If you are running on Mac OS X, a simple way of creating both versions is to use Virtual PC. This product, now owned by Microsoft, lets you run a complete Windows environment on your Macintosh. If you run FileMaker Developer in Virtual PC, it will in fact be running in Windows, and it will create a Windows standalone solution. For more information on Virtual PC go to http://www.microsoft.com/mac/.

Specify the Solution Name and the Files Needed

Figure 20.5 shows the Developer Utilities dialog; it appears after you choose File, Developer Utilities.

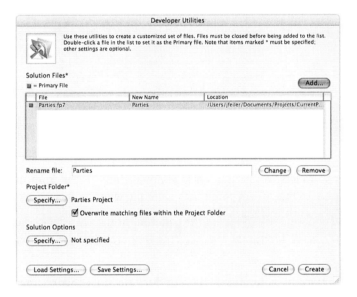

FIGURE 20.5
Create standalone applications with Developer Utilities.

Use the Add button at the upper right to add database files to the solution. Note that they must all be closed before being added. One file must be designated as the primary file. (You double-click its name to add the small rectangle to the left of its name.) This is the file that is opened when the solution is launched.

You can provide a new name for the file; you also need to specify a folder into which the solution and its files are placed. (These files include copies of the database files.)

Set Solution Options

Finally, you can click the Specify button under Solution Options to open the dialog shown in Figure 20.6.

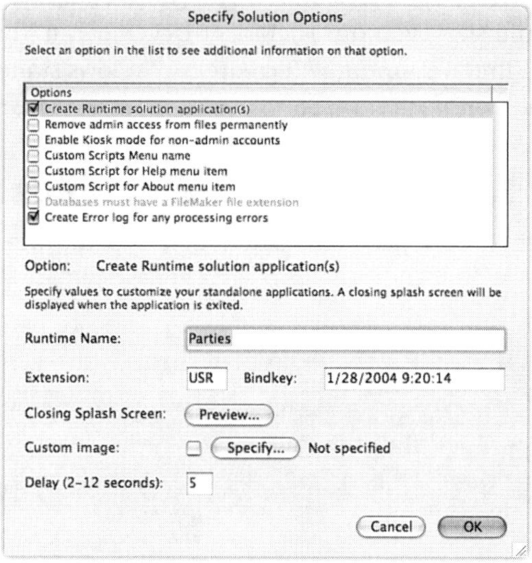

FIGURE 20.6
The Specify
Solution Options
dialog.

The first option needs to be checked to create a standalone runtime solution.

The second option lets you permanently remove admin access from the solution files; before you do this, make sure that you really want to do so.

You can next choose kiosk mode for the solution. In that case, the solution fills the computer screen, hiding the menus. This is appropriate for a public access solution.

Next, three options let you rename the standard FileMaker Scripts menu as well as the Help and About menu commands. You might want to rename the Scripts menu something like MySolution Scripts or MySolution Tools. Help might be renamed MySolution Help, and About might be similarly renamed. When you choose these options, your standalone solution will have its own look and feel.

Further down the Specify Solution Options dialog, you can choose a closing splash screen image and the length of time it appears. You can insert your own image, but the phrase "made with FileMaker" always appears above the image.

For a solution that runs on both Mac OS X and Windows, you need to create both as described previously in this hour. You also need to create a bind key that is identical for the two solutions. A default bind key is created with the date and time. You need to modify it so that it is identical for the two solutions. It is entered with the Specify Solution Options dialog shown in Figure 20.6.

When you are satisfied with your solution options, click OK. You can then use the Save Settings button at the lower left of the Developer Utilities dialog to save all those settings; they can be reloaded for that or another standalone solution with the Load Settings button.

> Be sure to read the FileMaker Developer documentation for guidance on preparing standalone solutions; if you are creating cross-platform solutions, note the recommendations for safe fonts and filenames.

By the Way

File Maintenance

Choosing File, File Maintenance from the menu opens the File Maintenance dialog shown in Figure 20.7.

FIGURE 20.7
Use file maintenance to improve database performance.

The two options let you reduce database file size as well as optimize it. You can perform file maintenance while the databases are open (unlike the Recover command). Most people use both options together to improve performance.

Note that the major improvements in performance will be noted in large files as well as those that frequently are used to find and sort data. If you have 100 records in a database file, file maintenance is not likely to be worth the effort.

Custom Functions

You can add custom functions to a database file using FileMaker Developer. Thereafter, people who open the database file using FileMaker Pro can use the functions (but they cannot modify them).

Start by choosing File, Define, Custom Functions from the menu to open the Define Custom Functions dialog shown in Figure 20.8.

FIGURE 20.8
Define custom
functions.

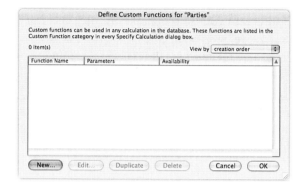

Click New to add a new function. As you can see in Figure 20.9, you are asked to name the function in the upper left of the dialog. You then add parameters by typing their names in the field directly below the function name. Click the + button to add each parameter; highlight a parameter in the list and click X to remove it. You can change the order of the parameters by sliding the double-arrow icons up and down. The custom function shown here produces a copyright line: You provide the year and the copyright holder; the function returns a string such as "Copyright 2005 Philmont Software Mill. All rights reserved."

FIGURE 20.9
Create the function.

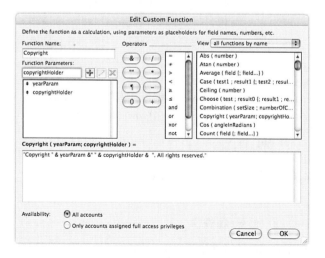

Thereafter, anyone opening the database file can use the function (subject to the security limitations you may have placed on it). It appears in the function list as shown at the right of Figure 20.10.

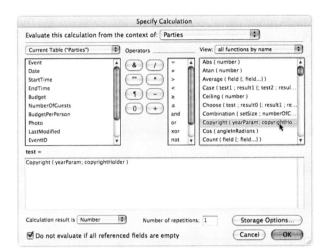

FIGURE 20.10
Anyone can use the function.

Summary

In this hour, you saw how to use the major features of FileMaker Developer. You can document FileMaker solutions (either made with FileMaker Developer or FileMaker Pro). You also can create standalone FileMaker solutions, perform file maintenance, and create custom functions.

In the final part of this book, you'll find information about sharing your FileMaker solutions. This includes networking FileMaker as well as publishing data on the Web.

Q&A

Q *When is the right time to run the Database Design Report?*

A Although it's an excellent idea to run the report at specific milestones of a project, it also makes sense to run the report periodically—including right after you have started the project.

  If you have inconsistent validation rules or potentially confusing field names, seeing them all on the report may immediately encourage you to fix the issues before they become serious problems.

Q *What is the easiest way to create several standalone solutions?*

A Create a database file that contains the common elements: custom functions, a graphic for the background of windows, and the like. Save this database file and then, whenever you want to create a new solution, make a copy of it, and all your standard elements will be ready to use.

Workshop

Quiz

1. How many primary files do you need in a standalone solution?

2. What performance issues does the File Maintenance command address most effectively?

3. Is there a limit to the number of custom functions in a database?

Quiz Answers

1. One and only one.

2. Large database files and those that use frequent Find and Sort commands.

3. No.

Activities

If you have FileMaker Developer, create a new database from one of the templates. Then create a standalone solution. Experiment with creating a kiosk version.

PART IV

Sharing FileMaker Solutions

Sharing Databases with FileMaker Pro

What You'll Learn in This Hour:

▶ About FileMaker Networking—Here is an overview of the variety of ways you can share FileMaker databases.

▶ Adjust Your Firewall—The first step is to configure your firewall to allow FileMaker to get through it.

▶ Set Up Sharing with FileMaker Pro—Sharing a database requires you to open it and indicate who can use it.

▶ Connecting to a Shared FileMaker Database—Use the Open Remote dialog to open a shared database.

▶ Locking Databases (Shared Database Etiquette)—Share a database and access it on one computer to see how sharing works. This section provides some tips on preventing problems when several people are accessing databases at the same time.

This part of the book is about sharing information. You will see how to network FileMaker to share databases, and you will see how to use Instant Web Publishing to share databases over the Web or a LAN. You will also see how to use XML to share data and to create dynamic database-driven Web sites.

This hour focuses on FileMaker itself: You use it both as a provider of shared data and as a consumer. Each person accessing the database has a copy of FileMaker.

Note that *host* and *client* refer to an individual database. You can host Database A, and someone else can host Database B. You can be a client of Database B while someone else is a client of your Database A. And, just to keep things lively, it is possible to host a database on your computer and access it from that same computer as a client.

About FileMaker Networking

With FileMaker 7, the product lineup has been simplified. There are now four FileMaker products:

- FileMaker Pro—The basic product, lets you create and use databases. Unless otherwise noted, everything discussed in this book with the exception of Hour 20, "Creating Solutions with FileMaker Developer," applies to FileMaker Pro. With FileMaker Pro, you can share databases over a network (even over the Internet). Each person who accesses your shared database needs a copy of FileMaker Pro.

    You also can use FileMaker Pro to publish databases using Instant Web Publishing. People can then use Internet browsers to access your shared database. FileMaker Pro allows only five users to share your database with Instant Web Publishing.

- FileMaker Developer—The product lets you produce standalone FileMaker solutions. It also has a variety of tools that let you document and manage complex FileMaker solutions. FileMaker Developer incorporates FileMaker Pro; as a result, you can do everything you do in FileMaker Pro in FileMaker Developer—and more.

- FileMaker Server and FileMaker Server Advanced—The workhorse application that you need to share databases among many people. It does not have the five-person limit for Instant Web Publishing that FileMaker Pro has; rather, its limit is 350. FileMaker Server is only a server product: You cannot design databases with it or use it as a client to access databases (shared or unshared).

- FileMaker Mobile—Designed to run on portable digital assistants, some cell phones, and other small devices. It is designed to share data with a desktop FileMaker database.

As you can see, sharing is a primary concern of FileMaker. This hour explores the use of FileMaker Pro as client and server; Hour 22, "Using FileMaker on the Web or an Intranet: Instant Web Publishing," looks at Instant Web Publishing with FileMaker Pro.

Database Sharing and Networking Terminology

A number of words and phrases are important for you to know before going further with database sharing. These are general terms, and they relate to database sharing with any database product, not just FileMaker:

▶ Contention—A multiuser database manager needs to detect and manage the situation in which two users are trying to update the same record. This situation is called *contention*.

▶ Concurrency—Relates to the simultaneous (or almost simultaneous) access to data by several users. Concurrency and contention are two sides of the same coin, and they can be used interchangeably.

▶ Locking—A database *locks* a record when it is being updated by a user. When the record is locked, it cannot be accessed by someone else. Various forms of locking are used in databases; some allow no access during the lock, whereas others allow read-only access during the lock. FileMaker automatically takes care of locking records for you. Database performance is fastest when locks are few and of short duration.

▶ Optimistic locking—Technique used to improve database throughput. Instead of locking a record when a user begins to edit it and retaining the lock until the user completes the edit, a copy of the data is obtained when the user begins editing. When the user completes the edit, the current data in the record is retrieved again and compared to the image obtained before the edit commenced. If the two images are identical, it means that no one has modified the record during this time, and the record is briefly locked while the user changes are applied. This is optimistic in the sense that in a large database, in most cases, it is likely that different people will be modifying different records. Occasionally, two people do try to modify the same record, and an update will fail with a message that the record has been changed by someone else. FileMaker uses optimistic locking with Instant Web Publishing, which is the topic of Hour 22.

▶ Host—The computer that shares a database is called a *host*. The process is called *hosting*.

▶ IP address (Internet Protocol address)—The quartet of numbers, such as 192.168.0.3, that identify a computer connected to a TCP/IP network such as the Internet or a LAN that uses TCP/IP. (Computers connected to networks with IP addresses are commonly referred to as *hosts*.) IP addresses can be assigned by your network coordinator or ISP. They can be *static* or *dynamic*.

▶ Dynamic IP address—These addresses may change each time you dial up; with a connection such as cable or DSL, your modem may negotiate automatically with the ISP to obtain a new IP address periodically (sometimes once a day). If you are on a LAN (and that includes a small network with a wired or wireless router that shares a cable or DSL modem), the router may automatically assign you a dynamic IP address.

▶ Static IP address—An address that does not change. Static IP addresses are commonly used to support Internet domain names or for reasons of security. In the case of domain names, the Internet's domain name system maintains a list of names (such as `filemaker.com`) and their associated IP addresses. When you type `filemaker.com`, the message is sent to the IP address in the routing table. For security, a static IP address can be used to identify a given computer for a long period of time. Access to certain data can be limited to computers with known IP addresses.

▶ MAC (Media Access Control)/Ethernet Address—Every Ethernet interface has a unique identifying number. If you have a single Ethernet port, you have one MAC address. If you have two (perhaps a wired port and a wireless card), you have two MAC addresses. You cannot change this address unless you replace the Ethernet interface. The address is usually shown as six pairs of hexadecimal numbers, such as `00:30:65:1f:eb:93`.

▶ Escape sequence—A hexadecimal representation of a single character using two or more characters, often in hexadecimal code. Normally, it is used for characters such as blanks that are illegal in URLs, but nothing prevents you from using an escape sequence for normal letters and numerals (although that would be strange). The most common escape sequence is `%20` for a blank. Escape sequences are introduced by the percent symbol.

TCP/IP: The Network Protocol

Today, FileMaker uses TCP/IP for its networking. In the past, various types of networking were supported, but as the Internet and the Web have become more common, FileMaker, along with many other software products, has standardized on TCP/IP.

The good news is that because of this standardization, you probably already have an appropriate network in place. If you can use email or the Web, you most likely have TCP/IP in place and properly configured. In addition, if your computer or its operating system is relatively recent, it's likely that TCP/IP support is built in and was configured during installation. If that is not the case, consult your operating system installation documentation or system coordinator.

By the Way

> If you use America Online with a dial-up connection, you might not be using TCP/IP for your email and Web browsing, but it probably has been set up for you during your operating system's installation.

To share a database using FileMaker, you need to set up your firewall and then choose the appropriate sharing options in FileMaker. The next two sections show you how to accomplish those tasks.

When you are connected to a network with a shared database on it, you can use FileMaker to access it. The final section of this hour shows you how to do that.

Adjust Your Firewall

Every computer on the Internet has its own unique address—an IP address. You may access a Web site using its domain name (such as www.filemaker.com), but in fact, Internet routing tables convert every domain name into an IP address (such as 216.168.46.10).

Because a computer connected to the Internet may be running a number of services (mail, Web, FTP, and more), it is necessary to have a mechanism to address requests to specific services. *Ports* are used for this purpose. Thus, a request for a Web page is sent to port 80—http://216.168.46.10). You can explicitly direct a request to a specific port—http://216.168.46.10:10, but the standard requests are automatically sent to the appropriate ports.

This section refers to messages sent to a computer over the Internet through a firewall. The same principles apply to messages sent from a computer through a firewall. Furthermore, local area networks not connected to the Internet often use the same technology.

By the Way

There are thousands of possible port numbers ranging from 0 to 65535; some of them are assigned for specific purposes such as mail or Web servers, but the vast majority are unassigned. Miscreants can gain access to a computer through an open port because the incoming message goes not to a specific application such as a mail program, but directly into the computer itself where it can cause problems.

For this reason, people use firewalls to block access to all but selected ports. If your computer is connected to the Internet—particularly with a persistent connection such as cable or some forms of DSL—it is essential that you have a firewall in place.

Firewalls can be implemented in software on your own computer; if you have a router or other network control device between your computer and your Internet connection, it can have a firewall built into it. Whether you implement the firewall for your own computer or your network, it should be in place. (Placing a firewall at the network level is often the best plan because it has to be set up only once, rather than for each computer.)

When FileMaker is sharing a database, it communicates over port 5003. (The number has been assigned by the Internet Assigned Numbers Authority and should not be used for other purposes.)

If you are behind a network firewall, you or your network administrator must make sure that port 5003 is open for any computer that will be hosting a FileMaker database.

By the Way

> If you are not behind a network firewall, are connected to the Internet, and do not have a firewall installed and enabled, you are courting disaster in today's world of hackers, viruses, trojan horses, and more. You should immediately enable the firewall that comes with most operating systems as described in the following sections.

Adjusting the Firewall on Windows

Start by going to Control Panel; then double–click Networking and Internet Connections and then click Network Connections. Select the connection to open the dialog shown in Figure 21.1.

FIGURE 21.1
Set up your firewall.

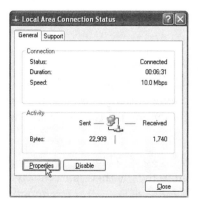

Click Properties to open the dialog shown in Figure 21.2. Choose the Advanced tab.

FIGURE 21.2
Enable the firewall.

The checkbox at the top is where you enable or disable the firewall software. Click it to enable the firewall software. If you are setting up a firewall for the first time, you may want to use the wizard with a link at the bottom of the dialog to do so. Manually configuring mail, Web, and other ports is tedious.

The FileMaker port needs to be set up explicitly. Click Settings to open the dialog shown in Figure 21.3.

FIGURE 21.3
Add FileMaker settings to the firewall.

Standard ports are listed here; click Add to set up the FileMaker port. When you click Add, you open the dialog shown in Figure 21.4.

FIGURE 21.4
Define FileMaker
port.

Complete the dialog as shown in Figure 21.4. Use the IP address of the computer that will be sharing FileMaker databases. Click OK here and on the other dialogs as you exit the setup software.

Adjusting the Firewall on Mac OS X

The process is the same on Mac OS X, but the dialogs look different. In System Preferences, click the Sharing icon to open the dialog shown in Figure 21.5.

FIGURE 21.5
Use the Sharing preferences to configure your firewall.

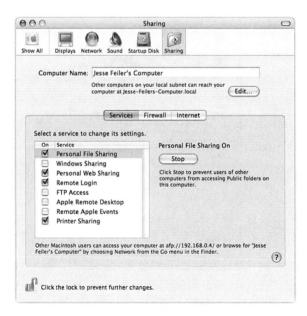

The Firewall tab lets you manually configure the firewall. (When you select services in the Sharing tab shown in Figure 21.5, the firewall is automatically configured.)

Figure 21.6 shows the Firewall tab; by default there will not be a FileMaker checkbox. If you have previously configured the port, you can open or close it by checking it as shown in Figure 21.6.

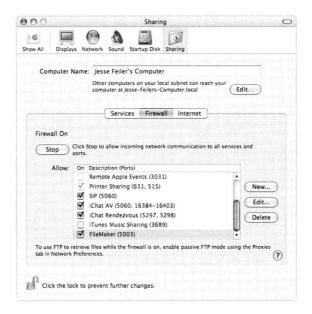

FIGURE 21.6
Use the Firewall tab to configure the firewall.

If you need to add the port, click New to open the dialog shown in Figure 21.7. Complete the information as shown here, and then you are finished.

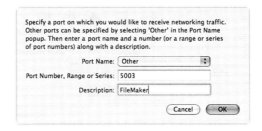

FIGURE 21.7
Add a new port if necessary.

Set Up Sharing with FileMaker Pro

With your firewall properly configured, you can now share FileMaker databases.

> You can use privilege sets (discussed in Hour 18, "Securing Your Solutions and Databases") to control access to your databases. If you want to use a privilege set in this way, set it up now before continuing with the steps in this section.

Open the database you want to share, and choose FileMaker Network from the Sharing submenu of the Edit menu (Windows) or the FileMaker Pro application menu (Mac OS X) as shown in Figure 21.8.

FIGURE 21.8
Choose FileMaker Network from the Sharing submenu.

The FileMaker Network Settings dialog opens as shown in Figure 21.9.

FIGURE 21.9
Use FileMaker Network Settings to configure the shared databases.

At the top of the dialog, you turn sharing on or off. Make sure that it is on. Beneath the radio buttons, you see your computer's IP address. If people will be accessing your databases over the Internet (rather than on a local area network), they need this address.

IP addresses are not random. As noted previously, every computer on the Internet has a unique IP address. There are several exceptions, however. IP addresses starting with 10 or with 192 are reserved for local networks. If you have an Internet hub for your local area network, chances are that you will use addresses starting with 192 by default; for a larger local network, usually 10 is the default. The hub manages your connection to the Internet using its own IP address; the various computers on your network with their own IP addresses are not visible over the Internet. Thus, there are many IP addresses starting with 192 active at any time; none of them is directly on the Internet.

At the lower left of the dialog box, you see a list of your open databases. For each database, you can set three types of access:

▶ All users

▶ No users

▶ Users based on a privilege set

If you have several databases open, you can choose to share each one in different ways (or not at all).

At the lower right, you can control whether a database is shown in the list of databases available to be shared. You see that list at the beginning of the next section. As far as setting up your databases to be shared, you are now finished.

Connecting to a Shared FileMaker Database

To connect to a shared database, choose File, Open Remote from the menu to open the dialog shown in Figure 21.10.

FileMaker attempts to find computers sharing databases on the local area network. If it finds any, it lists them as shown in Figure 21.10. Select a host, and you see a list of the sharable databases at the right of the dialog. (Any database indicated as being not shown will be omitted from this list.)

FIGURE 21.10
Use the Open
Remote command
to open a shared
database.

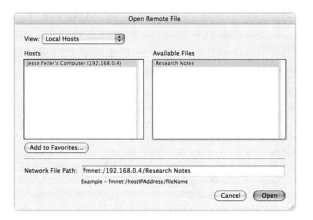

Select the host and database; then click Open to open it.

To open a sharable database that is not in the list, type in the network path as shown at the bottom of Figure 21.10. In this way, you can let people know what databases to open by providing your IP address and the name of the database, but people without those instructions will not see the database in the list of available databases.

By the Way

FileMaker URLs start with the schema `fmnet` as shown in Figure 21.10. If you are familiar with URLs in general on the Internet, you know that certain characters—including spaces—need to be handled with special escape sequences because spaces are not allowed in URLs. FileMaker makes this adjustment for you. However, in general, if you are sharing databases over the Internet, you might want to consider using names with no spaces to avoid complications with other software.

Because FileMaker is using TCP/IP for its networking, the shared database need not be on your local area network. If you have the IP address of a computer anywhere on the Internet that is sharing a database, you can type in the appropriate `fmnet` address to access it.

Locking Databases (Shared Database Etiquette)

You can share a database and access it all on one computer. Open the database you want to share and configure it for sharing as described previously. Then, use the Open Remote command to open it in a second window. Position the windows so that the shared database is at one side of the monitor, and the client database is at the other side.

Shared Databases Are Updated When You Commit Changes

Create a new record in the database using the client database. Note that the number of records in the shared database is unchanged. You can enter data into this record, and nothing changes in the shared database.

Now, commit those changes. You do so by moving to another record in the database or by using the `commit` script step. As soon as you do, you see that the shared database now has one more record than it had before.

Only One User Can Make Changes at a Time

As a second experiment, go to the same record in the shared database and the client database. Click in a data entry field in the client database. Without committing the change (that is, without clicking out—clicking in another field, in the background, or moving to another record), click in the same field in the shared database. As soon as you try to type anything, you get the message shown in Figure 21.11.

"Jesse Feiler (Admin)" is modifying this record. You cannot use this record until "Jesse Feiler (Admin)" is finished.

Send Message...   OK

FIGURE 21.11
FileMaker will not let two people modify the same record at the same time.

FileMaker locks the entire record until changes are committed. You can prove that by repeating this process. Start to edit a field in the client database; then, click in another field in the shared database and try to enter data. You get the same message. Note that any number of people can view the same record: The record is locked only when editing starts.

You can send a message to the person who has locked the record as shown in Figure 21.12.

This mechanism keeps the database consistent even as many people access it. But you need to do your part. If you start to edit a record in a shared database, you have locked that record until the change is committed (usually by moving to another record). If you go to lunch before the record is committed, no one else can access it. If you are in an office, that is not too big a problem; however, if you are working at another site and accessing the database using an `fmnet` URL, there will be no one to walk over to your desk to commit the record and unlock the database.

FIGURE 21.12
Send a message to
the user who is
locking the record.

Shared Databases to Which People Are Attached Cannot Be Closed

Another part of FileMaker's sharing system prevents you from closing a database that other people are using. If you attempt to close a shared database that others are using, you see the message shown in Figure 21.13. (Note that this is the shared database; if you close a database that you are accessing as a client, it does not affect the shared database, and you receive no message.)

FIGURE 21.13
You cannot close a
shared database
that people are
using.

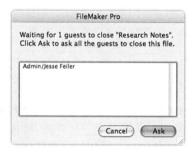

If you click Ask, the connected users receive the message shown in Figure 21.14.

If you click Cancel, the database does not close, and the dialog shown previously in Figure 21.13 remains on the computer that is sharing the database.

Note that the dialog shown in Figure 21.14 indicates that if the user does not act, the database will be closed in 25 seconds. That is no idle threat. If you are entering data but have not yet completed the process, the database will be closed, and your partially entered data will be stored with no indication that it is incomplete. (How could FileMaker know that you intended to type more keystrokes?)

FIGURE 21.14
FileMaker can ask the users to close their windows onto the database.

But there is a further wrinkle here. If you have set a validation rule that cannot be overridden, when FileMaker attempts to close the client database, a dialog appears with the error message. Until it is dismissed with the OK button, that client database remains open—and the shared database, too, remains open.

You can minimize problems by closing databases that you are accessing as a client as soon as you are finished with them. In this way, any records that you have locked will be committed and released; also, if the person sharing the database wants to close it, there will not be a problem because someone appears to be using it (but has actually left for the day).

On the server side, you can also minimize problems by recognizing that the bulk of the processing for the database is being done on the server. Only minimal interface processing is done on the client copies of FileMaker. Performance for clients will be degraded if you take this opportunity to do processor-intensive tasks.

Summary

In this hour, you saw how to use FileMaker networking to share databases. In this scenario, both host and client use copies of FileMaker Pro. (Hour 22 shows you how to use a browser as a client.)

You need to configure your firewall to allow FileMaker sharing. This can be as simple as checking a box, but it also can require discussions with a network administrator if your firewall is on the network rather than your own computer. Critically important is the possibility that you may be connected to the Internet and not have a firewall installed. To make it as simple as possible for people to connect to the Internet, many firewall products are shipped but not enabled. This has turned out to leave the door wide open to all sorts of malicious acts. Even if you have no intention of ever sharing a FileMaker database, you should use the firewall section to make sure that you do have some protection.

FileMaker provides sophisticated mechanisms for keeping multiple users from falling over one another. You saw some of them at work, and you also saw how to be a good colleague when sharing databases (close them when you are finished).

Q&A

Q *When do you need FileMaker Server for sharing databases?*

A There is no hard-and-fast rule for this (other than the limit on five concurrent users for FileMaker Pro), but there are some basic considerations. Any large-scale shared database will benefit from FileMaker Server's sophisticated management and diagnostic tools, which go far beyond those in FileMaker Pro. Also, some sharing features (such as ODBC) are implemented only in the Server product.

If you want to run a classic database operation, FileMaker Server is the right choice. Instead of running a copy of FileMaker Pro that allows you to update the shared database, with FileMaker Server the application that shares the database does only that and does not allow access to the data from the server computer (only from the clients).

Q *Are there design considerations for shared databases?*

A If you know that a database is going to be shared (and it is probably a good idea to assume that any database might be shared in the future unless you are sure that it will not be), you can design good sharing features into it. Perhaps the most important consideration is to remember that with a shared database it may be closed by the server under the circumstances described in this hour. Properly setting validation rules can set up a foolproof solution that cannot be closed with a database record that is inconsistent. (This can also set up a database that cannot be closed at all when the validation fails, and no one responds to the message.)

Q *How much of the solution is shared? What happens when the database is sorted?*

A Only the data is shared. The server does all the processing for each client, and it keeps track of separate sorts, finds, and other states for every user.

Workshop

Quiz

1. How do you open a shared database?

2. After you have set up a database to be shared, can it be accessed even if it is closed?

3. How many people can open a shared database?

Quiz Answers

1. Choose File, Open Remote from the menu (not the Open command).

2. No. The database must be running on the server (FileMaker Pro or FileMaker Server).

3. One person can open it with the Open command. All others must open it with Open Remote.

Activities

If you have not followed the examples in this hour, do so now. Create a database, share it, and then access it (either from your own computer as described here or from another computer). Experiment with making changes and closing the database. Sort it, enter data, and perform finds: See how the database status area is updated on the client and server windows.

Using FileMaker on the Web or an Intranet: Instant Web Publishing

What You'll Learn in This Hour:

▶ About Instant Web Publishing—Here is an overview of the simple process of publishing FileMaker databases on the Web with Instant Web Publishing.

▶ Using the Instant Web Publishing Interface—In this section, you will see how to use the status area for Instant Web Publishing. It is almost the same as the status area interface you find in FileMaker Pro itself, but there are some important differences.

▶ Publishing a Database Using Instant Web Publishing—Here are the few steps you need to take to publish a FileMaker database.

▶ Designing for Instant Web Publishing—Whether your database is designed solely for Instant Web Publishing or for both Instant Web Publishing and FileMaker clients, here are some considerations you should think about as you design your layouts.

In Hour 21, "Sharing Databases with FileMaker Pro," you saw how to share databases with FileMaker networking where everyone runs FileMaker. In this hour, you will see the first of two ways to use FileMaker databases on the Web; you use one copy of FileMaker as a database Web server, and the clients use standard Web browsers. (The other way of sharing databases on the Web—using XML—is discussed in Hour 23, "Using FileMaker and XML with Other Applications," and Hour 24, "Using FileMaker, XML, and XSLT.")

By the Way

Whether you publish your databases on the Web, on a local area network, or on an intranet, the techniques and technology are the same. In this hour, the phrase "on the Web" refers not only to the Web itself but also to LANs, intranets, and any other variation of network that uses Web protocols and standards.

About Instant Web Publishing

Instant Web Publishing made its debut in FileMaker 4. At that time, it provided a standard interface to FileMaker databases. Now, Instant Web Publishing has evolved into a much more powerful and flexible tool; its goal is not just to provide access to FileMaker databases but also to make the Web access look and feel as much like the experience you have when using FileMaker itself.

Figure 22.1 shows the Research Notes template with some data entered into it.

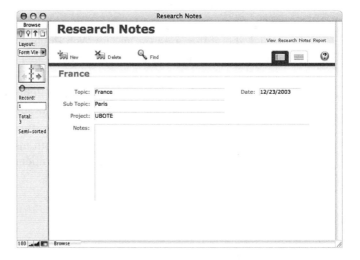

FIGURE 22.1
The Research Notes template shown in FileMaker Pro.

When you publish it using Instant Web Publishing, you can access it with a Web browser as shown in Figure 22.2.

Note that all that has been done here is to turn on Instant Web Publishing for the database. (You will see how to do that later in this hour.) The look and feel of the layout has been implemented successfully on the Web without your having to do a thing. There are some subtle differences, but not many. The following section, which describes how to use the Web client, highlights some of the differences.

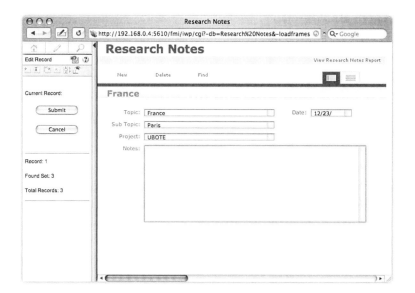

FIGURE 22.2
With Instant Web Publishing, you can access a database using a Web browser.

thers are described later in this hour in the section "Designing for Instant Web Publishing."

Using the Instant Web Publishing Interface

Although much of the look of the database is the same on the Web, some of the controls in the status area are different. This section shows you how to use the Instant Web Publishing interface. Specifically, you will learn:

▶ How to use the FileMaker Database Homepage

▶ How to use Browse mode

▶ How to navigate through a database

▶ How to edit and commit changes

▶ How to use Find

The FileMaker Database Homepage

To use a database with a browser, go to the IP address at which the databases are published. (The following section shows you how to publish a database and how to determine that address. As a client of the database, you are given the location of the database by the person who sets it up using the following section's instructions.)

You see a page like the one shown in Figure 22.3. This lists all the databases published on that computer with the exception of databases that have been published using the option to not display them on the FileMaker homepage. (These could be internal databases such as join tables; they are accessible, but not with a single click from the homepage.)

FIGURE 22.3
Select a database
from the FileMaker
homepage.

You are prompted to enter a name and password. These are processed in the unified security model; if you have access, you then see the database.

As you saw previously in Figures 22.1 and 22.2, the layout itself is similar in its presentation in FileMaker and on the Web. What is significantly different is the status area at the left. Figure 22.4 shows the status area in FileMaker on the left and the status area on the Web on the right. Both are shown in Browse mode.

Browse Mode in Instant Web Publishing

FileMaker Pro has four modes: Browse, Find, Layout, and Preview. On the Web, there are two: Browse and Find.

If you compare the top of the two status areas, you see the icons reflecting this difference. Note that on the Web, there is a Home icon to send you back to the FileMaker Database Homepage.

Next, you find a row of seven icons. From the left, they are the following:

▶ New Record

▶ Edit Record

▶ Duplicate Record

▶ Delete Record

▶ Sort

▶ Show All Records

▶ Show Additional Toolbar

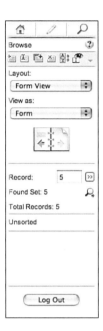

FIGURE 22.4
Compare the status area in FileMaker Pro (left) and the status area on the Web (right).

This last icon reveals a row of three further icons:

▶ Omit Record

▶ Omit Multiple Records

▶ Show Omitted

These icons are needed on the Web because the FileMaker menu commands are not available. (The menu bar is for the browser you are using, not for FileMaker.)

The Edit Record icon also represents a big difference between the Web and the desktop FileMaker application. On the desktop, you can edit data by simply clicking in the field and starting to type. After you have done so, the record is locked so that no one else can update it until your changes are committed (by clicking out of the field or by moving to another record). This process was described in Hour 21.

On the Web, as soon as you start to edit a record (or when you click the Edit Record icon), the status area changes to the display shown in Figure 22.5.

Just as on a network using FileMaker Pro for clients, as soon as one person starts to make changes to a record, that record is locked; no one else can make changes. If you try, you get an error message. Until the changes are committed (with the Submit button) or cancelled, the first person has the record.

FIGURE 22.5
The status area on
the Web lets you
commit changes.

After the record is released, another person can click in a field to start making changes. At this point, it is conceivable that the data shown will be refreshed, reflecting someone else's changes. In any event, the integrity of the data is preserved, just as it is on the desktop.

Toward the top of the status area, next to the text Edit Record, you find the Revert button. Click here to revert the data to what it was before you started editing it, but to retain your lock on the data. You can then re-edit the data and click Submit to commit your changes. If you click Cancel instead of Revert, the data reverts to what it was before you started editing it, but you lost your lock on the data.

Navigating Through a Database

The remainder of the status area on the Web functions much as it does on the desktop. You can select layouts, use the book to go from one record to the next, or type in a record number to which you want to go. (On the Web, you must click the small icon to the right of the record number rather than simply use the Return key as you do on the desktop.) Note, too, that on the Web, the choices to view the data as a form, list, or table are in the status area rather than in a non-existent FileMaker menu bar.

The Log Out button at the bottom of the status area is as critical on the Web as it is on a FileMaker network. Log out when you are finished using the database so that others can do their work.

Using Find Mode on the Web

Find mode on the Web works exactly as it does on the desktop. Clicking the Find icon at the top of the status area changes it to the view shown in Figure 22.6.

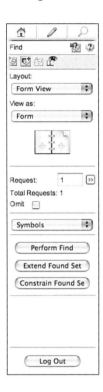

FIGURE 22.6
Find data on the Web in Find mode.

Publishing a Database Using Instant Web Publishing

As with databases to be shared over a network, start by setting up accounts and privileges to be used. (You can reuse settings you have already created, but often you want additional settings for the Web. If your database is on a closed network, reusing the settings is probably fine. However, if you are opening the database to everyone on the Web, you probably will want some new and more restrictive settings.)

People will normally use an IP address to access your published database if you are on a LAN; if you publish a database on the Web, they can use either an IP address or your domain name. You will need a static IP address for your Internet connection for people to be able to reliably get to your published databases. If your IP address changes from day to day (as it generally does with dial-up connections and as it may do with always-on connections), people will have to contact you each time they want to connect to your published databases to find out the address du jour.

With the database open in FileMaker Pro, choose Instant Web Publishing from the Sharing menu (in the FileMaker Pro application menu on Mac OS X and in the Edit menu on Windows). This opens the dialog shown in Figure 22.7.

(Note that if Instant Web Publishing is currently off, you will not see the IP address until you click the On button.)

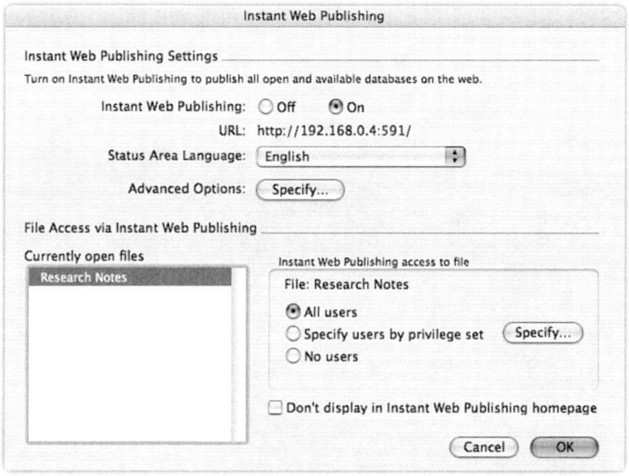

FIGURE 22.7
Configure a database for Instant Web Publishing.

Instant Web Publishing
Instant Web Publishing Settings
Turn on Instant Web Publishing to publish all open and available databases on the web.
Instant Web Publishing: ○ Off   ⊙ On
URL: http://192.168.0.4:591/
Status Area Language: [English ▼]
Advanced Options: (Specify...)
File Access via Instant Web Publishing
Currently open files	Instant Web Publishing access to file
Research Notes	File: Research Notes
	⊙ All users
	○ Specify users by privilege set (Specify...)
	○ No users
	☐ Don't display in Instant Web Publishing homepage
	(Cancel) (OK)

The top part of the window controls Instant Web Publishing for all the databases that you publish; the lower part controls settings for individual databases.

Start by clicking the On radio button to turn on Instant Web Publishing. You may likely get an error message such as the one shown in Figure 22.8.

FIGURE 22.8
You must have a unique port number for your Instant Web Publishing server.

FileMaker cannot share files over the Web because of a port number conflict. Please configure web publishing to use a different port.

(Change Port...)   (OK)

For any given IP address, only one application can be used for a specific port. That application listens at the port, and all incoming traffic on that port goes to that application. Port 80 is normally where a Web server application listens for incoming HTTP requests, and that is where FileMaker Pro tries to establish Instant Web Publishing. If you have a Web server running, port 80 will most likely be taken. This error message informs you of that, and it lets you select another port to use. You can use any port number that you want, provided that it does not conflict with another port that you have in use. FileMaker has registered port 591 as an alternative to port 80, so that is the preferred choice.

People who access your databases over the Web need the port number. Because 80 is the default port number for the Web, it need not be specified if you use it. If you use an alternative, you need to give it to people who will access your database. They will then type in an address such as `http://192.168.0.3:591` to send the request to port 591 of the designated IP address.

By the Way

The Specify button for Advanced Options opens the dialog shown in Figure 22.9.

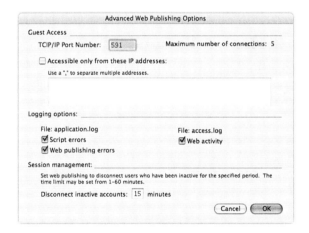

FIGURE 22.9
Set advanced options.

If you need to change the port number, here is where you can do it. Also, note that you can specify access only from certain IP addresses. This is useful if you are publishing a database on the Internet but do not want to make it truly public. You can specify the addresses that are allowed access, and no one else will see the database.

Return to the Instant Web Publishing dialog shown previously in Figure 22.7. For each open database, you can select it in the list at the lower left and set the access options you want to use in the lower right.

That is all there is to publishing a database on the Web with Instant Web Publishing.

Designing for Instant Web Publishing

If you are going to use Instant Web Publishing to publish your database, you should take certain steps during the design process to make the publication as smooth as possible.

These steps fall into three areas:

- ▶ Scripts
- ▶ Colors and graphics
- ▶ General design

Scripts for Instant Web Publishing

First, when creating scripts, note which script steps are compatible with the Web. In Figure 22.10, you can see the checkbox for Web compatibility checked; some of the script steps are grayed out.

FIGURE 22.10
You can disable script steps that are not compatible with the Web.

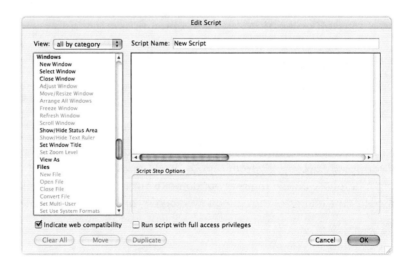

If you examine the grayed-out script steps, you can see that most of them are unavailable because they manipulate the FileMaker interface itself—windows or menus for the most part. Obviously, these are not available on the Web because you are using a browser and the window is the browser's window (not a FileMaker window).

If you are designing a solution for Instant Web Publishing alone, you can simply avoid these script steps. If you are designing a solution to run both on the Web and on FileMaker clients, you can construct your scripts so that the Web-only steps are in separate scripts from the others. Thus, you wind up with some scripts that are independent of the interface (that manipulate data only, not the interface), and then there will be other scripts that manipulate the FileMaker interface. These typically would be attached to buttons in the interface itself.

Colors, Fonts, and Graphics for Instant Web Publishing

Not all colors are usable on the Web. When choosing colors for the Web, make sure that they appear as you expect them to (within the rather wide range of color matching that occurs automatically). You can use the Web-safe palette in the Mac OS X color picker to help you as shown in Figure 22.11.

FIGURE 22.11
Use Web-safe colors.

Also, in choosing fonts, choose those that are likely to be available to all your users on whatever platforms they use and whatever browsers they use.

General Design Concerns for Instant Web Publishing

There is one overriding recommendation for producing good Instant Web Publishing interfaces: Constantly check your Web layouts as you proceed. Layouts that are to be used only on the Web or only on the desktop are generally easier to create than those that need to be used in both ways. In such cases, keep switching back and forth.

With practice, you may come to learn what features are most troublesome and learn to avoid them. Very precise space, for example, with very little space between interface elements can be problematic.

Another consideration is evident when you look back at Figures 22.1 and 22.2, which show the same template in FileMaker and using Instant Web Publishing. Because the FileMaker menu bar is not visible when you are using Instant Web Publishing in a browser, it is necessary for the status area to have icons for New Record, Sort, and so forth. Many modern interface designs have buttons on their layouts for these purposes. (The menu bar is becoming less important as displays get larger and there is room for more buttons.) Because the interface itself has buttons for New and Find, when it is shown in Instant Web Publishing, there are buttons in the layout for New and Find (and other tasks) alongside the buttons in the Instant Web Publishing status area. Although such duplication is not particularly confusing, still it does provide unnecessary repetition. You can get around this by using separate layouts for Instant Web Publishing and for FileMaker clients, but other solutions are also possible.

Summary

In this hour, you saw how to use Instant Web Publishing to publish FileMaker databases on the Web. The process is the same whether you are publishing on the Web itself or on a local area network or an intranet.

FileMaker allows you to configure your FileMaker Web server easily. The most important configuration steps you need to take are selecting the appropriate port and, optionally, setting allowable IP addresses for people using your database.

From the standpoint of your database users, the interface that they will use is almost the same as it is on the desktop. In most cases, if your database solution works properly on the desktop, it will work properly—and look almost the same—on the Web using Instant Web Publishing.

Q&A

Q *How much traffic can an Instant Web Publishing site handle?*

A Traffic for any Web site is constrained by the bandwidth of the connection, the speed of the computer running the Web server software, and external constraints. In the case of FileMaker, the chief external constraint is that Instant Web Publishing using FileMaker Pro is limited to five connections. This makes it appropriate for workgroups as well as for Web-based solutions that have relatively few connections. This last situation is far from rare: Many people publish information on the Web that is, to say the least, recherché. There may be very few hits on such a site, but more often than not, the people using the site are finding out information that they could not find out anywhere else on the Web (or in the real world, for that matter).

If you need more than five connections, you need to use FileMaker Server, which is designed for larger-scale sharing over the Web.

Q *Can you change the Instant Web Publishing status area?*

A No. Any customization requires the XML process described in Hours 23 and 24. Instant Web Publishing is particularly powerful because it does so much automatically for you. But the cost is that you must accept its interface.

Workshop

Quiz

1. Why do you need to worry about port numbers?

2. How do you control access to databases you share with Instant Web Publishing?

3. Can Instant Web Publishing handle portals and relationships?

Quiz Answers

1. Only one application can use a port at a time. If HTTP requests come into your computer, they normally come to port 80 and are directed to Web server software. If you are running a Web server (or are configured to do so), you need to use an alternative port such as 591 for incoming FileMaker Web server requests.

2. You control access with the unified security model of account names and privileges. However, you also have the ability to control access by the IP address of the user.

3. Yes. The only things it cannot handle are certain script steps that manipulate the FileMaker interface itself.

Activities

If you have not done so, open a database (perhaps one from the templates) and share it using Instant Web Publishing. Use the database for various tasks; watch it in FileMaker itself and in the Web browser. (You can do this on a single computer.) Look for the subtle differences in the interface.

Now take one of your own databases—particularly one with a graphically intense interface. Do the same thing. Does it look the same with Instant Web Publishing? Where are the differences?

Using FileMaker and XML with Other Applications

What You'll Learn in This Hour:

▶ The XML Difference—XML allows you to handle the complexity of related data with ease. Because it uses tags to delimit data, it also avoids some of the issues that arise in comma- and tab-delimited files when delimiters are part of the data.

▶ Setting Up the Example—Combine the Contact Management and Asset Management templates to track assets and the people to whom they are assigned. (This is also a good review of relationships.)

▶ Exporting XML—Here is how to actually export the data that you have set up.

▶ Inside an XML Document—This section examines the contents of XML documents in general.

▶ The XML Export File from the Example—Your new set of databases now has a portal in the Contact Management database. This section shows you how you can export the data with XML.

▶ What Next?—Tools such as XPath and XQuery can help you parse the exported data.

XML (eXtensible Markup Language) is rapidly becoming the standard for data interchange. FileMaker supports XML import and export. In this hour, you will see how to use them. (Although this hour shows you how to export data from FileMaker and then import it back in, in most cases, you export from FileMaker and import into another application or vice versa).

In addition to importing and exporting data, you can also use XML's companion technology, XSLT, to format data.

The XML Difference

You saw in Hour 11, "Importing and Exporting Data," how to import and export data to and from FileMaker. A variety of common formats including tab- and comma-delimited text files are supported and make it easy to work with other applications.

But there are some problems with these formats. They have been designed to work with many applications and to support many types of data, but FileMaker can support more sophisticated data structures than they can support. For example, consider the case of a portal in a data record. The portal can display any number of related records for the primary record. How should this be exported?

Using tab-delimited data, here is how a record with portal data is exported. These are the exported records for an individual to whom a variety of equipment has been assigned:

```
Jesse Feiler   Wireless Keyboard
               Wireless Mouse
```

The exported data looks exactly the same as would two records for two individuals, one of whose names has not been entered.

XML has been designed to represent complex data structures such as the related records in the portal. For that alone, it is an important addition to the existing import/export formats. There are many more reasons to use XML. (The description of XML later in this hour pinpoints many of them.)

Setting Up the Example

In this hour, two FileMaker templates are combined to create a hybrid solution. The Asset Management template is modified to identify the individual to whom an asset is assigned. This is done by adding a Contact ID field to the Asset Management table and then creating relationships in both directions—a one-to-many relationship from contact to asset and a one-to-one relationship from asset to contact. Figure 23.1 shows the relationship graph from the standpoint of the Contact Management table.

In the Asset Management database, modify the layout to add a field in which to enter Contact ID. If you want, you can further modify the database to show the related name of the contact as shown in Figure 23.2. (The field in which to enter Contact ID is not visible at the bottom of the window, but the displayed name is visible at the top of the data section.) Enter a contact ID number for a valid record in the Contact Management database, and you see the related data in the Asset Management layout.

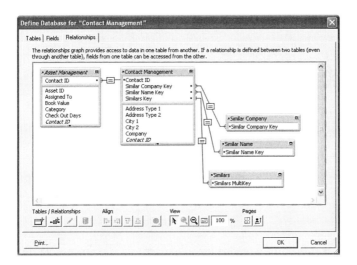

FIGURE 23.1
Create relation-
ships based on
Contact ID between
Asset Management
and Contact
Management data-
bases.

FIGURE 23.2
Add the Contact ID
field to the Asset
Management data-
base.

In Figure 23.3, you can see the modification made to the Contact Management database. At the right, the container field that in the template is used to display an image of the asset has been replaced with a portal displaying the related records from Asset Management.

FIGURE 23.3
Add a portal of
related assets to
Contact
Management.

If you want, at this point you can try to export tab- or comma-delimited data.
You will see the ambiguous results described in the previous section.

Exporting XML

Exporting the data using XML removes the ambiguity. Before looking inside the
file to see how it is done, begin by exporting the data to create the XML export
file.

By the Way

> This section shows you how to export the related portal data that appears in the
> one-to-many relationship in the Contact Management database. The ambiguous data
> situation noted previously only occurs in such portals. If you were to export data
> from the Asset Management database, the one-to-one relationship to the Contact
> Management database means that there is no ambiguity with the exported data.

Start by choosing File, Export from the menu. Name the file and select the XML
format as shown in Figure 23.4.

In the next dialog, select FMPXMLRESULT as the grammar as shown in Figure 23.5.
(The meaning of this is discussed later in this hour.)

Finally, just as you did in Hour 11, select the fields for export as shown in
Figure 23.6.

FIGURE 23.4
Select XML as the file format.

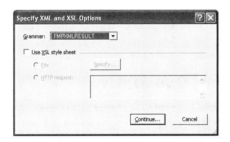

FIGURE 23.5
Use FMPXMLRESULT as the grammar.

FIGURE 23.6
Select the fields to export.

Having created the XML export file, you can now look inside it.

Inside an XML Document

This section provides an overview of XML itself. The actual XML document created in the previous section is described in the following section.

XML is one of the many markup languages derived from SGM (Standard Generalized Markup Language), which first appeared in the 1960s. These languages use tags—generally enclosed in brackets such as <this>—to add descriptive information to text in a file.

For example, in HTML, a paragraph is delineated as follows:

```
<P>
This is a paragraph.
</P>
```

Spacing in HTML does not matter; the following code is identical to the previous code:

```
<P>This is a paragraph.</P>
```

The text enclosed in brackets is called a *tag*; the entire construct is called an *element*.

XML Can Be Self-Descriptive

XML documents may use a document type definition (DTD) or an XML schema to describe their syntax. XML itself provides no standard tags such as the paragraph tag in HTML (<P>). It is not necessary to use a DTD or schema; in the examples in this hour, you'll see both usages. Note that any tags you see are given meaning within their own context—a DTD, a schema, or in the XML document itself.

XML Is Designed to Be Parsed and Generated Primarily by Software

The first line in any XML file contains the XML version and the encoding used in the file.

Plain Text

XML is plain text. That's why you need to specify the encoding in the XML declaration at the beginning of each file.

Elements Are Closed

Every XML element is closed; HTML elements do not always need to be closed. If an XML element has an opening tag—such as <p>, it is closed with a closing tag such as </p>.

Sometimes, an element can be closed without using a closing tag. For example, in FileMaker export files, a DATA element contains the data. Here is a data element consisting of the words "Wireless Keyboard." Note the opening and closing tags.

```
<DATA>Wireless Keyboard</DATA>
```

Here is a data element with no data in it. Note the single tag with the / to close it at the end:

```
<DATA />
```

Elements Can be Nested

Elements can contain other elements. Because elements must contain ending tags, there is no ambiguity over what is contained within what.

There Is Always a Root

The root element is the first element following the XML declaration. All other elements are contained within it. This further clarifies the nested structure of elements within an XML document.

Attribute Values Are Quoted

Unlike in HTML, values of attributes must always be quoted.

Using Quotes

You can use single or double quotes in XML. If you use double quotes to delimit an attribute value, you can use single quotes within it as normal quotes; you can also do the reverse.

White Space Matters

Because attributes are enclosed in quotes, XML parsers don't have to guess where one identifier begins and another ends (as is the case in HTML). Thus, white space within an element does matter.

XML Validation

Two validation concepts are important for XML.

Well-Formed XML

Well-formed XML adheres to the rules of XML; it can be parsed by a compliant parser. Because XML itself has no intrinsic elements, this parsing only checks that elements are properly opened and closed and other such concerns.

Valid XML

If an XML document contains a schema or DTD, a parser can check that the XML is valid. Although no elements are defined within XML itself, a schema or DTD does define elements.

Escaped Characters

XML defines general syntax and tries to avoid specific references to literals where possible. However, five symbols have specific meaning for XML parsers; if they are used in any other way (in text, for example), they need to be escaped. Table 23.1 lists the five symbols and their escape sequences.

TABLE 23.1   Escape Sequences for XML Characters

Escape Sequence	Character
&gt;	>
&lt;	<
&amp;	&
&apos	'
&quot	"

The XML Export File from the Example

The file from the example is shown here. XML is designed to be read and written by software, so you rarely have to look inside a file. However, if you do, you see how the features described in the previous section are used.

The entire document consists of an FMPXMLRESULT element. Within it, there are several introductory elements:

▶ The ERRORCODE element displays any error that has been encountered—0 means no error.

▶ The PRODUCT BUILD element provides information about the version of FileMaker used to create the file. (The PRODUCT BUILD element is self-terminating as is the DATABASE element, which follows.)

▶ The DATABASE element provides information about the database and the default date and time formats.

▶ The METADATA element contains the names of the fields that are exported.

When you exported data and chose the FMPXMLRESULT grammar (refer to Figure 23.5), you could have chosen a different grammar—FMPDSORESULT. That grammar does not list the field names in the METADATA element; rather each field name is repeated in each record. Those files are larger than FMPXMLRESULT files.

By the Way

Following these elements, the data is found. The RESULTSET element contains one ROW element for each row; each ROW element contains a COL element for each field. Finally, within the COL element, a DATA element contains the data for that row/column. That is how the ambiguity of the data in the portal is resolved. Note that in the second COL element there are simply two DATA elements representing the related values.

```
<?xml version="1.0" encoding="UTF-8" ?>
<FMPXMLRESULT xmlns="http://www.filemaker.com/fmpxmlresult">
  <ERRORCODE>0</ERRORCODE>
  <PRODUCT BUILD="12-10-2003" NAME="FileMaker Pro" VERSION="7.0v1" />
  <DATABASE
    DATEFORMAT="M/d/yyyy"
    LAYOUT=""
    NAME="Contact Management.fp7"
    RECORDS="1"
    TIMEFORMAT="h:mm:ss a" />
  <METADATA>
    <FIELD EMPTYOK="YES" MAXREPEAT="1" NAME="Full Name" TYPE="TEXT" />
    <FIELD EMPTYOK="YES" MAXREPEAT="1" NAME="Asset Management::Item"
➥ TYPE="TEXT" />
  </METADATA>

  <RESULTSET FOUND="1">
    <ROW MODID="0" RECORDID="1">
      <COL>
        <DATA>Jesse Feiler</DATA>
      </COL>
```

```
<COL>
  <DATA>Wireless Keyboard</DATA>
  <DATA>Wireless Mouse</DATA>
</COL>

</ROW>

</RESULTSET>

</FMPXMLRESULT>
```

What Next?

You have seen how XML exports from FileMaker can retain the structure of a relationship. (Simple exports—that is, from a single table or from a table with only one-to-one relationships—are easy both with XML and with the simpler technologies described in Hour 11.)

By their nature, these complex data exports need careful attention when you want to import them into other applications. A variety of tools is available specifically designed to work with XML files and to locate data within them. Two of the most common are XPath and XQuery. You can pair them with XML to quickly write code to parse your XML files.

Summary

XML provides a means to easily export complex data from FileMaker to other applications (or to FileMaker itself). As more applications support XML, it is rapidly becoming the tool of choice for data transfer—not just for the relatively complex issue of related data shown here, but even for the simplest data. Its self-documenting features and rigorous grammar make it ideal for cross-platform and cross-application data sharing.

In this hour, you saw how to use XML to share data among applications where computer software reads and writes the data. But what if you want to import or export data in a human-readable format? Hour 24 shows you how to pair XML with XSLT to create Web pages, RTF files, and more.

Q&A

Q *Isn't XML much more complicated than simple tab- and comma-delimited files?*

A All those formats are designed for data transfer, not for human readability. XML could be even more complicated than it is (and it really is not very complicated), and it still would shine as a data transfer tool in view of the fact that it is designed for application programs to read and write it. Some programs (such as Microsoft Internet Explorer) format XML with colors and indentations so that it is easy to read when you are debugging it.

Q *Can you import the example XML file back into FileMaker?*

A Importing related data generally requires some massaging. The simplest way is to work from a flattened table—that is, one with no relationships or with only one-to-one relationships. In this case, the table would be the Asset Management table. There are several strategies you could pursue. One would be to do two imports: one into the Asset Management table and the second into the Contact Management table. (Using the relationship, you can access all the Contact Management fields from Asset Management.) You would have to eliminate duplicate contacts.

Workshop

Quiz

1. What are some of the ways in which XML differs from HTML?
2. What tools can you use to read XML?
3. How do you export data from a portal?

Quiz Answers

1. Capitalization matters, spaces count, attributes must be quoted, and every element must have a closing tag.

2. Applications such as Microsoft Internet Explorer can display XML in a colored and indented format. Tools such as XPath and XQuery can parse XML easily.

3. Portal data (one-to-many data) can be exported using any export format; however, to have unambiguous exported data, you should use XML for this purpose.

Activities

If you have not already done so, set up the example shown here and experiment with exporting data. Use only two or three records so that the XML file is short and can be read.

Experiment with moving the data back into FileMaker. If you export data from the Asset Management database, you will wind up with duplicate Contact Management records. How can you avoid this? (There are several ways; one of them involves a script.)

Using FileMaker, XML, and XSLT

What You'll Learn in This Hour:

▶ Transforming XML Exports into HTML—You can take the XML files that you exported from the Hour 23, "Using FileMaker and XML with Other Applications," and turn them into Web pages.

▶ A Look at XSLT—This section looks at the details of XSLT, the tool that does the transformation.

▶ Modifying the Simple Table Transformation—In this section, you see how to make several modifications to the simple table style sheet that ships with FileMaker.

▶ Using XPath Expressions to Select and Manipulate Text—This section introduces you to more advanced programming for XSLT. It is only a taste of what is available, but it can start you thinking and doing new things.

In Hour 23, you saw how to export data using XML. This process is the most reliable way to export data that may contain delimiter characters (such as quotes or commas) as well as complex related data structures. The export process is totally data-related: No formatting is done. To read the data, you need to use am XML-savvy application or write code using XPath, XQuery, or another XML manipulation language.

In this hour, you will see how to use XSLT to transform XML into properly formatted HTML. You will be able to apply the principles shown here to other formats such as RTF easily.

This is the last hour in the book, and it is designed not only to cover the material involved with XSLT style sheets, but also to provide you with a range of possibilities for further exploration.

Transforming XML Exports into HTML

In this section, you see how to use standard XSLT style sheets provided with FileMaker to

▶ Format simple tables.

▶ Sort and summarize tables with related data.

For starters, use the same databases you used in Hour 23 (the modified Contact Management and Asset Management databases). You can use two XSLT files included with FileMaker Pro to automatically transform them into HTML. Here is what you do.

This section uses the provided XSLT files. The following sections look inside those files to show you how they work.

Exporting Simple Tables to HTML

Start from the Asset Management database. When asked for the grammar, again choose FMPXMLRESULT. However, unlike the steps in the Hour 23, choose to use an XSL style sheet. Select simple_table.xsl, which is installed automatically with FileMaker. Inside the FileMaker folder, you will find it in English Extras/Examples/XML Examples/Export. The dialog should look as it appears in Figure 24.1.

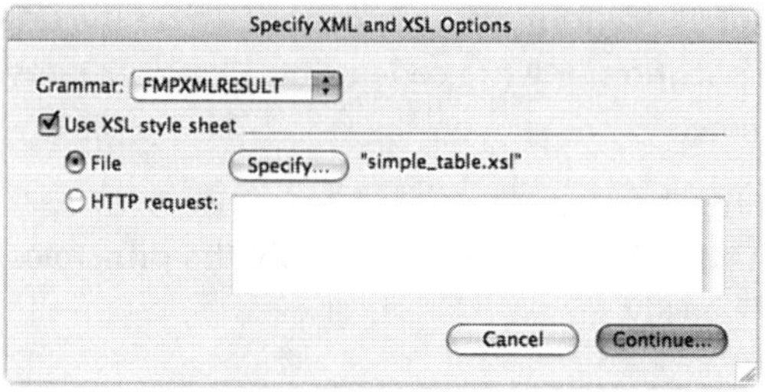

FIGURE 24.1
Select the
simple_table.xsl
style sheet.

This style sheet displays a flattened table (that is, one without a portal) in an HTML table.

Next, select the Contact Management::Full Name and Item from the current table, Asset Management, for export as shown in Figure 24.2.

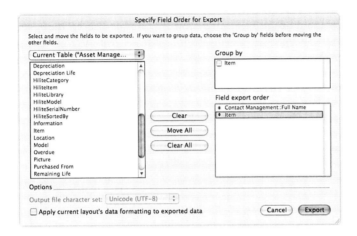

FIGURE 24.2
Select the fields.

The export is completed, and you can open the resulting file using a browser or any other software that can interpret HTML. (You may need to change the extension to .html.) Figure 24.3 shows the result.

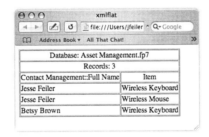

FIGURE 24.3
The XML data is transformed into an HTML table.

This style sheet works for any FileMaker table with any number of rows or columns. It is probably the simplest way to transform your exported XML data. (You see in the following section how to modify the style sheet to change the HTML formatting.)

Exporting Subsummary Tables to HTML

You can use another standard style sheet to summarize data. As you can see in Figure 24.3, the three records of the Asset Management database are presented in the order they are found in the database; one person has two assets, and they appear on two separate lines.

To summarize the data, use the subsummary.xsl style sheet when you export the data. (It, too, is provided in the standard FileMaker installation, and it is in the same folder as simple_table.xsl.)

With no other action on your part, you create the table shown in Figure 24.4.

FIGURE 24.4
Sort and summarize data automatically.

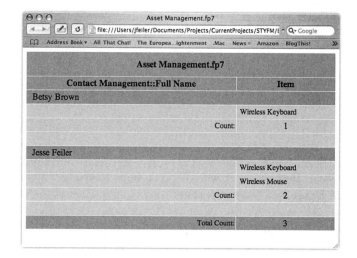

This style sheet not only summarizes the data, but it also sorts it (note the sequence of records is different from that shown in Figure 24.3—nothing was done in FileMaker to sort or summarize the data).

A Look at XSLT

Just using those two style sheets, you can format your FileMaker data for printing without further ado. In this section, you will look inside them.

This section covers

▶ XSLT basics

▶ The top of the style sheet: basic declarations

- ▶ Displaying the data in an HTML table
- ▶ The bottom of the style sheet: ending up

XSLT Basics

XSL (Extensible Stylesheet Language) is a set of recommendations for defining XML document transformation and presentation. It includes XSLT (XSL Transformations), XML Path Language (XPath), and XSL Formatting Objects (XSL-FO). For more information see `http://www.w3.org/Style/XSL/`.

XSLT is a powerful language, but at its core is a simple concept: Template rules are defined that transform the incoming XML document into another XML document. Each template rule has two components:

- ▶ Pattern—This is a pattern to be found in the incoming XML document.
- ▶ Template—If the pattern is found, the template is instantiated in the result XML document. The template may combine text from the incoming XML document with constants.

You can create an XSLT style sheet from scratch; more often than not, you modify an existing style sheet such as the two used in the previous section. The simple_table.xsl style sheet is described in this section. You can use it and the description to begin to create your own style sheets. It has been reformatted in some places, and some of the comments have been removed so as not to duplicate the text.

The syntax for XSLT is common programming syntax: calling routines, loops, and the like. The representation of that syntax may be new to you, but the concepts should not be if you have done any programming.

XSLT uses the expression language from XPath. You can find out more about XPath at `http://www.w3.org/TR/xpath`.

The Top of the Style Sheet: Basic Declarations

The top of the style sheet consists of standard declarations. You will probably not change this. It is followed by a comment that you should change to indicate what you are doing in the style sheet.

```
<?xml version="1.0" encoding="UTF-8"?>

<xsl:stylesheet version="1.0"
  xmlns:xsl="http://www.w3.org/1999/XSL/Transform"
  xmlns:fmp="http://www.filemaker.com/fmpxmlresult"
  exclude-result-prefixes="fmp">

  <xsl:output method="html" version="1.0" encoding="UTF-8" indent="yes"/>
```

Now comes the heart of the style sheet. It is a template rule invoked when the pattern fmp:FMPXMLRESULT is found in the incoming XML file.

This is right at the beginning of the XML file, and the template is instantiated in the result XML file. Everything within the xsl:template element is simply placed into the result XML file. Compare the beginning of the template rule with the result XML. First, the template rule:

```
<xsl:template match="fmp:FMPXMLRESULT">
  <html>
    <body>
      <table border="1" cellPadding="1" cellSpacing="1">
```

Here is the result. The three lines of HTML are exported:

```
<html>
  <body>
    <table border="1" cellPadding="1" cellSpacing="1">
```

Next, the template calls a template to display the header. The header template displays the title information. (This hour focuses on the data itself and does not discuss the header template. However, if you look at the file, you see that it is simply a matter of picking up fields from the XML file and emitting them as HTML.)

```
<xsl:call-template name="header"/>
```

Displaying the Data in an HTML Table

To display the data from the XML file, a standard HTML table is created with rows (the <tr> elements)and data cells within the rows (the <td> elements). The XSL code loops through each row and each column; it then exports the value of the data. Interspersed with the XSL code are HTML elements.

To follow this, you will find three snippets here:

▶ The XSLT loops

▶ The XML input document

▶ The resulting HTML

Looping Through the Data

First, the XSLT loops:

```
<xsl:for-each select="fmp:RESULTSET/fmp:ROW">
  <tr>
    <xsl:for-each select="fmp:COL">
      <td>
        <xsl:value-of select="fmp:DATA"/>
      </td>
    </xsl:for-each>
  </tr>
</xsl:for-each>
```

The XML Input Data

Next the relevant XML input (the full document was described in Hour 23):

```
<ROW MODID="0" RECORDID="1">
  <COL>
    <DATA>
      Jesse Feiler
    </DATA>
  </COL>
  <COL>
    <DATA>
      Wireless Keyboard
    </DATA>
  </COL>
</ROW>

<ROW MODID="0" RECORDID="2">
  <COL>
    <DATA>
      Jesse Feiler
    </DATA>
  </COL>
  <COL>
    <DATA>
      Wireless Mouse
    </DATA>
  </COL>
</ROW>

<ROW MODID="0" RECORDID="3">
  <COL>
    <DATA>
      Betsy Brown
    </DATA>
  </COL>
  <COL>
    <DATA>
      Wireless Keyboard
    </DATA>
  </COL>
</ROW>
```

The Resulting HTML Table

Finally, the resulting HTML:

```
<tr>
  <td>
    Jesse Feiler
  </td>
  <td>
    Wireless Keyboard
  </td>
</tr>

<tr>
  <td>
    Jesse Feiler
  </td>
  <td>
    Wireless Mouse
  </td>
</tr>

<tr>
  <td>
    Betsy Brown
  </td>
  <td>
    Wireless Keyboard
  </td>
</tr>
```

The Bottom of the Style Sheet: Ending Up

At the bottom of the template, the HTML that completes the table and document is emitted:

```
      </table>
    </body>
  </html>
</xsl:template>
```

Modifying the Simple Table Transformation

The simple_table.xsl style sheet works for any tabular data that you export from FileMaker. You can modify it for specific purposes so that you have a style sheet customized for a single database (or for a group of similar databases). This section shows you one type of customization.

Before starting work, make sure that you have made a copy of simple_table.xsl so that you can return to the generic version.

The modification shown here is simple: The first column is italicized, and the second column is boldfaced as shown in Figure 24.5.

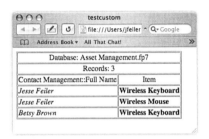

FIGURE 24.5
Customize the simple table style sheet.

The heart of the style sheet is the loop that runs across all rows and then across all columns:

```
<xsl:for-each select="fmp:RESULTSET/fmp:ROW">
  <tr>
    <xsl:for-each select="fmp:COL">
      <td>
        <xsl:value-of select="fmp:DATA"/>
      </td>
    </xsl:for-each>
  </tr>
</xsl:for-each>
```

This needs to change so that it runs across all rows and then explicitly references each column in that row (because the columns will be treated differently).

Here is the revised code. It contains the row loop, and it shows you how to explicitly reference each cell within a column.

```
<xsl:for-each select="fmp:RESULTSET/fmp:ROW">
  <tr>
    <td>
      <xsl:value-of select= "fmp:COL[1]/fmp:DATA"/>
    </td>

    <td>
      <xsl:value-of select= "fmp:COL[2]/fmp:DATA"/>
    </td>
  </tr>
</xsl:for-each>
```

At this point, it is easy to add the tags to control italics and boldfaced text.

```
<xsl:for-each select="fmp:RESULTSET/fmp:ROW">
  <tr>
    <td>
      <i>
      <xsl:value-of select= "fmp:COL[1]/fmp:DATA"/>
      </i>
    </td>

    <td>
      <b>
      <xsl:value-of select= "fmp:COL[2]/fmp:DATA"/>
      </b>
    </td>
  </tr>
</xsl:for-each>
```

Using XPath Expressions to Select and Manipulate Text

There is almost no limit to the manipulations that you can perform in a style sheet. The subsummary.xsl style sheet sorts and sums data: You can use it as a model for your own complex style sheets.

Even for simple style sheets, you can use a host of other functions. Particularly useful are the editing and conditional functions. A full description of XSLT is beyond the scope of this book, but here is a code snippet to whet your appetite. (If you are experienced with programming—in any language—you can modify it for your own purposes.)

Remember that the data exported with XML is not formatted by FileMaker. As a result, numbers may not be displayed with a uniform number of decimal places. This code uniformly displays two digits to the right of the decimal point.

It starts by emitting the value of the fifth column of data. (This is an arbitrary choice, selected to show you how to access an individual column by number.) It then uses the choose construct (similar to a case statement in other languages). Each element of the choose statement is a when statement. The first test tests the length of the substring of that column that follows the decimal point. If it is 0, the string .00 is emitted. In the next test, it adds a single 0 after the string so that a number with one digit following the decimal point now has two. It does nothing in other cases. (If you have data that might have more than two digits to the right of the decimal point, you would have to truncate it.)

```
<xsl:value-of select="fmp:COL[5]/fmp:DATA"/>
<xsl:choose >

  <xsl:when test = "string-length(substring-after (fmp:COL[5]/fmp:DATA, '.'))=0">
    <xsl:text>.00</xsl:text>
  </xsl:when>

  <xsl:when test = "string-length(substring-after (fmp:COL[5]/fmp:DATA, '.'))=1">
    <xsl:text>0</xsl:text>
  </xsl:when>

  <xsl:otherwise>
  </xsl:otherwise>

</xsl:choose>
```

In addition to the XPath expressions and the XSL choose and when expressions, note the xsl:text element. This element contains any text that is to be emitted to the result XML document. The text within the xsl:text element is copied exactly as it is typed—spaces and all—to the output document. It has not been used previously in this hour because the text that has been used in the simple table style sheet consists of HTML tags that do not need to be placed in an xsl:text element.

Summary

In this hour you were introduced to the power of XSLT, which can let you turn your XML exports into Web pages, RTF files, or any other type of document that you can define in XSLT. When you experiment with XSLT, you will find that it is a remarkably powerful tool that, with some practice, you can use to greatly extend FileMaker. (Note, too, that many people use XSLT for many purposes. You can create your FileMaker solutions and export an XML file so that someone with a knowledge of XSLT but not of FileMaker can carry on from there.)

Because you can use XSLT for formatting XML output as HTML, you can use it as the basis for an interactive Web site. This requires the use of FileMaker Server Advanced, discussed briefly in Appendix D, "Using FileMaker Server."

As FileMaker enters its third decade, it remains a rare combination of ease-of-use and industrial-strength power. Whether you use the templates out of the box without customizing them, create a brand-new database from scratch, or build a totally customized solution based on some combination of these along with imports and exports from and to other applications, you will find that FileMaker quickly becomes an indispensable part of your life.

Q&A

Q *How significant is FileMaker 7?*

A This book was written from the ground up for FileMaker 7. Most of the concepts in the book and in FileMaker are not new; they have stood the test of time. But other features of FileMaker 7 are radical departures—particularly the idea of having several tables in one file. Also important and different in FileMaker 7 are the unified security model and the handling of file references. Major enhancements to scripting and Instant Web Publishing also are present.

If you are an old hand at FileMaker, you can adopt FileMaker 7 in most cases by simply opening your old databases in FileMaker 7: It does the conversion for you automatically. However, you will not automatically take advantage of the new features. Take some time to look at the new features so that when you start your next project (or do maintenance work on an existing project) you can use these new features.

Q *As you develop solutions with FileMaker and become more and more dependent on it, what is the best way to protect that investment?*

A There are several answers to this. The first one is document, document, document. Use comments (including the new comment feature for fields in the database) all over the place. A year from now, you will not remember why you did things one way or another.

Nor will you remember the difference between the field SalesTotal and TotalSales. Comments can help, but standard naming conventions can also help. A script that edits data but has no user interaction might be called EditLineItem. The script that runs EditLineItem and provides a message dialog to display whatever message was generated could be DoEditLineItem. If you adopt such a naming convention, make it consistent. (And as you modify your existing solutions, start to rename fields, scripts, and layouts without modifying them to bring the nomenclature into a standard form.)

And finally, treat your FileMaker solutions like the valuable tools that they are. FileMaker makes it easy to make modifications, but even if you are a one-person operation, resist the temptation to tweak the solution every time you run it. If you are the developer as well as the user, try to keep those two roles distinct.

Workshop

Quiz

1. What text goes into `xsl:text` elements?

2. What is the limit on the number of rows and columns that the simple table style sheet can handle?

Quiz Answers

1. All text except for HTML or XML elements and tags.

2. There is none. It handles whatever is there. (From a practical point of view, there are limits to the size of files on your hard disk, but they are very large.)

Activities

In previous hours of this book, activities have been suggested for you to test your skills and expand your knowledge. Now, at the end of the book, you should be feeling confident about your FileMaker skills. Some areas may be a little uncertain (maybe you are an old FileMaker hand and the idea of multiple tables in a database is a little unnerving, or maybe XML/XSLT seems somewhat daunting). Consider the areas in which you need more practice and then set some tasks for yourself to increase your skills in those areas.

But do not forget that in most areas, your skills are now probably quite strong. From here on, your activities should be the productive and useful ones of developing FileMaker solutions for yourself and others.

You may want to go back to some of the test databases you created while working through this book. Maybe now you have different ways to approach them—perhaps you would even like to start over. Polish them up so that you can build on robust solutions in the future.

If you intend to develop FileMaker solutions seriously, also consider joining the FileMaker Solutions Alliance (FSA), which can be accessed through `http://www.filemaker.com`.

Finally, there's one last activity, but it's not for you: It's for the author. Welcome to the FileMaker community! It's a great group of people, doing imaginative things for all types of businesses and organizations. There's a great deal of sharing on the FSA mailing list, and you'll find that your FileMaker colleagues are always welcome to help. FileMaker brings out the best in people and their database solutions.

PART V

Appendices

Converting from Previous Versions of FileMaker

This appendix provides some tips for converting databases and solutions from previous versions of FileMaker to FileMaker 7. A default conversion takes place when you open an old database file in FileMaker 7. In most cases, that conversion is ready to use immediately. However, the default conversion retains the structure of the old database. New FileMaker 7 features are not used in most cases. This appendix describes how you can use the new features in FileMaker 7 to go beyond the default conversion.

FileMaker provides a lot of information and documentation on its Web site to assist you with conversion. This appendix does not attempt to duplicate that documentation. Rather, it pinpoints some of the features that the author found himself using repeatedly as he created and converted literally dozens of databases in researching this book.

By the Way

Getting Started with Conversion

A new version of FileMaker is an opportunity to review your databases and solutions. Most of the time, routine maintenance is devoted to fixing bugs and adding features. If your FileMaker database is more than a few years old, chances are that a general review—even without upgrading to FileMaker 7—will reap benefits.

FileMaker is now more than 20 years old. Many databases are nearly that old. Over the years, they have been modified and enhanced; it is a tribute to FileMaker that it is easy to protect your investment in FileMaker solutions. To keep your FileMaker databases running efficiently, it's a good idea to plan for routine maintenance over and above enhancements and bug fixes. (This is true for all software products.)

Begin by collecting your solution and its documentation. Before moving to FileMaker 7, check out the solution in your current version of FileMaker. Make sure that everything works correctly. (You don't want to track down a FileMaker 7 "bug" that has been there for years.)

You may want to clean up the data, deleting old records and correcting errors. Whether you do this in the old or new version is up to you. If a lot of data clean-up needs to be done, you can argue equally well that it should be done before and after conversion. If you are new to FileMaker 7, one argument for doing it after conversion is that it will help you to become familiar with using FileMaker 7 (although the basic data entry and finding mechanisms are essentially unchanged).

In addition to data clean-up, you may want to take this opportunity to revise layouts; standardize naming for fields, tables, scripts, and layouts; and create new graphics with external applications such as Photoshop. Whether this is done before or after the conversion is up to you.

Whatever approach you take, make sure that you

- ▶ Keep one or more duplicate copies of the preconversion database (along with your old copy of FileMaker and its registration information) in case you need to reinstall it.

- ▶ Run whatever reports that you can so that you will have something to check the converted database against (for example, know that the total of outstanding balances is X, that there are Y records in the clients database, and so forth.

Hiring a Consultant

One of the great attractions of FileMaker is that it allows people with domain-specific knowledge to create databases and solutions with ease. However, there are times when an experienced consultant can be helpful. Perhaps you need just a little bit more expertise; or maybe you just don't have the time to spare. Fortunately, FileMaker consultants are easy to find: Go to http://www.filemaker.com/solutions/find_consultants.html to search for members of the FileMaker Solutions Alliance. You can search by name, telephone area code, address, and the like.

In hiring a consultant (for FileMaker or another project), here are a few points to consider.

- ▶ Make sure that you both understand the scope of work. Who will install the software? Who will test it?

- ▶ In the case of a conversion, is it a straight conversion or do you expect preexisting bugs to be fixed and enhancements to be made?

- ▶ In many cases, old FileMaker solutions need a bit of rehab. This is normal. When a consultant makes suggestions, don't be defensive (but see the next point).

> ▶ Don't be afraid to ask "why," and "what does this mean?" Your job is to explain your domain-specific logic to the consultant; the consultant's job is to understand that and to provide the best FileMaker solution possible within the budget.
>
> ▶ Most FileMaker consultants have FileMaker Developer. Ask your consultant for a full range of database reports (as described in Hour 20, "Creating Solutions with FileMaker Developer"). It's your data and your solution; you need to have all the reference materials.
>
> ▶ Make sure that you and the consultant understand how future maintenance will be handled. Are you turning over all maintenance to the consultant (sometimes a cost-effective approach), or are you simply asking for a one-time consultation after which you or your staff will take over?
>
> ▶ Using actual data for testing is almost always the best way to ensure a good result. Most consultants will be glad to sign a nondisclosure agreement that binds them to keeping your data confidential.

Remove Calculations for Relationships

Before FileMaker 7, relationships could only go to an adjacent table. Consider the case of three tables: A, B, and C. If A was related to B and B was related to C, it was not possible to access data in C from A. As a result, calculation fields proliferated. You could create a calculation field in B that contained the related value from C. Then, from A, you could access the adjacent field—the calculated value in B—and through it a value in C.

This was a common practice. It is no longer necessary in FileMaker 7. If the relationship graph shows a path from A to any other table (no matter how many intervening tables and relationship are involved), you can access the distant field from A.

Removing these no-longer-needed calculations and verifying that the database graph is correct can simplify your FileMaker 7 solutions.

Replace Finds with Nonequal Relationships and Self-Joins

To find all the records that fulfill a certain criterion, you often needed to use a Find. Often, in FileMaker 7, you can now do this with a nonequal relationship and a self-join.

Figure A.1 shows a sample of how this can work.

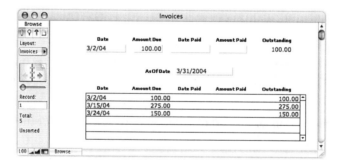

At the top of Figure A.1, you see this record's data: an invoice with its date and amount due along with fields to enter the amount paid and the payment date. The outstanding balance is a calculation field.

A global lets you enter an as-of-date for the table. Then, in a portal at the lower part of the window, all the invoices with a date less than or equal to the as-of-date are shown.

In Figure A.2, you see the result of changing the as-of-date: Fewer records are displayed in the portal.

All this is done with a single table joined to itself. Figure A.3 shows the table's fields.

Use the New Table button at the lower left of the Relationships tab of the Define Database dialog to create a second table based on Invoices. Create a relationship from Invoices to Invoices 2 based on the AsOfDate (Invoices) and the Date (Invoices 2). Figure A.4 shows the relationship when it is complete.

FIGURE A.3
Create invoice fields and a global as-of-date field.

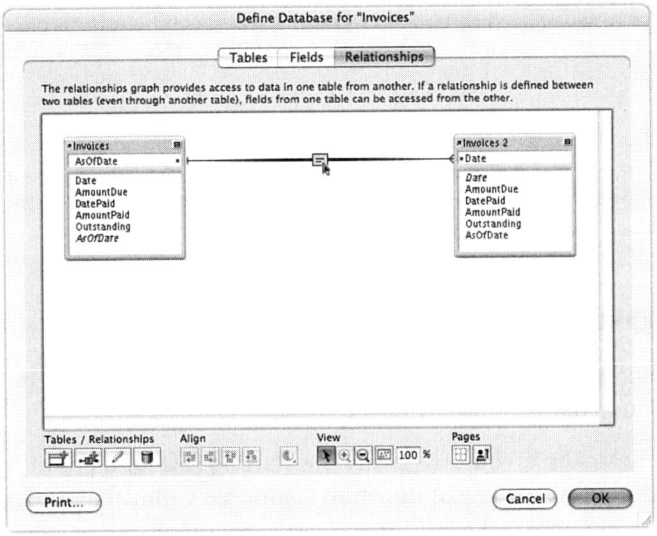

FIGURE A.4
Create a relationship.

When first drawn, the relationship will be one of equality. Double-click the relationship to open the Edit Relationship dialog shown in Figure A.5. Change the relationship to less than or equal.

Rather than procedurally find records in the table, you now can create a self join relationship that automatically maintains the appropriate records. As with the calculations used for distant relationship, the use of nonequal relationships lets you remove code.

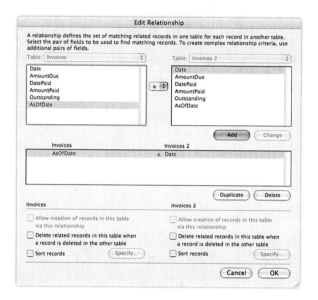

This example shows a self-join. You can achieve comparable results using additional tables so that the control field (the as-of-date) is located in another location.

Use Row Numbers in Portals

As the table grows, the portal in which it is displayed may need to be enlarged. Figure A.6 shows a layout with a larger portal.

Starting in FileMaker 7, you can specify the starting row for a portal. You may be able to replace the single portal shown in Figure A.6 with two portals as shown in Figure A.7. The portal on the left shows rows 1 through 5; the one on the right shows rows starting with 6. Note that only the one on the right has a scroll bar.

The data shown in Figure A.7 is also reduced. Sometimes using multiple portals can make the amount of data you display less critical—not just in terms of the rows displayed but also the fields.

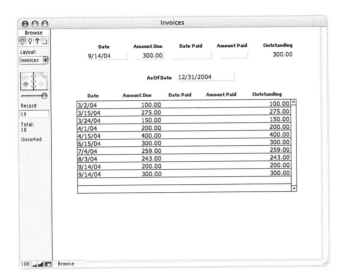

FIGURE A.6
Portals can take up a lot of space.

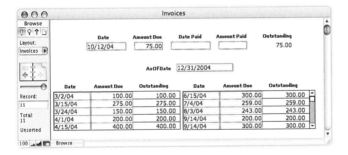

FIGURE A.7
Use multiple portals.

Sort Portals

Another new FileMaker 7 feature lets you control the sort order for portals (not just relationships). Some workarounds (such as multiple otherwise identical relationships) can be removed.

Use Timestamp Fields

A single field can now contain a date and time. Many databases contain separate fields for modification date and modification time (and perhaps another pair for creation date and time). By converting to a timestamp field, you can save space. Note that in converting old data, you need to write a script to map the double fields into a single timestamp field. The Timestamp function can do this.

Use XML

Although not new in FileMaker 7, XML is an extraordinarily powerful tool for data export and display. If you have complex reports, you may want to consider moving to XML and allowing the complex formatting to be done in a spreadsheet or word processor.

Explore the Instant Web Publishing Script Steps

Instant Web Publishing now interacts more completely with FileMaker 7. If you previously dismissed a Web interface to your FileMaker solution as too much work, reconsider it.

Use Field Comments

In the Define Database dialog's Fields tab, use comments to identify each field and the assumptions behind it. It may be a lot of work now, but with the passage of even more time over the next few years, the logic behind the field (and its inherent assumptions) will only become more obscure.

APPENDIX B

FileMaker Functions

This appendix lists the FileMaker 7 functions by category. Where parameter names are not self-explanatory, they are described. Likewise, if the result is not self-explanatory, it is also described. For parameters, the following conventions are used:

- ▶ ...—Indicates any number of occurrences of the previous item
- ▶ {}—Indicates an optional term

Thus, Sum (*field1* {; *field2...*}) allows the following:

- ▶ Sum (*field1; field2*)
- ▶ Sum (*field1; field2; field3*)
- ▶ Sum (*field1*)

Aggregate Functions

All these functions have similar syntax. They take one or more fields and aggregate them. If the field is a repeating field, all the repetitions are aggregated. A list of fields can include repeating fields, local fields, or related fields; it can also include a function (such as if) that returns 0 or 1 field. If the fields in the aggregation list are repeating fields and the result of the calculation is a repeating field, the aggregation is done for each of the repetitions. However, if the result of the calculation is not a repeating field, the values are simply aggregated.

TABLE B.1   Aggregate Functions

Function	Result
Average (*field1* {; *field2*...})	Number
Count (*field1* {; *field2*...})	Number
Max (*field1* {; *field2*...})	Number
Min (*field1* {; *field2*...})	Number
StDev (*field1* {; *field2*...}) (Standard deviation for sample: n-1)	Number
StDevP (*field1* {; *field2*...}) (Standard deviation for population: n)	Number
Sum (*field1* {; *field2*...})	Number
Variance (*field1* {; *field2*...}) (Variance for sample: n-1)	Number
VarianceP (*field1* {; *field2*...}) (Variance for population: n)	Number

Date Functions

The formats of dates in FileMaker are determined by the date settings in layouts as well as by the settings for your computer. To avoid ambiguity, always use four-digit years.

Several functions take a parameter named date. In those cases, date can be a FileMaker date field, an expression that evaluates to a date, or a text string or field that evaluates to a date. From that date, a day number, month, or year can be derived in the appropriate functions.

TABLE B.2   Date Functions

Function	Result
Date (*month*; *day*; *year*)	Date
Day (*date*)	Number
DayName (*date*)	Text
DayNameJ (*date*) Japanese version of DayName	Text
DayOfWeek (*date*)	Number
DayOfYear (*date*)	Number
Month (*date*)	Number
MonthName (*date*)	Text
MonthNameJ (*date*) Japanese version of MonthName	Text

TABLE B.2 Continued

Function	Result
WeekOfYear (*date*)	Number from 1–54 Number of weeks (including partial weeks) after January 1
WeekOfYearFiscal (*date*; *startingDay*) startingDay is 1-7, with 1=Sunday	Number from 1–53 Week 1 is the first week with 4 or more days in it.
Year (*date*)	Number
YearName (*date*; *format*) Japanese year name	Text

Design Functions

These functions return information about databases, fields, and layouts. Functions returning lists of interface elements return those names separated by carriage returns unless otherwise noted.

Database filenames are simple filenames: They do not include paths, and they do not include extensions. Database files must be open for you to use design functions that access them. A valid database filename for a design function is something like "Expense Report."

Field names in related tables should be specified as *tableName*::*fieldName* for the *fieldName* parameter.

TABLE B.3 Design Functions

Function	Result
DatabaseNames () Open databases only.	Text
FieldBounds (*fileName*; *layoutName*; *fieldName*)	Text. Four values separated by spaces of pixels for left, top, right, bottom coordinates (LTRB).
FieldComment (*fileName*; *fieldName*)	Text
FieldIDs (*fileName*; *layoutName*)	Text. Numeric file ID including table IDs for related fields.
FieldNames (*fileName*; *layoutName*)	Text

TABLE B.3   Continued

Function	Result
FieldRepetitions (*fileName*; *layoutName*; *fieldName*)	Text. Number of repetitions followed by "horizontal" or "vertical." Layout information, not field information (that is, may be fewer repetitions than exist in the table itself).
FieldStyle (*fileName*; *layoutName*; *fieldName*)	Text. One of: Standard, Scrolling, Popuplist, Popupmenu, Checkbox, or Radiobutton.
FieldType (*fileName*; *fieldName*)	Text. Four values, separated by spaces: 1: Standard, StoredCalc, Summary, UnstoredCalc, or Global. 2: Text, number, date, time, timestamp, or container. 3: Indexed or Unindexed. 4: Number of repetitions.
GetNextSerialValue (*fileName*; *fieldName*)	Text
LayoutIDs (*fileName*)	Text
LayoutNames (*fileName*)	Text
RelationInfo (*fileName*; *tableName*)	Text. Four values, separated by carriage returns: 1: Database file for tableName. 2: Related field name. 3: Field name in this table. 4: Any of Delete, Create, or Sorted, separated by spaces.
ScriptIDs (*fileName*)	Text
ScriptNames (*fileName*)	Text
TableIDs (*fileName*)	Text
TableNames (*fileName*)	Text
ValueListIDs (*fileName*)	Text
ValueListItems (*fileName*; *valueList*)	Text
ValueListNames (*fileName*)	Text
WindowNames ()	Text

Financial Functions

These are standard financial functions; they are found in many databases and spreadsheets.

TABLE B.4   Financial Functions

Function	Result
FV (*payment*; *interestRate*; *periods*)	Number
NPV (*payment*; *interestRate*)	Number
PMT (*principal*; *interestRate*; *term*)	Number
PV (*payment*; *interestRate*; *periods*)	Number

Get **Functions**

These functions replace and expand the old status functions in earlier versions of FileMaker. A few functions may return different results when evaluated on host or client machines sharing FileMaker databases. These are indicated with *.

Many Get functions operate on the currently open database. Some operate on the active window. For example, Get(FoundCount) returns the number of records in the find set for the active window.

TABLE B.5   Get Functions

Function	Result
Get(AccountName)	Text
Get(ActiveFieldContents)	Any
Get(ActiveFieldName)	Text
Get(ActiveFieldTableName)	Text
Get(ActiveModifierKeys)	Number. The sum of Shift (1), Caps Lock (2), Control (4), Alt/Windows Option/Mac OS (8), Command/Mac OS (16), depending on which keys are pressed.
Get(ActiveRepetitionNumber)	Number
Get(ActiveSelectionSize)	Number. Expressed in number of characters selected.
Get(ActiveSelectionStart)	Number

TABLE B.5   Continued

Function	Result
`Get(AllowAbortState)`	Number. 1 if Allow User Abort is on; Otherwise, 0.
`*Get(ApplicationLanguage)`	Text
`Get(ApplicationVersion)`	Text
`Get(CalculationRepetitionNumber)`	Number
`Get(CurrentDate)`	Date
`Get(CurrentHostTimestamp)`	Timestamp
`Get(CurrentTime)`	Time
`Get(CurrentTimestamp)`	Timestamp
`Get(ErrorCaptureState)`	Number. 1 if Set Error Capture is on; otherwise, 0.
`Get(ExtendedPrivileges)`	Text. Values include `fmnet`, `fmxdbc`, `fmiwp`, `fmmobile`.
`Get(FileName)`	Text
`Get(FilePath)`	Text
`Get(FileSize)`	Number
`Get(FoundCount)`	Number
`Get(HighContrastColor)`	Text. Windows only.
`Get(HighContrastState)`	Text. Windows only.
`Get(HostName)`	Text
`Get(LastError)`	Number
`Get(LastMessageChoice)`	Number. The number of the button clicked in a custom dialog.
`Get(LastODBCError)`	Text
`Get(LayoutAccess)`	Number. 0 for no access, 1 for view only, 2 for modifiable.
`Get(LayoutCount)`	Text
`Get(LayoutName)`	Text
`Get(LayoutNumber)`	Number
`Get(LayoutTableName)`	Text
`Get(LayoutViewState)`	Number. 0 for Form view, 1 for List view, 2 for Table view.

TABLE B.5   Continued

Function	Result
Get(MultiUserState)	Number. 0 for no network sharing, 1 for sharing and accessing the database on the host, 2 for sharing and accessing the database from a client.
Get(NetworkProtocol)	Text
Get(PageNumber)	Number. Valid only in Preview mode or when printing.
Get(PortalRowNumber)	Number
*Get(PrinterName)	Text
Get(PrivilegeSetName)	Text
Get(RecordAccess)	Number. 0 for neither View nor Edit access, 2 for both View and Edit access; 1 otherwise.
Get(RecordID)	Number. This is the number that never changes for a record.
Get(RecordModificationCount)	Number
Get(RecordNumber)	Number. Record number within a found set.
Get(RequestCount)	Number
Get(ScreenDepth)	Number
Get(ScreenHeight)	Number
Get(ScreenWidth)	Number
Get(ScriptName)	Text
Get(ScriptParameter)	Text
Get(SortState)	Number. 0 for not sorted, 1 for sorted, 2 for semisorted.
Get(StatusAreaState)	Number. 0 for hidden, 1 for visible, 2 for visible/locked, 3 for hidden/locked.
*Get(SystemIPAddress)	Text
Get(SystemLanguage)	Text
*Get(SystemNICAddress)	Text
Get(SystemPlatform)	Number. -1 for Mac OS X, -2 for Windows.
Get(SystemVersion)	Text
Get(TotalRecordCount)	Number
Get(UserCount)	Text

TABLE B.5   Continued

Function	Result
*Get(UserName)	Text
Get(WindowContentHeight)	Number
Get(WindowContentWidth)	Number
Get(WindowDesktopHeight)	Number
Get(WindowDesktopWidth)	Number
Get(WindowHeight)	Number
Get(WindowLeft)	Number
Get(WindowMode)	Number. 0 for Browse, 1 for Find, 2 for Preview, 3 for printing.
Get(WindowName)	Text
Get(WindowTop)	Text
Get(WindowVisible)	Number. 1 for visible, 0 for hidden.
Get(WindowWidth)	Number

Logical Functions

These functions are described in Hour 8, "More on Calculations and Functions." They are presented here for completeness without the explanations that appear in Hour 8.

TABLE B.6   Logical Functions

Function	Result
Case (test1;result1{;test2; result2;defaultResult...}))	Any type.
Choose (test;result0{;result1; result2...})	Text, number, date, time, timestamp, or container.
Evaluate (expression{;[field1; field2;field3;...]})	Text, number, date, time, timestamp, or container.
EvaluationError (expression)	Number
GetField (fieldName)	Text, number, date, time, timestamp, or container.
If (test;result1;result2)	Text, number, date, time, timestamp, or container.

TABLE B.6   Continued

Function	Result
IsEmpty (*field*)	Number. Returns 0 if the field contains anything; 1 if it is empty, a table is missing, or it otherwise cannot be evaluated.
IsValid (*field*)	Number. Returns 1 if it is valid, 0 in all other cases (see IsEmpty).
IsValidExpression (*expression*)	Number. Returns 1 if expression is valid, 0 in all other cases.
Let ({*[]var1=expression1* {;*var2=expression2...]*}; *calculation*)	Text, number, date, time, timestamp, or container.
Lookup (*sourceField* {;*failExpression*})	Text, number, date, time, timestamp, or container.
LookupNext (*sourceField*; *lower/higherFlag*)	Text, number, date, time, timestamp, or container.
Quote (*text*)	Returns text surrounded by quotes.

Number Functions

Many of these functions take a number as a parameter; as with other functions, an expression that yields a number is also a valid parameter. Also, note that for functions that take a parameter such as precision, you can use an if function to vary the precision based on data or other choices.

TABLE B.7   Number Functions

Function	Result
Abs (*number*)	Number or time.
Ceiling (*number*)	Number
Combination (*setSize*; *numberOfChoices*)	Number
Div (*number*; *divisor*)	Number
Exp (*number*)	Number
Factorial (*number*{;*numberOfFactors*})	Number
Floor (*number*)	Number
Int (*number*)	Number
Lg (*number*)	Number

TABLE B.7   Continued

Function	Result
Ln (*number*)	Number
Log (*number*)	Number
Mod (*number*; *divisor*)	Number
Random (*number*)	Number
Round (number; precision)	Number
SetPrecision (*expression*; *precision*)	Number
Sign (*number*)	Number. -1 for negative numbers, 0 for zero, and 1 for positive numbers.
Sqrt (*number*)	Number
Truncate (*number*; *precision*)	Number

Repeating Functions

Repeating fields were described fully in Hour 7, "Working with Calculations, Formulas, Functions, and Repeating Fields."

TABLE B.8   Repeating Functions

Function	Result
Extend (*nonrepeatingField*)	Text, number, date, time, timestamp, or container. The function doesn't actually return anything. It uses the nonrepeating value as many times as necessary to evaluate a calculation with a repeating field.
GetRepetition (*repeatingField*; *repetitionNumber*)	Text, number, date, time, timestamp, or container.
Last (*repeatingField*)	Text, number, date, time, timestamp, or container.

Summary Functions

The GetSummary function is similar to an aggregate function that references a related field (even in a self-join).

TABLE B.9   Summary Functions

Function	Result
GetSummary (*summaryField*; *breakField*)	Number, date, time, or timestamp.

Text Functions

These functions operate on text (text expressions, fields containing text, or text literal strings). See the following section, "Text Formatting Functions," for functions that change the appearance of text (text styles).

TABLE B.10   Text Functions

Function	Result
Exact (*originalText*; *comparisonText*)	Number. 1 if the strings are identical except for styling such as font); 0 otherwise.
Filter (*textToFilter*; *filterText*)	Text. Characters in filterText are retained in textToFilter. Case matters; style does not. Use to easily drop spaces, -, or () from phone numbers.
FilterValues (*textToFilter*; *filterValues*)	Similar to Filter, but filterValues contains text strings separated by carriage returns rather than individual characters to filter.
GetAsCSS (*text*)	Text. The text returned is the Cascading Style Sheet description of the font an style.
GetAsDate (*text*)	Date
GetAsNumber (*text*)	Number
GetAsSVG (*text*)	Text. The text returned is the Scalable Vector Graphics description of the font and style.
GetAsText (*data*)	Text. If the parameter is a container field, the text may be the path to the file.
GetAsTime (*text*)	Time
GetAsTimestamp (*text*)	Timestamp
Left (*text*; *numberOfCharacters*)	Text

TABLE B.10   Continued

Function	Result
LeftValues (*text*; *numberOfValues*)	Text. Values are separated by carriage returns.
LeftWords (*text*, *numberOfWords*)	Text. Words are separated by spaces, &, or -.
Length (*field*)	Number
Lower (*text*)	Text
Middle (*text*; *start*; *numberOfCharacters*)	Text
MiddleValues (*text*, *startingValue*; *numberOfValues*)	Text. Values are separated by carriage returns.
MiddleWords (*text*, *startingWord*; *numberOfWords*)	Text. Words are separated by spaces, &, or -.
PatternCount (*text*; *searchString*)	Number
Position (*text*; *searchString*; *start*; *occurrence*)	Number
Proper (*text*)	Text
Replace (*text*; *start*; *numberOfCharacters*; *replacementText*)	Text
Right (*text*; *numberOfCharacters*)	Text
RightValues (*text*; *numberOfValues*)	Text. Values are separated by carriage returns.
RightWords (*text*; *numberOfWords*)	Text. Words are separated by spaces, &, or -.
SerialIncrement (*text*; *incrementBy*)	Text
Substitute (*text*; *searchString* *replaceString*)	Text
Trim (*text*)	Text
TrimAll (*text*, *trimSpaces*; *trimType*)	Text. Use for removing spaces in text that mixes Roman and non-Roman characters.
Upper (*text*)	Text
ValueCount (*text*)	Number. Values are separated by carriage returns.

TABLE B.10   Continued

Function	Result
WordCount (*text*)	Number. Words are separated by spaces, &, or -.
Hiragana (*text*)	Text
KanaHankaku (*text*)	Text
KanaZenkaku (*text*)	Text
KanjiNumeral (*text*)	Text
Katakana (*text*)	Text
NumToJText (*number*; *separator characterType*)	Text
RomanHankaku (*text*)	Text
RomanZenkaku (*text*)	Text

Text Formatting Functions

The functions in the preceding section deal with text without regard to its appearance. These functions let you manipulate fonts, colors, and sizes.

TABLE B.11   Text Formatting Functions

Function	Result
RGB (*red*; *green*; *blue*)	Number. Use in TextColor function.
TextColor (*text*; *RGBcolor*) or TextColor (*text*; *RGB* (*red*; *green*; *blue*))	Text
TextFont (*text*;*fontName* {;*fontScript*})	Text
TextSize (*text*; *fontSize*)	Text
TextStyleAdd (*text*; *styles*)	Text. See Table B.12 for values for styles.
TextStyleRemove (*text*; *styles*)	Text. See Table B.12 for values for styles.

TextStyleAdd and TextStyleRemove take as their second parameter an expression that is a list of styles to add or remove. Styles are combined with + (as in Underline+Bold).

TABLE B.12   Values for Styles

Value
Plain (ignored for TextStyleRemove)
Bold
Italic
Underline
Condense
Extend
Strikethrough
SmallCaps
Superscript
Subscript
Uppercase
Lowercase
Titlecase
WordUnderline
DoubleUnderline
AllStyles (all available styles)

Time Functions

These are similar to the date functions described previously.

TABLE B.13   Time Functions

Function	Result
Hour (*time*)	Number
Minute (*time*)	Number
Seconds (*time*)	Number
Time (*hours*; *minutes*; *seconds*)	Time

Timestamp Functions

New in FileMaker 7, timestamp functions can replace separated date and time fields and let you clean up your databases.

TABLE B.14   Timestamp Function

Function	Result
Timestamp (*date*; *time*)	Timestamp

Trigonometric Functions

These are the standard geometric functions you find in spreadsheets and other applications.

TABLE B.15   Trigonometric Functions

Function	Result
Atan (*number*)	Number
Cos (*angleInRadians*)	Number
Degrees (*angleInRadians*)	Number
Pi ()	Number
Radians (*angleInDegrees*)	Number
Sin (*angleInRadians*)	Number
Tan (*angleInRadians*)	Number

FileMaker Script Steps

The FileMaker 7 script steps are listed in this appendix. Remember that you use the ScriptMaker dialog to construct script steps, selecting them from the list at the left and using the Specify button and other interface elements to complete the script step and its parameters. You don't directly type the script step.

Conventions used in this appendix (and in the FileMaker documentation) are

- ▶ <some text> indicates a variable or other text that you type in (usually with the Specify button).

- ▶ [and] surround the options for a script step.

- ▶ Within the options, [and] surround optional syntax.

- ▶ | indicates that the two adjacent items are mutually exclusive.

- ▶ All other text represents itself.

Because you build FileMaker scripts using the point-and-click interface in ScriptMaker, you don't have to worry about the order of variables and the details of syntax that are necessary when you are typing a command in another programming language. Thus, although the syntax descriptions in this chapter would allow you to type illegal commands in some cases, ScriptMaker prevents you from doing so. The goal is to provide the most succinct listing of FileMaker script steps in a format that most closely matches what you see in ScriptMaker as you build a script.

Also, note that <field name> implies <table::field name> for fields in related tables unless otherwise indicated.

By the
Way

Script steps that are not Web-compatible are labeled with *.

Control Script Steps

These are the basic programming script steps to manage control of scripts.

```
Perform Script ["<script name>"[; Parameter: <parameter>]]
Pause/Resume Script [Indefinitely|Duration (<seconds>)]
Exit Script
Halt Script
If [<Boolean calculation>]
Else If [<Boolean calculation>]
Else
End If
Loop
Exit Loop If [<Boolean calculation>]
End Loop
Allow User Abort [on | off]
```

When on, users can stop a script with Esc (Windows) or Command-. (Mac OS).

```
* Set Error Capture [on | off]
```

When on, FileMaker alerts and some dialogs are suppressed. Handle errors in your script by using Get (LastError).

Navigation Script Steps

These script steps let you navigate through the database.

```
Go to Layout [original layout|<layout name>|<layout number>|<name/number from
calculation>]
Go to Record/Request/Page [First|Last|Previous|Next|<by calculation>]
Go to Related Record [[Show only related records] From table: <table name>
  Using layout: Current layout|<name/number by calculation>|<layout name>
  [; New window]
Go to Portal Row [[Select] First|Last|Previous|Next|<by calculation>
Go to Field [[Select|Perform] <field name>]
Go to Next Field
Go to Previous Field
Enter Browse Mode [[Pause]]
Enter Find Mode [[Restore][Pause]]
* Enter Preview Mode [[Pause]]
```

Editing Script Steps

These are the standard editing script steps. Note that Find/Replace is for text find/replace, not the FileMaker Find mode, which is accessible from the Enter Find Mode and Perform Find script steps.

```
Undo
Cut [[Select] <field name>]
Copy [[Select] <field name>]
Paste [[Select] [Nostyle] <field name>]
Clear [[Select] <field name>]
Set Selection [<field name> [Start Position: <number or calculation>]
  <End Position: <number or calculation>]
Select All
* Perform Find/Replace [[No dialog] "<text to be found>" "<text to be replaced>"
  Find Next|Replace & Find|Replace|Replace All]
```

Fields Script Steps

These steps let you enter data in fields. You may want to use the Go to Field
navigation script step to move out of a field after you have set its data. Also see
Commit in the records script steps.

```
Set Field [<field name> <calculation>]
Set Next Serial Value [<field name> <calculation>]
Insert Text [[Select] <field name> "<text to insert>"]
Insert Calculated Result [[Select] <field name> "<calculation>"]
* Insert From Index [[Select] <field name>]
Insert From Last Visited [[Select] <field name>]
Insert Current Date [[Select] <field name>]
Insert Current Time [[Select] <field name>]
Insert Current User Name [[Select] <field name>]
* Insert Picture [[Reference] <field name>]
* Insert QuickTime [<field name>]
* Insert Object (Windows) ["<object type>]
* Insert File [[Select] <field name> "<file name>"]
Update Link (Windows) [<field name>]
Replace Field Contents [[No dialog]
  <field name> Current contents|Serial numbers|<calculation result>]
Relookup Field Contents [[No dialog] <field name>]
* Export Field Contents [<field name> "<file name>"]
```

Records

These script steps work on records. See also the navigation script steps for moving
from one record to another.

```
New Record/Request
Duplicate Record/Request
Delete Record/Request [[No dialog]]
Delete Portal Row [[No dialog]]
Delete All Records [[No dialog]]
Open Record/Request
Revert Record/Request [[No dialog]]
```

```
Commit Records/Requests [[Skip data entry validation][No dialog]]
Copy Record/Request
Copy All Records/Requests
* Import Records [[No dialog] <source or file name>
  Add|Update existing|Update matching <platform and character set>]
* Export Records [[No dialog] <output file name>]
```

Found Sets

After you perform a Find, you can manipulate the found records with these script steps:

```
Perform Find [Restore]
Constrain Found Set [Restore]
Extend Found Set [Restore]
Modify Last Find
Show All Records
Show Omitted Only
Omit Record
Omit Multiple Records [[No dialog] <number of records>]
Sort Records [Restore; [No dialog]]
Unsort Records
```

Windows

These script steps manipulate windows. Note that many of them are not compatible with the Web, because on the Web you are using a browser window, not a FileMaker window.

```
New Window [Name: <name>; Height: <n>; Width: <n>; Top: <n>; Left: <n>]
Select Window [Current window|<window name>]
Close Window [Current window|<window name>]
* Adjust Window [Resize to fit|Restore|Maximize|Minimize|Hide]
* Move/Resize Window [Current window|<window name>]
* Arrange All Windows [Tile vertically| Tile horizontally|
  Cascade window|Bring all to front]
* Freeze Window
* Refresh Window
* Scroll Window [Home|End|Page up|Page down|To selection]
Show/Hide Status Area [[Lock;] Show|Hide|Toggle]
* Show/Hide Text Ruler [Show|Hide|Toggle]
Set Window Title [Current window|<window name> New title:"<window title>"]
* Set Zoom Level [[Lock;] 25%|50%|75%|100%|150%|200%|300%|400%|Zoom In|Zoom Out]
View As [View as Form|View as List|View as Table|Cycle]
```

* Files

None of these script steps is compatible with the Web.

```
* New File
* Open File [[Open hidden;] <file reference name>]
* Close File [Current file | <file reference name>]
* Convert File [[No dialog] <file or data source name>]
* Set Multi-User [On|Off|On (hidden)]
* Set Use System Formats [On|Off]
* Save a Copy as [<file name> copy|compacted|clone]
* Recover File [[No dialog] <file name>]
* Print Setup [Restore [;No dialog]]
* Print [Restore [;No dialog]]
```

Accounts

Use these script steps to manage security. Note that most of them are available both on the Web and on a local FileMaker computer; you use the unified security model for both.

```
Add Account [Account Name: "<account  name>"; Password: "<password>";
  Privilege Set: "<privilege set>" [; Expire password]]
Delete Account [Account Name: "<account  name>"]
Reset Account Password [Account Name: "<account  name>;"
 New Password: "<password>" [; Expire password]]
* Change Password [Old Password: "<password>" New Password: "<password>"
 Perform with dialog|No dialog]
Enable Account [Account Name: "<account  name>" Activate|Deactivate]
* Re-Login Account Name: "<account  name>"; Password: "<password>
  No dialog|Perform with dialog]
```

* Spelling

None of the spelling script steps is available on the Web.

```
* Check Selection [[Select] <field name>]
* Check Record
* Check Found Set
* Correct Word
* Spelling Options
* Select Dictionaries
* Edit User Dictionary
```

* Open Menu Items

These script steps manipulate the FileMaker menus; thus, none is available on the Web where you only have your browser's menus.

```
* Open Preferences
* Open File Options
* Open Define Database
* Open Define File References
* Open Define Value Lists
* Open Find/Replace
* Open Help
* Open Remote
* Open ScriptMaker
* Open Sharing
```

Miscellaneous

Most of these script steps are not available on the Web:

```
* Show Custom Dialog [<title> <message> [<field 1> [;<field 2> [; <field 3>]]]]
* Allow Toolbars [On|Off]
* Beep
* Speak (Mac OS) ["<the text>"]
* Dial Phone [[No dialog] <the number>]
Open UR[[No dialog] "<the URL>"]
* Send Mail [[No dialog;] To: <to>; [CC: <CC>;] [BCC: <BCC>;]
  [Subject: <subject>;] [Message: <message>;] ["<attachment file name>"]]
* Send DDE Execute (Windows) [<topic text or file name> <service name>]
* Perform AppleScript (Mac OS) [<AppleScript commands>|<Calculated commands>]
* Execute SQL [[No Dialog;] DSN: <datasource name>; SQL Text:<SQL>|
  Calculated SQL Text: <calculation>]
* Send Event "<Target Application>"; "<Event Class>"; "<Event ID>",
  "<document>|<calculation>|<script text>"]
Comment [<comment text>]
* Flush Cache to Disk
Exit Application
```

Using FileMaker Server

There are two versions of FileMaker Server: FileMaker Server and FileMaker Server Advanced. FileMaker Pro itself allows you to share databases both to FileMaker clients and to browser clients (with Instant Web Publishing). However, it is limited to five concurrent users. The FileMaker Server products allow up to 350 concurrent users.

FileMaker Server

FileMaker Server differs from the other products (FileMaker Pro, FileMaker Developer, and FileMaker Mobile) in that it is not designed for interactive use. All FileMaker Server does is run the databases that you create with FileMaker Pro or FileMaker Developer.

It contains industrial-strength utilities to manage databases and back them up. It provides those databases to users accessing them over FileMaker networking using FileMaker Pro or FileMaker Developer as well as users accessing them over the Web or another network that uses Web technology.

You cannot edit a database with FileMaker Server directly, although you can connect to FileMaker Server from FileMaker Pro to edit the database (provided that you have the appropriate security).

FileMaker Server is generally not required for a small group of users—under 5. It is essential for large numbers of users.

If you are in the middle, you might consider some of the FileMaker Server features and decide whether they are important to you. Perhaps most important is the ability to schedule database backups in advance. If you are using FileMaker Pro to host a few users, you are responsible for backing up the databases on a regular basis (perhaps using a standard backup procedure that you have already implemented on your network). With FileMaker Server, you can set the backups within FileMaker Server.

FileMaker Server Advanced

In addition to the features of FileMaker Server, FileMaker Server Advanced allows you to publish databases on the Web using either Instant Web Publishing or Custom Web Publishing with XML and XSLT. On Windows, it also allows you to use FileMaker databases as ODBC and JDBC data sources.

Index

U - V